Psychology Revivals

The Scientific Study of Social Behaviour

Originally published in 1957 this title was an up-to-date account of psychological research into human social behaviour of the time. There are chapters on interaction between pairs of people, behaviour in small social groups, and human relations in industry. The author avoided the adoption of any particular theoretical position, and concentrated on the established empirical findings of the time. The results of several hundred investigations are summarised and compared, so that the principal generalisations which emerge can be seen. Stress is placed on rigorous methods of research, and a critical account is given of current techniques of social research, showing the importance of experimental and statistical methods. Careful consideration is given to the danger of the investigator disturbing what is being investigated. Use is made of recent ideas about theory and explanation, and the different kinds of theory used in experimental psychology were considered for the first time as possible ways of accounting for group behaviour.

This book was intended not only for students of psychology and of the other social sciences, but also for industrialists, administrators and indeed all who were interested in the laws underlying social behaviour. Today it can be read and enjoyed in its historical context.

The Scientific Study of Social Behaviour

Michael Argyle

LONDON AND NEW YORK

First published in 1957
by Methuen & Co. Ltd

This edition first published in 2013 by Routledge
27 Church Road, Hove, BN3 2FA

Simultaneously published in the USA and Canada
by Routledge
711 Third Avenue, New York, NY 10017

Routledge is an imprint of the Taylor & Francis Group, an informa business

All rights reserved. No part of this book may be reprinted or reproduced or utilised in any form or by any electronic, mechanical, or other means, now known or hereafter invented, including photocopying and recording, or in any information storage or retrieval system, without permission in writing from the publishers.

Publisher's Note
The publisher has gone to great lengths to ensure the quality of this reprint but points out that some imperfections in the original copies may be apparent.

Disclaimer
The publisher has made every effort to trace copyright holders and welcomes correspondence from those they have been unable to contact.

A Library of Congress record exists under LC Control no.: 57003243

ISBN: 978-0-415-83874-0 (hbk)
ISBN: 978-0-203-77940-8 (ebk)

THE SCIENTIFIC STUDY
OF SOCIAL BEHAVIOUR

The Scientific Study of Social Behaviour

MICHAEL ARGYLE
*Lecturer in Social Psychology in the
University of Oxford*

METHUEN & CO LTD
36 ESSEX STREET LONDON WC2

First published February 7th, 1957
Reprinted 1959

CATALOGUE NO. 5881/U

PRINTED IN ENGLAND BY
HAZELL WATSON AND VINEY LTD
AYLESBURY AND SLOUGH

FOR
SONIA, MIRANDA
AND
NICHOLAS

CONTENTS

	Preface	xi
	Acknowledgments	xiii
I.	INTRODUCTION	1

PART I. METHODOLOGY

II.	METHODS OF STUDYING SOCIAL BEHAVIOUR	
	Introduction	13
	Measuring instruments	14
	The logic of measurement	26
	The design of social investigations	38

III.	THE EXPLANATION OF SOCIAL BEHAVIOUR	
	Introduction	54
	Two preliminary stages to theory-construction	58
	Different types of theory	63
	Two alternative approaches	84

PART II. GENERALISATIONS AND THEORIES

IV.	INTERACTION BETWEEN TWO PEOPLE	
	The perception of other people	95
	The effect of the presence of other people	105
	The influence of one person's behaviour on another	108
	Continuous interaction between two people	112

V.	SMALL SOCIAL GROUPS	
	The influence of certain group dimensions on group behaviour	118
	Individual personality and group behaviour	135
	The influence of the environment on small groups	145
	Spontaneous changes with time	151

CONTENTS

VI. HUMAN RELATIONS IN INDUSTRY AND OTHER SOCIAL ORGANISATIONS
   The dependent variables 161
   Relations between the dependent variables 171
   The organisational structure 174
   Supervision and management 194

References 204

Author Index 229

Subject Index 236

FIGURES

1 Pavlov's theory of conditioning	*page* 71
2 Lorenz's model for instinctive behaviour	75
3 Deutsch's theory of motivation	77
4 The phenomenal field and behaviour	86
5 The distribution of participation in small groups	141
Table I Validation studies of systematic selection methods	179

PREFACE

THIS book is intended for students of psychology and of the other social sciences, to give a guide to the procedures and results in this rapidly growing field. I hope that it will not be regarded as a 'textbook of social psychology', of which there are many already—often illustrating a particular theoretical viewpoint with a congeries of experiments, quasi-experiments, and other people's opinions. Here only part of social psychology is dealt with— the part dealing with the study of social interaction—the fields of socialisation and personality being excluded. An effort has been made to put facts before theory, and to set out what facts have been discovered about social behaviour by reference to a substantial proportion of the valid research which has been done. The various theories are then examined in the light of this evidence.

It is hoped that the book will also be of interest to others outside the strict category of 'students', since many of the results reported are of direct relevance to social administrators, while the methods of research described could be readily applied to the solution of practical problems.

If I had not written this book I could have spent more time interviewing, observing, and calculating. Nevertheless I have learnt a great deal myself, and hope that this attempt to survey an important new field will be of some interest and value to others.

MICHAEL ARGYLE

Institute of Experimental Psychology, Oxford
May 1955

ACKNOWLEDGMENTS

MANY people have helped me with this book, directly or indirectly. Perhaps I should record a debt to two of my teachers at Cambridge, Sir Frederic Bartlett and Dr. R. H. Thouless, for first interesting me in the scientific study of social behaviour. My colleagues at Oxford have taught me a great deal, in addition to reading chapters and discussing particular problems. I am particularly indebted to Dr. J. A. Deutsch, Mr. Frank Cioffi, Dr. Godfrey Gardner, Dr. Harry Kay and Mr. Alan Watson (now at Cambridge). Several others have given me the use of their expert knowledge, in particular Professor R. B. Braithwaite of King's College, Cambridge, Mr. John D. Handyside of the N.I.I.P., Dr. Alistair Heron of the M.R.C. Ageing Unit at Liverpool University, Dr. Terence Lee of the University College of the South West, and Dr. John Mogey of University College, Oxford. Finally, I am indebted to my wife who has put in a great deal of therapeutic work on the style and grammar, and to Mrs. D. M. Pushman for typing the various drafts.

CHAPTER I

INTRODUCTION

MEN HAVE ALWAYS been deeply interested in problems of social behaviour, as is testified by the writings of many philosophers and moralists, novelists and dramatists. It is only recently however that any systematic or 'scientific' methods have been applied: previously it was just a matter of simple observation and individual experience, acute and insightful though the results very often were. Scarcely any of the research quoted in these pages was published before 1930, and most of it has appeared since 1940. It is not surprising, therefore, that this work is little known to those outside the social sciences. More surprising is the fact that the scientific approach is still not accepted by some scientists in this country, who favour subjective, intuitive methods in this particular field, though demanding the usual rigorous procedures in their own.

It is in a way surprising that the systematic investigation of this field should have been neglected for so long, while less familiar and less important areas of study have been thoroughly investigated. What is the reason for this unwillingness to apply scientific procedures to the study of social behaviour? It may be because precise means of measurement did not exist; in other fields of knowledge measuring instruments have had to be invented, though progress is impeded until the necessary procedures have been devised. Possibly the subject-matter of social behaviour seemed too complex for analytical study; but the phenomena studied in biochemistry and atomic physics could hardly be described as simple. Another reason is perhaps that social behaviour is so immediate and familiar that it is not clear what remains to be 'discovered'; this point is dealt with later in the chapter where the notion of discovery in the social sciences will be discussed.

A final reason is that people often require no explanation of the problems involved, both on account of their very familiarity, and because they can be accounted for in other ways. In particular it is common to accept as an explanation for a social phenomenon the presence of certain conscious processes in the people involved. This is the way of the novelist and of common sense, and serves to allay curiosity. It has even become the basis for a form of psychological theory,[1] while the interpretations of abnormal behaviour made by psychoanalysts consist of the postulation of further 'repressed' processes accompanying the behaviour and making it understandable.

Why did the scientific study of social behaviour ever develop at all? Part of the reason was no doubt the growth of suitable research techniques devised in other branches of psychology, such as special kinds of interview and questionnaire, systematic observation, and various statistical tests. In addition to this there were a number of problems in which people became interested, and which demanded a causal answer for the reliable prediction of future events.

The result is that to-day the study of social behaviour forms a fairly coherent field, though it overlaps in places with sociology and with the psychology of personality. The field is concerned primarily with the causal conditions and effects of behaviour towards other people—i.e. how the behaviour of one person influences the behaviour of others. This is taken here to include not only two-person situations pure and simple, but the study of small social groups and the investigation of interactions within social organisations. Just as experimental psychology is regarded as the fountain source of fundamental ideas and first principles for the various branches of applied psychology, so perhaps the study of social behaviour may come to be looked upon as being of especial importance among the social sciences, not only in view of its rigorous methods of research, but because its problems are of fundamental importance and may throw light on events in other fields.

The Problems of Social Behaviour

Some of the problems which have been studied were investigated simply because they were interesting in themselves. Others arose out of practical questions which demanded a precise answer. Once the subject was started, of course, one problem followed another, until to-day the stage is being reached where many investigations test predictions from theories. In this section the origin of some of the classical problems in the field will be listed, following roughly the organisation of the second part of the book.

Many of the problems of interaction between two people arose out of the interview situation—the hitherto universal method of selecting candidates for jobs. It became suspected that the interview was not particularly good for this purpose, and research was carried

[1] The phenomenal field approach. See p. 84 ff.

out to find out just how good it was. Meanwhile, quite different selection procedures were being devised, which proved to be better. All kinds of interesting problems emerged, such as how well one can judge the personality of another just by looking at him, which sort of person is the best judge of others, and how well we can judge ourselves. As interviewing began to be used for investigating attitudes and beliefs in social surveys, research was directed towards the best methods of obtaining accurate information. It was discovered that the appearance of the interviewer and the way the interview was conducted influenced the answers that were obtained, and ways of avoiding these difficulties were explored. Rather similar problems have arisen in connection with psychotherapy, and interest has also arisen in the interaction processes which occur during treatment.

Another problem about the interaction between pairs of people concerns suggestion. It is familiar that people will change their minds as a result of persuasion, and investigations have been performed to find out what sorts of people can be most influenced in this way, and under what conditions they can be influenced most. In addition it has been asked why they should give way to suggestions at all.

One of the earliest questions which was asked about social behaviour was what difference it made to someone working at a task if another person was watching him: this was the social psychologist's approach to 'stage-fright', and in a way it is one of his fundamental problems, since it is concerned simply with the presence or absence of other people in the situation. The research on this question is of great importance, since it shows how the test-scores of people being tested, and of subjects being experimented upon, depend on the presence of other people.

Interest in small social groups has grown very rapidly during the last few years, and they have now become an object of research in their own right, regardless of any practical application. The investigations of several groups in the Hawthorne plant of the Western Electric Company, though far from satisfactory, drew attention to the curious interactions within groups, producing effects which were inexplicable if one just treated people as isolated individuals. Research was then carried out upon the characteristics of different kinds of groups—large and small, co-operative and competitive, more and less friendly—and it became possible to say what sort of group would be the most satisfactory for a given purpose.

It has long been known that social groups develop their own internal hierarchies and throw up their own leaders; early researchers were very keen to find out what sort of person became a leader. The largely inconclusive results of over a hundred investigations led to the realisation that leadership depends to a great extent upon the demands of the situation. It is nevertheless of great interest to be able to predict individual behaviour in groups from personality measurements, and research on group therapy is beginning to throw light on this.

One of the most striking features of small groups is their power to modify and control the behaviour of their members: it is familiar how even the lawless members of delinquent gangs submit to the rules of the gang. A number of ingenious experimental situations have been devised for research on this problem, and more is now known about it than about almost any other part of the field. The 'sociometric' method of disclosing friendship patterns has proved to be a useful instrument of research, though its exponents have been somewhat overenthusiastic. Much has been found out about which people become friends, who is popular, and how this affects their behaviour and treatment.

The third area of social research to be considered is that of interactions within social organisations like industry and the Services. Much unsystematic research had been carried out here, and it is only recently that any adequate research has been done. One difficulty has been in the measurement of output and other aspects of efficiency. This has largely been achieved, and the blanket term 'morale' has been broken down into measurable components. The famous laboratory experiment by Lewin and Lippitt on leadership in boys' clubs stimulated not only a host of laboratory experiments using similar methods, but also several industrial studies following up similar ideas. The investigation of the effects of different kinds of leadership at various levels is now a major research topic.

The influence of the formal organisation on behaviour had been much discussed by sociologists in connection with 'roles'. Investigations have been carried out which show how role behaviour is a result of selection and training processes of varying degrees of efficiency, and how there is residual variation due to personality. Other organisational research has been directed towards comparing the efficiency of different kinds of organisational structure—different spans of control, degrees of delegation, etc. Other workers have looked into the effects of different kinds of incentive systems. All this work is only beginning, but already sufficient information has been accumulated to show that most of the books on 'management' and 'administration' are obsolete, and must be replaced by exact studies of the problems concerned.

Relation to Other Fields of Research

The study of social behaviour grew out of experimental psychology; it is often conducted in laboratories of experimental psychology, though in America separate departments have sometimes branched off; the majority of social psychologists were trained in experimental psychology. In many ways social behaviour is simply a field of experimental psychology with a special subject-matter—the behaviour of people when others are present. Where the one deals with the perception of shapes, moving lights, etc., the other deals with the perception of emotions, attitudes, and intelligence in other people; where one is interested in motivation by hunger and thirst, the other is interested in the needs for status and acceptance. Social behaviour draws on experimental psychology for many of its research techniques and as a valuable factual and theoretical foundation for explaining the results of social research. However, it may be suggested that the fields have less in common now that their methods have become refined and specialised, and that the growth of separate departments is inevitable.

The study of social behaviour must also be distinguished from the psychology of personality—both of them being parts of that rather broader area of study often called Social Psychology.[1] One aspect of research on personality is the relation between the behaviour of people in different situations: where experimental psychologists are concerned with the causal effects of changes in the situation regardless of individual differences, personality psychologists are interested in seeing whether people behave similarly in successive experimental situations, and which groups of situations produce the same ordering of subjects. The two kinds of research are complementary, and although we are primarily concerned with the first type, use will be made of a number of findings of the second kind, in cases where individual differences are important. Personality study is also concerned with the origins of personality in inheritance and social learning, whereas the two other fields investigate the behaviour of the finished product, though often at different stages of completion.

Sociology and anthropology at first glance appear to be concerned with the same subject-matter as the study of social behaviour. There

[1] The scope of social psychology may be taken to be defined by the contents of the *Handbook of Social Psychology* (Lindzey 1954).

are however two important differences. In the first place the great bulk of research in sociology and anthropology is of the descriptive survey type. The social life and institutions of particular towns, primitive tribes, or social groups are described with reference perhaps to economic, political, or religious matters. There is very little attempt to arrive at generalisations about the causal relations between variables. There are however two ways in which these are occasionally produced—by analysis of social-survey results, showing for example that the middle classes are more conservative or more ambitious, and secondly, by the systematic comparison of a number of towns, primitive tribes, or social groups. The other respect in which sociology is different is that the basic unit of analysis is the group, whether it be a social class, an age-sex category, a town, or a culture: sociologists are not concerned with individuals save as they contribute to an average for a social group or category. Here, too, the line is difficult to draw, as there is a certain amount of discussion of the behaviour of small groups of different types in Chapter V, and of social organisations of different structures in Chapter VI. The contribution of the study of social behaviour to sociology is that it can provide precise generalisations about individual social behaviour which may be used to explain sociological findings.[1] The contribution of sociology is to provide information about the institutional and historical setting against which social behaviour takes place. In an industrial context the study of Industrial Relations can be of great assistance in this way. Again the material provided by anthropology is of great value in showing just how much of our behaviour may be culturally conditioned (cf. Kluckhohn 1954).

Apologia for the Scientific Approach

The pre-scientific way of dealing with social behaviour was often to observe particular events or social groups and to interpret what happened by reference to the conscious processes of the participants. The scientific approach consists in the first place in establishing empirical generalisations about the relations between a number of measurable variables: this entails the use of exact methods of measurement, the study of a number of cases from the comparison of which the generalisation can be deduced, and the use of statistical tests to show that the results could not have occurred by chance. The first stage of the explanation of a social event is to show that it is an instance of one or more such generalisations, and could have been predicted from

[1] See Chapter III on the explanation of sociological generalisations.

INTRODUCTION 7

knowledge of the values of the antecedent variables. The second stage of explanation consists in deducing the generalisation from a series of postulates, from which other testable predictions also follow. These two stages are described in Chapters II and III respectively. Two concrete examples of the whole procedure will now be given, drawing on material which is given in greater detail later.

The first example is: Are friendly work-teams more efficient than others? One difficulty is how to measure friendliness and efficiency. The first can now be done by the sociometric technique (see p. 21), the second by a variety of measures used by industrial psychologists. Of the latter, the measurement of 'output' alone is a highly complex matter, since different work-teams are usually engaged upon different work. There have now been a number of investigations of the main problem, and it appears that friendly groups do more work when their activities are interdependent, though not when they are on separate jobs. Similarly, absenteeism and labour turnover are less in friendly groups. The explanation of these results is very simple, and can be carried out simply by postulating a need to be liked by other people which is satisfied by interacting with friends. Since interdependent work entails social interaction, members of friendly groups will be motivated to work: when their work is independent they will still be motivated to interact, but this may well be an alternative to working. Similarly, absenteeism and labour turnover will be less, since members will want to continue to be with one another. This explanation is supported by the higher job satisfaction found in friendly teams. A further aspect of this research is that a great deal is now known about the conditions under which friendly groups are formed.

The second example is concerned with the problem of differential participation in discussion groups, though this is still at the research stage. One of the greatest difficulties facing a discussion-group leader is the fact that about a third of the group do all the talking. Systematic observation methods have been developed for recording discussion within a group, and records of large numbers of groups show that a very asymmetrical distribution of participation is a universal characteristic of such groups; furthermore, the mathematical form of the distribution is known. It has been found that participation will be more equally shared in smaller groups, when the range of intelligence is small, and when none of the members possesses specialised knowledge of the matter under discussion. Those who talk most will be of high intelligence and will also differ in personality from the others. The best style of leadership behaviour for flattening out the distribution is not yet known, but is an obvious topic for research. Little has been done as yet by way of explanation, though the individual differences scarcely require it, being extensions of behaviour in other situations.

What Constitutes a 'Discovery' about Social Behaviour

It was suggested earlier that one reason why scientists had avoided the study of social behaviour was that the field was so familiar that no discovery seemed possible. The discovery of anything like new nebulae seems to be impossible in such a familiar field. The real analogy to this, however, is to find people behaving in a very unusual manner; this is constantly being done by workers in the adjacent fields of anthropology and psychiatry and is a discovery at the level of fact-finding. There are several more interesting kinds of discovery which may be made in the study of social behaviour just as well as elsewhere.

To begin with there may be classificatory discoveries—showing that it is convenient to subdivide a set of phenomena into certain categories which are easily discriminable and which embody a number of important common properties. The example to be given is from the field of personality. Eysenck (1952) has shown that it is convenient to classify individuals along the dimensions of introversion-extroversion, neuroticism, and psychoticism, and he has shown that all three dimensions are relatively independent of one another.

Another type of discovery is in the development of measuring instruments. A great deal of research has been carried out, for example, in connection with the measurement of attitudes by questionnaire methods. Several different kinds of scale have been devised, which are discussed later. One kind, that due to Guttman (Stouffer et al. 1950), makes use of a 'scalogram board' for arranging questions as well as subjects in order of extremity of attitude; it is possible to select a small number of questions so that they form a series in which a person answering 'yes' to any one question will answer 'yes' to all those below it in the series.

A third form of discovery, and probably the most important, is simply the establishment of empirical generalisations. Part II of this book summarises the known generalisations in this field. Sometimes they are obvious, sometimes not. Even when they are obvious it is important for them to be firmly established, and more important to know the precise empirical conditions under which they do and do not hold. Take for example the generalisation that members of groups who hold different opinions from the other members will be rejected. It is now known that this only happens if the opinion is on a matter that is relevant to the group's purposes, and that rejection is stronger in more friendly and co-operative groups. Current problems about the limits of this generalisation are whether it applies to leaders and high-status members less than to others, and whether there are cross-cultural variations.

A fourth kind of discovery is concerned with the invention of theories to explain generalisations which have been established. In experimental psychology and physics, theory-construction is associated with the postulation of physiological and sub-atomic entities respectively, a development which has attracted a lot of attention. In the study of social behaviour, theory-construction is often carried out by making use of findings in experimental psychology, and may include the postulation of new processes, such as various secondary drives. An example of such a theory is Deutsch's theory (1949*a*) of co-operation and competition, from which a large number of predictions follow, many of these now being confirmed.

Lastly, there are mathematical and statistical discoveries which may be of immense value in opening up knowledge in the field. The development of statistical tests which do not require the data to be normally distributed (cf. K. Smith 1953) will enable more rigorous calculations to be made in the future. Again, the creation or application of new areas of mathematics may enable deductions from theories to be made with much greater facility. The Theory of Games in economics, and Information Theory in experimental psychology, are instances of this.

The fear that the material of social behaviour is too familiar for discovery to be possible is unfounded. Though one spectacular variety of discovery is largely ruled out (it occurs in anthropology and psychiatry), other and more fundamental discoveries can be made in much the same way as in other sciences.

Part I

METHODOLOGY

CHAPTER II

METHODS OF STUDYING SOCIAL BEHAVIOUR

INTRODUCTION

THE STUDENT OF social behaviour is fortunate in many ways: he does not need to travel to Polynesia or to the bottom of the sea, he does not require animal houses or complex apparatus. Nevertheless the development of a science of social behaviour has been held up through a complete lack of adequate techniques. Some people still have doubts as to whether social behaviour is really capable of being treated scientifically. It is true that it raises a number of unique problems, though probably no more than any other branch of science. In this chapter these difficulties will be indicated, together with the attempts which have been made to overcome them. The position taken here is that it is just as possible to find valid empirical laws in the social sciences as it is in physics and chemistry. In the following pages a concise account will be given of the methods of research as they have been perfected so far, with particular reference to their logical features.

There are perhaps two groups of people who will disagree with this approach—plain sceptics, and exponents of 'Action Research'.

Many people outside social science are rather sceptical of what it can do, and they sometimes maintain that it is not possible to obtain valid empirical laws in this field. Their argument is supported by reference to the special difficulties of research here—the influence of the investigator on the behaviour studied, the difficulty of social experimentation, the intermediacy of the human instrument in measurement, etc. These and other questions are dealt with in this chapter.

By 'Action Research' is meant any investigation in which social change or therapy is the prior object, and the discovery of scientific results a subordinate one. From a belief in the greater importance of social change, together with an awareness of the difficulty of obtaining objective empirical laws, some writers go on to say that the scientific aim should, in effect, be abandoned. ". . . the experiment tends to submerge its classical objective, the search for proof, and becomes instead a miniature form of social action" (Madge 1953,

p. 287). This is to regard objective empirical laws as a fetish of merely academic interest. The point is that they are of direct and universal application, whereas immediate results are not. The Action Researcher ought to obtain objective results of at least two kinds: firstly, he should prove that what he is doing is genuinely effective—for example, in increasing output, reducing inter-group hostility, or curing neurotics. Secondly, he should show the precise conditions under which these successful results can be obtained, so that others can do the same. It is not suggested that he should go further and take an interest in testing theoretical hypotheses, for these are largely the concern of the research worker.

MEASURING INSTRUMENTS

The student of social behaviour has two measuring instruments which are particularly his own, though he may borrow the tools of others. These two are the different kinds of interview and questionnaire, and the techniques of controlled observation. The questions about the logic of measurement, the disturbance created by the investigator, and the design of the research will be discussed in later sections of the chapter.

Interview and Questionnaire

Modern psychologists are more concerned with behaviour than with states of consciousness. Nevertheless one kind of behaviour is verbal behaviour, and what a person says or writes is of great interest to the psychologist in several ways. One way in which the interview or questionnaire may be used is for obtaining knowledge about objective facts known to the informant but not to the investigator. For example, an anthropologist who arrived too late for a rare ceremony, such as a coronation, in a society which kept no records would have to use this method. Likewise an investigator of behaviour which he was not allowed to observe, such as sexual behaviour, would use this approach (cf. Kinsey et al. 1948). It is however familiar to the experimental psychologist that perceptions are liable to selection and distortion according to interest and mood, and that memory continues this process. If any more direct method is available, it is preferable to the interviewing of informants. Another use of the interview and questionnaire is in personality assessment. From a person's answers to certain questions and his general behaviour in the test situation, predictions are made about his behaviour in other contexts. The accuracy of this method of assessment is discussed later (p. 95 ff.).

A third use of the interview is to change a person's behaviour, as in psychotherapy and social case-work. This will be discussed later as a form of social interaction (p. 112 f.), but is not a means of measurement and will not be pursued here further.

The most important use of verbal methods in the study of social behaviour is for the analysis of perceptions, attitudes, and motivation, since this cannot be carried out so well in any other way. By *perception* is meant the sum total of material open to introspection, about some part of a person's present physical environment, and which can be obtained from subsequent verbal reports. For social psychology the term is used in a somewhat broader sense than in experimental psychology (see p. 95). In general the best way of investigating perceptions is with open-ended questions, but it is possible to use closed multiple-response questions or rating scales. Two investigators, for instance, have measured 'perception of the attitudes of others to oneself' by this means: Horowitz and others (1951) used a graphic scale, and Pepitone (1950) a set of verbal categories. Another method of assessing perceptions is to compare the situation or stimulus with a number of standard stimuli, as in classical psychophysics. This method has not yet been used in the study of social perception proper—the perception of social objects—though Bruner and Goodman (1947) used it in their investigation of the influence of economic background on perception of the size of coins. It could be used in social perception if one had a graded series of pictures, recordings, or actual personalities against which to match the person being judged.

Attitudes are patterns of behaviour in response to particular people or objects, or classes of these. The most familiar kinds of attitude are political, religious, and inter-racial ones, though attitudes towards specific individuals can also be measured. An attitude resembles a personality trait, save that it refers to a narrower class of responses, and as in the case of traits the class of behaviours comprising the pattern is defined by the correlation together[1] of these responses over a large number of people. An important logical difference between perceptions and attitudes is that attitudes refer primarily to overt behaviour, while perceptions do not. Thus verbal measures of attitudes can be validated against behaviour, but this is not the case with perceptions. Similarly if *beliefs* are defined as verbal assent to certain propositions, there is no further criterion beyond interview-questionnaire data.

[1] Their association may be indicated by some other scaling method.

The third kind of empirical variable which can be measured by interview and questionnaire is *motivation*. This differs from perception in that its operational definition does not rest in verbal reports, and from attitudes in that, while it may be defined in terms of behavioural criteria, these are not yet agreed upon. Motivational states may be defined as (*a*) the result of a certain period of deprivation, as in experiments on animals, (*b*) biological states of the organism, in the case of primary drives, or (*c*) certain kinds of behaviour, such as on the 'activity wheel' used for rats. What is required is research on deprived humans, after the model of the Minnesota starvation study (Keys et al. 1945), to find the concomitants of motivational states and to develop convenient means of testing for these states. The measurements could take the form of records of behaviour in certain situations, or of some kind of interview or questionnaire. One such method which has been used is assessment of fantasy by content analysis of Thematic Apperception Test protocols (McClelland et al. 1953). A second is to offer choices of activity to the subject, as in the Allport–Vernon values questionnaire (1931). A third is the use of self-rating scales such as Swanson used (1951), with questions like "How much does it mean to you to be one of the leading members of the group?".

There are a number of types of interview and questionnaire, the more important of which will be described here, together with brief notes on their advantages and disadvantages for measuring perceptions, attitudes, and motivation.

Many kinds of information can be obtained either by interview or by questionnaire—the questions are spoken in one case and written in the other. (The unstructured and psychoanalytic types of interview cannot of course be given in questionnaire form.) When an interviewer obtains answers to a number of definite questions it is called a *schedule*. The questionnaire has the great advantage of anonymity, making for more truthful answers, though it was found in the course of investigations in the U.S. Army that Negro soldiers thought that their answers would be read by a white audience (Hyman 1951, p. 209), indicating that 'audience effects' are not always eliminated in the questionnaire. The more standard situation of the questionnaire also serves to cut out uncontrolled personal influences, and there is less likelihood of bias in the coding of replies.

The interview, on the other hand, although suffering from the corresponding disadvantages, is in general more flexible and can produce more illuminating results. It has been shown, for example, that the same question can have different meanings to different people (Crutchfield and Gorden 1947), and such misunderstandings should be avoided. The interviewer can probe for the true significance of replies, and make ratings based on the whole of the subject's behaviour. He can vary the order of the questions, and prevent the subject looking over the whole list before answering.

The following five types of interview and questionnaire will be discussed below: the social-survey interview or questionnaire, the non-directive interview, the psychoanalytic interview, attitude scales, and sociometry.

(1) Social surveys are generally conducted by a standardised interview, since not everyone who receives a questionnaire under these conditions will return it; a high-percentage return is required if the results are to be at all representative, whereas, for example, 10% to 40% is typical for a postal ballot.

This kind of interview is necessarily short, since a large number[1] have to be completed, and consequently it consists of a series of direct questions, often with a limited range of possible answers. The use of this kind of question has been criticised by McNemar (1946) on the grounds that the answers are very unstable and liable to be influenced by such peripheral factors as emotionally charged words, the order of the questions, and so forth. Furthermore, the use of fixed alternatives may force an answer before one has crystallised, and direct questions have a way of suggesting their own answers, even when this would not be expected (Muscio 1916). However, most of these difficulties may be countered in some way—by careful pre-testing of the questions, by 'filter' questions to ascertain if the respondent possesses the knowledge or opinion in question, and by the inclusion of a number of open-ended questions permitting a free answer in the subject's own words. A great deal is known about the best ways of wording the questions; this is discussed by Cannell and Kahn (1953) and Cantril (1944). In carrying out a social survey it is usual to train the interviewers so that they all adopt a quite standardised approach, and variation due to the interviewer is eliminated.

(2) The non-directive interview is the opposite of the above method, and allows spontaneous conversation on the part of the subject, with the minimum of questioning on the part of the interviewer. The method was first used in the Hawthorne investigations (Roethlis-

[1] The British Social Survey uses a sample size of two thousand.

berger and Dickson 1939, pp. 272–86), and was developed as a method of therapy by Carl Rogers (1942). Rogers has devised skills of interviewing which enable the interviewer to elicit answers by putting extremely vague questions, by asking for fuller information, and by making encouraging noises. This method avoids the suggestion of answers to the subject and the misinterpretation of questions, allows him to reply in his own words instead of confining him to set alternatives, and encourages him to say what seems important to him; it seeks for his reasons and will reach areas of personal importance ('depth'). (Krech and Crutchfield 1948, pp. 276–88.)

There are two drawbacks to this method of interviewing—the subject may fail to talk about the subjects in which the interviewer is interested, and the results are difficult to score. The first difficulty may be overcome by means of semi-structured questions, so that increasingly direct questions may be asked in a 'funnel structure' to obtain answers on the required subjects. In the 'focused interview' developed by Merton and Kendall (1946), semi-structured questions are used in relation to a specified range of material to be covered, while attempts are made to discover what precise experiences and feelings are being reported. The difficulty of scoring may be overcome by the interviewer making ratings on the spot—of the extent to which certain attitudes, for example, are displayed; or he can take full notes which are afterwards rated by judges or subjected to a formal content analysis, along lines to be described later. This method is valuable for measuring drives, attitudes, and perceptions both quantitively and qualitatively; its length, however, restricts it to purely research purposes or to the pilot stage of a survey.

(3) The psychoanalytic interview is the now quite familiar process wherein the patient lies on a couch and free-associates with the help of the analyst, usually starting from memories of childhood and the recall of dreams. As will be mentioned later in this chapter, the patient is more highly motivated towards frank disclosure than are most subjects in social research, and he may become aware of material that was initially not open to conscious introspection. The method aims to disclose unconscious motivations and memories. It is claimed by psychoanalysts that this method gives results unobtainable by any other means, and that they are of greater importance for understanding a person's motivations. There are, however, grounds for comparing this method unfavourably with other kinds of interview. Firstly, no attempt is made to ask questions which are either standard (like the questionnaire and

schedule) or free from suggestiveness (like the non-directive interview). Secondly, no attempt is made to obtain objective records of what is said, and it is clear that the analyst is selective in what he records, while his interpretation (which is the basis for later questions) is based on a particular theory. Thirdly, there is a somewhat complex social relationship between analyst and patient, and this may be expected to lead to particular kinds of concealment, invention, and distortion. As will be seen later, the relation between interviewer and subject is a matter of great importance. Furthermore, it is difficult to validate the psychoanalytic interview, for the following reasons: (i) The material obtained is not normally used to predict future behaviour, as for example are attitude scales, though there is no reason in principle why this method of validation could not be used, (ii) there is usually no way of checking the facts reported, e.g. about early childhood, and it is as a matter of fact recognised that many of these reports are fictitious (Ezriel 1951), (iii) the efficacy of psychoanalytic therapy would not prove the validity of the technique of interviewing, and in any case the efficacy of the therapy has yet to be demonstrated (Eysenck 1952, p. 25 f.). On the other hand, there are certain other criteria for the validation of psychoanalytic interpretations, i.e. of unconscious motivations. These will be discussed in the section on Case-studies (p. 40 ff.). It may be concluded that although the psychoanalytic interview motivates the subject towards frank disclosure, there are other factors which are liable to diminish its validity, and that the method has not been validated.

Some social scientists have tried to apply the psychoanalytic method to social research. The most notable attempt has been made at the Tavistock Institute of Human Relations in London (Cook 1951, Jaques 1948). The team enter a social organisation only when requested to do so—that is to say, when the organisation feels that some need may be met by the research. The analogy of the sick patient calling in the doctor is sometimes used. The method is for the team to enter straightforwardly in the role of industrial psychiatrists, and to sit in on committees and joint consultations, during the course of which they make the kind of interpretative comment that a group therapist might make. By this means unconscious hostilities and the rest are brought to light and 'worked through', so that beneficial changes of organisation can take place. This whole notion of the therapy of social organisations is a fascinating one, but here we are simply concerned with research methods. It should be pointed out in the first place that the whole procedure is daring, unorthodox, and necessarily disturbing in an unknown way: it is admitted that great resistance is shown (Wilson 1947). It is not likely that the motivation to frank disclosure under the conditions described will be very great. Furthermore the social situation here is so complex that it is impossible even to guess at the forces likely to influence what comes out: the behaviour of the therapists is not recorded. The remarks made about validation in connection with the psychoanalytic interview apply equally well here. Thus, while there is no evidence for the validity of material obtained by the Tavistock method, there are obvious grounds for assuming that it will not be very great. (It is also possible to criticise the work of the Tavistock Institute on the grounds that they use only the case-study design: this is discussed later.)

(4) Attitude scales are generally administered by questionnaire and consist of a combination of closed multiple-response questions, from the answers to which a single score can be calculated. The measurement of attitudes in this way is probably one of the most important developments in social psychological measurement. The three most familiar kinds of scale are those due to Likert, Thurstone, and Guttman. The Likert scale consists of a series of statements to which five degrees of agreement are possible; the latter are numbered 1 to 5 and the scores added to give a total score. The scale is purified by item analysis to give a consistent scale. In the Thurstone scale the items are selected by judges in such a way as to have 'equal intervals' between them; this claim is discussed later in the chapter. The Guttman scale is also designed so that the questions are of graded strength—a person agreeing with one question will agree with all those below it—but the questions are chosen by the results of a trial run rather than by judges. Excellent discussions of all these scaling methods may be found elsewhere, so they will not be pursued further here. (Peak 1953; Krech and Crutchfield 1948.)

The great advantage of these scales is that they have a high degree of validity (against behaviour) and reliability, and that they give fairly differentiated measurements. For these reasons much social research has been concerned with the determinants and correlates of attitudes—they have become a kind of universal dependent variable. These scales do however suffer from one of the disadvantages of the fixed-alternative question—that they may force answers into an unnatural frame of reference, and will often seem silly to educated people. On the other hand, they do not depend on the unstable answers to single questions and are unlikely to suggest their own answers. (5) Sociometry is the most widely used means of measuring the attitude of one person towards another. Very little progress has really been made in the conceptualisation or measurement of such attitudes. Theorists have made various suggestions—Freud's interpersonal mechanisms of identification, transference, and projection, Horney's attitudes of moving towards, away from, and against other people (1945)—but no satisfactory means of operational definition have been developed for them. The only concerted attempt at measurement has been Sociometry, which uses the technique of asking people whom they would like as companions for some activity (Moreno 1953). It is believed that the choices will be more genuine if the subjects think that their choices will actually affect social arrangements. Various calculations can be made, using the distribution of choices as data: (i) The total number of choices a person receives (sometimes subtracting rejections) is taken as a measure of his 'sociometric status', which is however more akin to popularity than to status as normally understood. 'Isolates' and 'stars' are indicated, while a powerful person may be one who, though not necessarily a star himself, is closely linked to others who are. (ii) Cleavages in the group due to stratification or racial discrimination are shown. (iii) The formation of cliques can be detected by matrix analysis (Proctor and Loomis 1951). (iv) Group cohesiveness[1] can be measured by some index such as percentage of choices made to others within the group.

The sociometric method is simple and reliable, and has been used to good purpose. However it measures only one aspect of interpersonal attitudes, shows relations only two at a time, and is not quantified.

The Observation of Behaviour

The experimental psychologist studies things like skilled movements of the limbs, most of which can be recorded with some precision, usually mechanically. The anthropologist and sociologist carry out far vaguer and more general descriptions of such things as crowds, ceremonials, and the customs of particular communities. The interests of the social psychologist lie somewhere in between, both as regards the size of units measured and in degree of precision. His interest is in the social behaviour of individuals, ranging from somewhat detailed studies of face-to-face interaction to investigations of whole social groups and organisations. It must be emphasised that

[1] See p. 123 f.

any level of analysis is legitimate so long as it adheres to rigorous methods of measurement. Two kinds of record of social behaviour will be considered—the use of message slips, and interaction recording and rating methods.

The use of message slips in laboratory experiments was first introduced by Festinger and has been used in a number of experiments carried out under his direction (Festinger et al. 1952). Communication in these experiments takes place by the subjects' passing messages on slips of paper instead of talking. The great advantage is that the difficulties of training observers for interaction recording, which will be described below, are avoided. Furthermore, permanent records of the interaction are produced, and they can be analysed at leisure by as many judges as desired, so that there are no difficulties about reliability. There should of course be the usual calculation of reliability, unless it is simply the sheer number of messages which is being measured. Other minor advantages are that the subjects are able to communicate 'anonymously' if required, while the messages can be traced by distinctive stapling; it is also easy to prearrange the messages which any subject is going to receive, as in Schachter, Ellertson and Gregory's experiment (1951), thus opening up a wide range of experimental possibilities. The disadvantage of this whole method is that it makes the situation artificial, and the influence of different modes of communication on behaviour is not known: it may be a very important variable.

Thirdly, we come to interaction recording and rating methods proper. In these a judge observes the behaviour to be recorded and decides in which of a series of categories it shall be placed. The human observer is not a mechanical or a perfect instrument, but it is possible to turn his selectivity of perception to good account. If an observer is trained in the use of a set of categories he can observe that dimension of behaviour very consistently. The observer may record the whole sequence of behaviour as a number of separate small units, he may sample it in various ways, or he may rate the sequence as a whole. The relative advantages of these procedures are discussed by Heyns and Zander (1953). Ratings may of course be used for any product of a subject—verbal or non-verbal behaviour, protocols of questionnaires or projection tests, or personal documents (Krech and Crutchfield 1948, pp. 234–45). It is the rating of social interactions which particularly concerns the social psychologist, and which will be dealt with here. This process of interaction recording was first developed by child psychologists like Thomas

(1929), and now constitutes one of the most powerful instruments of the social psychologist. The dimension of behaviour which is to be recorded is selected, and skilled observers are chosen: child psychologists for instance are used with children's groups, and observers must at all events be well steeped in the culture of the group members, or their interpretations will be incorrect. Most investigators have preferred to sacrifice a certain amount of reliability and have made use of skilled interpretation instead of using concretely defined categories.

While some investigators have attempted to record all aspects of group life, this entails either the use of several observers and an elaborate piecing together (e.g. Lippitt 1940), or the use of more categories than an observer can really handle (e.g. Carter et al. 1951a). One interesting feature of Lippitt's method is that it recorded changes in the group as a whole in addition to the behaviour of individuals. It is probably best to reserve the use of interaction recording for a late stage of investigation where there are definite hypotheses to be tested, and when it is necessary to record only certain selected aspects of the group process. There are several sets of categories of proved reliability which are suitable for general use. Of particular interest is that of Bales (1950), developed for recording group discussions and consisting of the following twelve categories: (1) Shows solidarity, (2) shows tension release, (3) agrees, (4) gives suggestion, (5) gives opinion, (6) gives orientation, (7) asks for orientation, (8) asks for opinion, (9) asks for suggestion, (10) disagrees, (11) shows tension, (12) shows antagonism. These categories can be grouped in several ways to make further categories. Other category sets of interest are the one used by Lippitt (1940) for aggressive behaviour, that devised by Fouriezos and co-workers (1950) for self-oriented needs in groups, and that of Snyder (1945) for the study of psychotherapy. Many others are listed by Bales in his bibliography (op. cit.).

When a new set of categories is being developed they should be clearly defined, mutually exclusive, of the same order of generality, and preferably homogeneous—for example in that all categories are aspects of problem-solving (Guetzkow 1950). The nature of the situation and of the hypotheses tested will suggest a number of categories. One can refine such a list and increase its reliability by trying it out and combining or subdividing, and redefining the categories. They should be communicable to others not directly instructed in their use.

For continuous recording it is best to have either a moving paper, divided into columns, as with Bales's 'interaction recorder' (Bales and Gerbrands 1948), or a typewriter adapted to printing categories and persons concerned, as used by Carter and his collaborators (1951a); with the latter the observer need not look down. In each case time is recorded automatically. The units of action recorded may be purely temporal, as in the early child studies—an entry being made for each time interval, or the material may be naturally divided, as in group discussion. Barker, Dembo and Lewin (1941) found that different information could be obtained by the use of different lengths of unit.

The observers must be trained in the use of the categories and unitising method adopted. While it may be advantageous to conceal from them the hypotheses to be tested, Bavelas has found that they learn faster if they help in the development of the categories. Training is conducted by post-mortems and discussion of difficulties, with the help of films if possible (Heyns and Zander 1953). Observers are considered trained when their reliability is high enough.

Reliability between observers can be calculated in several ways. Bales compares the number of acts placed in each category by different observers; Carter and his collaborators (1951b) correlate between the observers the number of acts in each category for each subject. Neither of these methods is very sensitive and the reliabilities found may be artificially enlarged by null categories. Better is Guetzkow's method (1950) of finding the percentage of all items categorised on which two observers agree. Reliability is reduced by the observers' responding to different symptoms, requiring different degrees of confidence before using a given category, and being influenced by their own needs, and also when there are too many categories or when these are not clearly defined.

One problem raised by the observation of behaviour is, what exactly is meant by 'behaviour'. To most experimental psychologists behaviour is the sum of physical movements made at any time; to Lewin and to Steinzor (1949) it is the 'meaning' of the action to the agent, while to Bales it is the impression made on others. Thelen and Withall (1949) compared the records of observers who responded to the 'objective' facts, of observers who tried to record from the point of view of the subjects, and records made by the agents themselves. They found that there was very little difference on the average, though there is no doubt that there is sometimes a difference for two people in the meaning of an act.

Interaction recording may be studied through the medium of tape-recordings and film strips. For a group with relatively little overt non-verbal behaviour a tape-recording probably supplies all that is needed, but it does omit expressions and gestures which may be important in the interpretation of behaviour: the observer on the spot uses all this material in his categorisation. The advantages of tape-recordings and film strips are that they remove the observer from the scene of the interaction, and that they can be played through more than once, so that the test-retest reliability of an observer can be computed.

There is one method of interaction recording which must be mentioned, because a whole school of thought has embraced its use. Chapple and Arensberg (1940) originally introduced the method of simply recording the order and duration of successive communications, regardless of their content. It is assumed that the originator of a series of acts will be in some way directing the behaviour of the others, though there seems little ground for this assumption. Several investigators have used this method, and the concepts implied in it are central to the thought of the so-called 'interaction theorists' (Homans 1951; Argyris 1952). It may be objected however that the concepts of order and duration are much too crude for the erection of a theory of interaction. Even if empirical laws can be found in their terms, as some have been, these will tell us relatively little, and we shall want to know what type of interaction took place. For this some form of interaction recording is needed.

Another approach to the measurement of social interaction is for those involved to record their own behaviour. Thelen and Withall (1949), as mentioned above, found considerable agreement between the records of observers and those made by subjects pushing buttons during a group discussion. Carlson (1951) has made use of a similar technique for recording interactions between industrial managers: after each meeting or communication with someone else a standard form is filled in, and these are collected and analysed for a period of time. This method is discussed further in Chapter VI (p. 167 f.).

The Use of Records

The only investigations to be reported in this book in which use has been made of records are certain industrial studies described in Chapter VI. There is a separate discussion in that chapter on the measurement of output, absenteeism, and labour turnover from the records kept by firms. Other kinds of records are used extensively in more 'sociological' research—census tracts, various economic indices, lists of membership, etc., of organisations. There are many pitfalls in the use and interpretation of records, and in addition the raw data may suffer from the usual errors of collection, owing to the unwillingness of informants, the lack of skill of the collectors, or to variations in method (Angell and Freedman 1953).

THE LOGIC OF MEASUREMENT

The various measuring instruments used by the social psychologist have been mentioned above. Several questions must now be asked about the use of these instruments. In what sense of 'measurement' do they measure anything? What concepts constitute the dimensions of measurement? Have such methods any objective validity, mediated as they are by human judgments?

What Kind of Measurements can be Obtained of Social Behaviour?

In everyday life and in physics, measurements are usually on interval scales[1]—that is, scales on which the points are in a definite order, and the intervals between successive points equivalent. The scales of length, time, and weight, for instance, are of this kind. Measurements in experimental psychology are either in terms of physical scales, or sheer number, or on physiological scales; these are all interval scales. The investigator of social behaviour however is rarely able to use measurements of this type, and falls back on *ordinal* and *nominal* scales. The ordinal scale has a series of points in fixed order, but where the intervals between the points are not assumed to be equal. Rating scales and attitude scales are like this. The nominal scale is not really a scale at all, but just a series of categories which are distinct, though not in any order. Most systems of interaction recording are of this type. With the ordinal scale there is measurement along conceptual dimensions; with the nominal scale there is categorisation, the concepts being related either to the categories themselves or to relations between them like frequency distributions, or sequences. The only interval scales in social psychology are those of time, distance, or number, when they are part of the data.

It is claimed that the Thurstone attitude scale gives measurements

[1] Actually, with the exception of most temperature scales, they are on 'ratio' scales; that is, interval scales with zero points so that ratios are meaningful. This distinction will not be discussed further here.

on an interval scale, and investigators making use of this scale have often used statistical methods appropriate to interval scales (Thurstone and Chave 1929). It would be so valuable to be able to obtain equal-interval measurements from interview data that this claim demands some examination. To construct a Thurstone scale a large number of statements expressing attitudes towards the object in question are ranked by a large number of judges. They place the statements in eleven groups so that the 'attitudinal distances' between adjacent groups are felt to be equivalent; this adaptation of the 'equi-appearing interval method' of classical psychophysics is the basis for the claim that this is an interval scale. Those statements with the smallest standard deviation between the judges—i.e. whose scale position is most agreed on—are kept, and the scale value of each is its median position among the heaps. To use the scale, a subject ticks those statements with which he agrees, and his attitude is represented by the average scale number of these statements. It is clear that there are equal intervals here in the sense of equi-appearing intervals, but is this sufficient to justify calculating means and standard deviations?[1]

There are two objections to treating the Thurstone scale as an interval scale in the latter sense. The first is an empirical objection. It was found that the method of scaling by equi-appearing intervals in the case of pitch was not always self-consistent (Stevens and Davis 1937, pp. 121-3). (Thus if successive equi-appearing intervals AB and BC are bisected by D and E respectively, and if the interval DE is then bisected, this mid-point does not turn out to be B.) This shows that, however else it may be possible to chart subjective dimensions, this particular operation is not adequate to do it. The second objection is methodological. Bergmann and Spence (1944) point out that the operation for showing when units are equal is performed by the subject, whereas a true operational definition is always in terms of operations carried out by the scientist. It might, of course, be possible to devise operations which would provide a criterion for equality of units. One might be to call equal the average shifts of attitude at different points of the scale when the same amount of propaganda (or other pressure to change) is experienced. There is a practical objection to this, that propaganda from different extremes of the scale would be sure to produce different patterns of change, while it may be felt odd to make equal by definition a series of such shifts at different attitudinal distances from the source of

[1] cf. Guilford (1950), Chapter V.

propaganda. It would be necessary to devise some other operation which would not be open to these difficulties. Thus, while it is not in principle impossible to find an acceptable criterion for equal units of attitude, it seems on balance that the Thurstone scale does not constitute an equal-interval scale.

To conclude this section, the statistical methods which it is possible to use with the different kinds of scale will be reviewed. The great importance of statistical methods will be emphasised in the section on Design of Investigations, when it will be shown that no valid conclusions can be drawn in the social sciences without them.

There are two principal ways in which statistics are used in social investigations—for comparing the scores of two batches of individuals (or other units), and for finding correlations between two sets of scores. Under ideal conditions, that is to say assuming equal-interval scales and normal distribution of the data, it is possible to compare the means of two sets of scores and to find out the chances that the scores are drawn from two different populations—that the means are 'significantly different'.[1] With the same assumptions, the correlation or degree of association between two sets of scores can be calculated quite simply.[2] When equal-interval scales are not in use, or where it is not possible to assume normality of distribution,[3] so-called 'non-parametric' methods have to be used. A variety of methods for testing the significance of difference of two sets of scores has now been developed.[4] For correlations under these conditions the various methods of rank correlation are available.[5] There are many examples in the literature where investigations using data which are really ordinal have been worked out as if interval scales were being used. When data are not measured along dimensions at all but simply obtained as frequencies in categories, as is the case with interaction-recording data, the degree of association between the categories can be assessed by a further type of calculation.[6]

There are many other statistical procedures for other purposes and other arrangements of the material. This is just an outline of the tests available, depending on the kind of measurements made and whether correlations or means are being examined.

[1] The *t* test. See Guilford (1950), p. 227 f.
[2] Product-moment correlation. See Guilford, op. cit., Chapter VIII.
[3] It is sometimes possible to normalise a set of scores by expressing them as multiples of the standard deviation. See Guilford, op. cit., Chapter XII.
[4] e.g. The Sign Test. See K. Smith (1953).
[5] *rho, tau*, etc. See Guilford, op. cit., Chapter XIII.
[6] *chi square*. See Guilford, op. cit., p. 273 f.

What Concepts are Measured in Social Psychology?

The empirical laws of a science consist of functional relationships between the values of two or more concepts. These concepts are related to actual observations by 'operational definitions' which state how their values are found. The empirical status of the various kinds of theoretical construct used in explanation will be considered in the next chapter. The needs of theory or of practice lead to attempts to measure certain empirical variables—as in the case of human motivation and intelligence respectively. On the other hand, the invention of new measuring instruments leads to the possibility of new concepts and empirical laws—such as the various uses of Sociometry and the measures which Bales (1950) derives from his method of recording behaviour. This two-way interaction between discovery of methods and the demands of theory and practice leads gradually to more useful concepts. The study of social behaviour is not sufficiently developed as a science for an agreed set of concepts to have developed yet, and different schools have emphasised different variables and measuring instruments.

Helen Peak (1953) has emphasised the importance of empirical variables having some kind of 'functional unity'. That is to say, measurements should stand for stable psychological entities, revealed by methods of scaling, correlation, or factor analysis. Investigators who have simply used the answers to single questions as their dependent variables ought to demonstrate that they have measured psychological entities of general significance and not mere artefacts of the measuring method.

There are as many concepts for describing social behaviour as there are systems of interaction recording. Bales (1950) made a notable attempt to produce a set of categories which could be used universally as a standard way of recording social behaviour in small groups. This system however is particularly oriented towards problem-solving in discussion groups and does not for instance measure 'self-oriented' and 'group-oriented' needs as does the system due to Fouriezos and others (1950). On the other hand, the category set of Carter and others (1951a), which attempts to be universal, has too many categories for normal use. Perhaps the best approach would be to develop several instruments, each of which measured one aspect of social behaviour with precision and could be regarded as the standard way of recording that variable. This would at the same time standardise the corresponding concepts for describing social behaviour. Such concepts could be derived from the records in various ways—they could be operationally defined by the frequency of acts in a certain category, as is most usual, or by ratios of frequencies, as with Bales's 'Index of Difficulty of Communication' (op. cit., p. 141), or by analysis of the sequences in a series of interactions.

Interview material is used to measure a great variety of concepts. Many dimensions of perception, attitudes, and motivation have in fact been measured, as was indicated in a previous section, so that concepts of these three types can be included in a theory of social behaviour. There is as yet however no agreed set of concepts in general use.

The concepts derived from political and religious attitudes, and from personality measures in general, are in a more satisfactory position. There are, in the first place, plenty of familiar dimensions for such attitudes and traits, and in the second place it is possible by factor analysis to find the clusters of such attitudes or traits, so that attention can be focused on the more important ones. Examples of this are the Authoritarian Personality study of race prejudice (Adorno et al. 1950), and the factor analysis of personality traits by Eysenck (1952). There are two criteria for the selection of such clusters—the intercorrelation of many measurements and the psychological meaningfulness of the result. If a factor analysis fails to produce dimensions which are psychologically meaningful it is always possible to 'rotate the axes' until meaningful dimensions are found.

Various concepts and measurements concern not single personalities but groups of people *qua* groups. The objection is often made that this or that group concept is 'invalid' in some way: the answer to this is that any concept for which a satisfactory form of operational definition exists is admissible. Consider, for instance, the concept of 'group needs' implied by some exponents of 'functional' explanations, like Roethlisberger and Dickson (1939, Chapter XXII) when they say that an output restriction norm serves the function of protecting the group against outside interference. No one has ever measured group needs, and it is difficult to see how it could be done. Possibly a behavioural criterion could be found in terms of joint goal-seeking and quiescence when the goal has been reached. On the other hand, Cattell's 'group syntality' (1948)—the group equivalent of 'personality'—seems valid enough. It may however be questioned how far the dimensions arrived at via factor analysis of group behaviour are sufficiently meaningful. An alternative is to use concepts built from simpler elements such as 'group cohesiveness', measured as the percentage of sociometric choices which are made to other members of the group (Festinger et al. 1950). Again there are few concepts in common use for describing groups, apart from attributes of the individual members. There is no agreed way of measuring 'degree of stratification', for example, or 'degree of conformity to norms'. Further research is needed before a satisfactory set of concepts comes into common use.

The Use of the 'Human Instrument'

In all the methods of measurement using interviewers, judges, or observers, a human being is part of the measuring instrument, and the combination has sometimes been referred to as a 'human instrument'. This includes all measurements of social behaviour with the exception of questionnaire results with multiple-response answers which can be scored mechanically, direct physical or physiological measurements, and some objective records. In this section the scientific status of measurements involving human instruments will be examined.

Methodologically, there is no great difference between these measurements and those obtained mechanically—for the investigator has always to read the final pointer reading in whatever way this is obtained. However, there is not likely to be much variation between observers in their reading of the same pointer, whereas the phenomena to be studied in the field of social behaviour are far more complex and difficult to score. In the case of the interviewer too, the investigator does more than merely read off the score: in a very real sense he *is* the instrument itself. The human instrument can be examined in exactly the same way as any other measuring device. It is simply a question of assessing its accuracy in the usual way—by finding its reliability and validity. Reliability in this case is interpreted as the amount of agreement between different people as observers or interviewers. It is, then, a measure of the extent to which the measurements are objective and public. As will be shown later, it is difficult to calculate the 'validity' of methods of observing behaviour, since there is no external criterion. Thus reliability is sometimes the only measure of the adequacy of the human instrument, and there are grounds for supposing that this is not enough. In the first place, although it is possible to train different people so that their results correlate—so that they have a high inter-observer reliability—yet they may all be suffering from a common error or bias of some kind. The answer to this is that even so, the instrument in use, complete with bias, is adequate within the limits of the investigation in question. All that is affected is the extent to which the results are communicable to others out of contact with the actual measurements, or comparable with other results obtained ostensibly by using the same instrument. The only way to escape from this difficulty is to make quite clear in detail the principles guiding the activity of the human instrument. Bales has attempted to do this for his twelve categories of behaviour (op. cit., Appendix).

The second way in which measuring instruments are often assessed is by finding their validity. The usual way of measuring the validity of a measuring instrument is by comparing it with a better measure—the defining criterion—of the same quantity: thus an attitude questionnaire can be validated against overt behaviour, and an aptitude test by its success in selection. A second method of validation is by testing the prediction of a theory: if the expected measurements are obtained, they validate both the theory and the measuring instrument to some extent. For instance, Luria validated his method of detecting unconscious complexes by inducing them hypnotically and finding the effect on the measurements made (White 1944, p. 226). A third method is to assert that the measurement in question *is* the defining criterion or operational definition for the empirical variable in question. The test is then said to have 'face validity', and the variable is named in accordance with the obvious nature of the test. A final method is that of internal validity, which does not establish any relation with independent criteria but simply shows that the index in question correlates highly with other indices. This is the same process as the establishment of functional unity considered previously.

Interview material referring either to facts or to behaviour can clearly be validated against an external criterion. Interview material referring to perceptions and beliefs cannot be validated in this way. While reports of perceptions could, in principle, be validated by the experimental method, it is hard to see how this could be done in practice for beliefs. The only alternative is to award face validity to such verbal reports. On the other hand, it is well known that people will say different things to different interviewers, so that we need grounds for deciding which answer has the face validity. These could be provided by knowledge of the situations which are of minimum constraint in terms of influencing verbal statements which *can* be validated, e.g. about attitudes.

Methods of observing behaviour cannot be validated against an external criterion, though various investigators thought that they were doing so. If the criterion is another measuring device, they are merely comparing two instruments; if it is a test, they are simply seeing how far social behaviour can be predicted from test scores; if it is contemporary introspections, they are just comparing conscious representations of behaviour with categorisation from outside. Heyns and Zander (1953, p. 408 f.) suggest the use of the experimental method of validation, but as yet this has not been done and investigators rely on the face validity of their instruments.

The Disturbance of the Behaviour to be Studied by the Investigator

One disadvantage of human beings as experimental animals is that they are generally aware of the fact that they are being studied, and may change their behaviour in order to impress the investigator in one way or another. This effect varies with the situation and diminishes with time. The sort of behaviour studied by the experimental psychologist is not so open to influences of this sort since he usually studies behaviour which is involuntary, or behaviour which is motivated by the desire to do well and impress the investigator. It is hard to see how either of these types of behaviour could be used by the social investigator, and that which is usually studied is open to all manner of influences—the desire to be seen in a certain light, the desire to appear not to have been influenced by the experimental variable, and so on. In physics this is a familiar problem—the ammeter introduced to a circuit to measure a current changes the current as a result of its own resistance—but this resistance is a known quantity and so correction can be made. Social psychology is not sufficiently far advanced for the 'stimulus value' of human investigators to be calculable, though it is obvious that some are more disturbing than others, and in ways that are sometimes understood.[1] The only way out is to try to minimise these effects—the equivalent of using ammeters of very small resistance. The possible roles of the observer will be discussed from the point of view of minimal disturbance of the behaviour studied. In addition to the question of the disturbance of behaviour there is the involvement of the observer in the behaviour that he is watching. Horowitz and others (1951) found for instance that social perceptions were affected by a person's attitude to the people perceived. The distortions introduced via the involvement of the observer may be regarded as

[1] The influence of an audience on behaviour is discussed on p. 105 ff.

providing a second criterion for assessing the various observer roles which are possible.

In the case of the interview the equivalent problem is the extent to which different interviewers get the same results, and how the answers vary as a function of the behaviour of the interviewer. It is generally assumed that the kind of interview or questionnaire which enables the best prediction of overt behaviour is the most valuable, though it must be realised that this would mean in the case of antisocial attitudes that the interview should impose as much restraint on verbal expression as society normally imposes on overt expression of the attitude in question. This is not the same as finding the person's conscious desires.

In addition to these problems of the disturbances created by the investigator, there is the question of the morality of various kinds of investigation. In order to minimise these disturbances resort is often made to the one-way screen, and to the disguised or 'participant' observer. Some maintain that these practices are to be condemned on moral grounds. In evaluating the rightness of an act it is however necessary to consider not only the nature of the act itself as an act of deception, etc.—but also the consequences of the act. It is maintained here that in the case of a responsible investigator who ensures that no harm comes to his subjects, the scientific and ultimately humanitarian fruits of his research will be the weightier consideration. Various kinds of deception are of course common both in psychological research and in medical practice. With regard to the one-way screen, it may be said that laboratory subjects frequently suppose they are being secretly observed when they are not, and this is felt to be part of the legitimate art of the psychologist. So far as the participant observer is concerned, it should be pointed out that he really *is* employed in the job (or whatever the role entails) and that a common reason for taking a job is to gain experience. It may be concluded that while the social scientist has obligations to his subjects, these are quite compatible with what in other contexts might appear as deception.

(i) *Observer Roles*

There are three possible roles for the observer which will be discussed—the concealed-observer role, the participant observer, and the observer as undisguised social scientist.

The concealed investigator role includes the use of one-way vision screens, the taking of tape-recordings unknown to the subjects, and the subsequent examination of records collected for other purposes. The first two methods have been extensively used in laboratory experiments and studies of children. On the first criterion this method has the enormous advantage that the observed behaviour is undisturbed by the investigator, unless the subjects are suspicious. Lack of disturbance is extremely important in the detailed analysis of social behaviour where every social influence is important, and a group of three quite different from a group of two.

Secondly, the observer is remote from the object of study and his involvement minimal. Benne and Sheats (1948) describe how training in objectivity is given by group members taking the 'observer role' and not participating; this would obviously be increased by concealment of the observer. On the other hand he may, if inexperienced, feel anxiety or guilt over his anomalous position and this may affect his perceptions, especially of the emotions and intentions of the subjects. Murray (1933) has shown how emotional states can affect perception in this way. This can be overcome by means of films and tape-recordings. As regards the areas of research for which the concealed-observer role is suitable, it is clearly limited on the whole to laboratory studies. While obviously unsuitable in industry and primitive society, there are a number of field situations where it might be valuable.

The second observer role to be considered is that of the participant observer who is disguised as a member of the society or group being studied. As mentioned above, social behaviour is very sensitive to an observer, the particular form of this influence depending on how he is perceived, and how the subjects wish to impress an audience of this type. The disturbance would be expected to be minimal if the observer (*a*) appears to be an ordinary member of the society or group, and (*b*) keeps passively in the background and does not show an ostentatious interest in what is going on. He will feel probably more anxiety than the concealed observer, since he must act a part if he is not to be found out. He cannot take notes, and some investigators have used mnemonic systems to help their memories when writing up the events afterwards (Lindgren 1935). There may also be difficulty in the publication of results, save in a very general or disguised form. The records of the participant observer may gain in areas of covert behaviour; he will share the experiences of the people studied and gain greater insight into the emotional significance of the behaviour (Kluckhohn 1940). The investigator who engages in 'functional penetration', i.e. who occupies specific positions in a social organisation, has a unique opportunity to observe how people behave towards the occupant of those positions. One observer can hold only one such position at a time, and sometimes a whole team of investigators has entered a community at different levels (Oeser 1939). It may be concluded that the participant-observer method of observing behaviour in the field can be of considerable value in making possible the study of behaviour in social organisations, without disturbing it.

The third observer role is that of the undisguised social scientist, the role normally adopted by anthropologists and sociologists. The great problem is how to minimise the disturbing effect of a scientific observer. Most writers agree that it is necessary to enter at the top and gain acceptance by the leaders of the society or organisation being studied (cf. Gardner and Whyte 1946). This helps with acceptance at lower levels. Another good plan is to prepare the community by straightforward advance notice of the nature and aims of the investigation, while Mann (1951) has suggested a general education of public opinion with regard to social research. Despite such preparations, the initial entry of the observer is bound to affect the behaviour of those observed, though experience suggests that after a few weeks the society settles down (Roethlisberger and Dickson 1939, p. 399 f.). It cannot be assumed however that the final state of the social system will be identical with the first. As for the second criterion, the observer can avoid becoming involved with particular individuals or groups, is free from the worries of subterfuge, and may even be able to take notes. It may be concluded that this observer role, while imperfect on the first criterion, has considerable advantages, and if used with care and tact can yield useful results.

(ii) *Interviewer Roles*

The interview raises different problems, and a single criterion may be used: how valid are the subject's replies, in the sense of 'valid' defined above? The principal focus of discussion may be taken as the influence of various kinds of interviewer on the answers to questions. The motivation of the subject and the effect of the interaction sequence *per se* will be considered afterwards.

With regard to the influence of an audience on verbal replies, much the same principles apply as in the case of an observer. People are unwilling to disclose intimate or socially disapproved matters to an interviewer: Kinsey (1948) used special techniques, such as placing the onus of denial on the subject, in his study of sexual behaviour; this method is of course open to the objection that it encourages certain answers. On the other hand, there is some evidence that people will sometimes tell a stranger things they would not admit to their associates, and so it seems desirable for an interviewer to have no connection with a respondent's ordinary life. In a similar way an interviewer should not be in any authoritative or official relationship with the subject, or the replies will be influenced by the desire to produce some impression. For example, Doob (1937) found that taking the role of a social relief worker produced a great readiness to talk about money, while it is notorious that an investigator suspected of connection with the management is distrusted by industrial workers. On the other hand, it may be advantageous for the interviewer to be of high social status: while people are glad to be consulted by those higher in the social stratum they may feel they are wasting their time in giving their views to a person of lower status (Riesman and Glaser 1948). This last consideration does not apply to the study of political opinions, since subjects tend to alter their replies to 'please' the interviewer, and middle-class interviewers tend to produce a conservative bias in the replies. In the same way Negro or Jewish interviewers will elicit less racially prejudiced answers (Cantril 1944).

These face-to-face influences can largely be eliminated by use of the questionnaire, though this is subject to the various disadvantages mentioned above, and as was indicated does not altogether avoid all audience effects. There are two interviewer roles which do succeed to some extent in obviating these difficulties. One is simply the role of social scientist under conditions in which the subjects have been suitably informed about the objects of the research—as with the equivalent observer role. They should not, of course, be told anything which will enable them to modify their answers through the wish to prove or disprove the hypotheses being tested. Another general strategy is to disguise the investigator, as in the case of the participant observer. 'Total immersion' is least disturbing, but makes too much questioning difficult—casual questioning and listening must suffice. The 'student' role is easier to act and permits questioning; Whyte (1943) took the role of 'local historian', which comes in this category. The 'student' may however be of too high a status for some groups.

The motivation of the subject to distort answers in particular ways has been discussed above. There is a further question concerning the motivation of the subject to answer at all, and to answer truthfully. The ordinary social investigator must rely on such incentives as persuading the subject to co-operate in a piece of research, and one which might lead to desirable social changes, the provision of a sympathetic listener, or actually paying him (Cannell and Kahn 1953). It is here that the psychoanalytic interview does have great advantages, for clearly a patient has a greater incentive for frank disclosure than the ordinary subject, and it is possible to explore the most intimate topics for long periods. Against this however must be set the drawbacks mentioned in the discussion of this form of interview in a previous section. In the social application of the psychoanalytic method by the Tavistock Institute it is hard to see that under those conditions there is really any incentive for truthfulness, and in any case the enormous complexity of the conditions makes any particular results hard to evaluate.

THE DESIGN OF SOCIAL INVESTIGATIONS

Introduction

Some writers on the social sciences maintain that there are three methods of social research—observation, interview, and experiment; they say that these are in order of increasing rigour, with the proviso that experiments are of course impossible in this field. The real situation is that interview and observation are the major techniques for obtaining measurements of the raw data, but that to draw conclusions in the form of empirical laws there must be an adequate research design. It is certainly true that there are various kinds of preliminary or exploratory study useful for forming or sharpening hypotheses (cf. Jahoda et al. 1951, p. 32 f.), but the real scientific work of testing hypotheses and finding empirical laws must be conducted with a proper design. Such designs include not only experiments, but in addition various kinds of valid non-experimental design. It is contended here that any investigation which does not employ one of these designs cannot yield results of a scientific character. While this contention will be accepted by psychologists and by natural scientists, many sociologists apparently think differently, so the grounds for making it will be set out in the course of this section.

Experiments will be defined as investigations in which the situation or subjects are systematically manipulated by the investigator, and controlled observations made, so that a definite hypothesis about the relation of variables can be tested (Underwood 1949, pp. 11–14). In *valid non-experimental studies* the events under investigation take place without interference by the investigator. The design may be the same as that of an experiment, the experimental variable being introduced in other ways, or it may take the form of finding a correlation between pairs of measurements of a series of events, individuals, or groups. Some social scientists maintain that valid scientific influences may be made from *case-studies*, which may be defined as investigations of an individual or group in which the variables studied are characteristics of the individual or group, and not of any sub-units of it. This claim will be further examined and the definition further elucidated in the following section. The designs of valid non-experimental, and of experimental, studies will be discussed in later sections.

The positive argument for the sole validity of the first two groups of designs may now be stated. The generally accepted criteria for saying that one phenomenon is causally related with another are the methods originally formulated by Mill (1851) (cf. Cohen and Nagel 1939, Chap. VIII). These are methods of disproof, that is of eliminating causal propositions. It is impossible to prove a causal relation; all that can be done is to obtain repeated confirmations by means of these methods. Of the various methods two are the most important. The Method of Difference states:

"If an instance in which the phenomenon under investigation occurs, and an instance in which it does not occur, have every circumstance in common save one, that one occurring only in the former; the circumstance in which alone the two instances differ is the effect, or the cause, or an indispensable part of the cause, of the phenomenon" (Mill 1851, **1,** p. 397).

The experimental designs are applications of this method. The other important method due to Mill is the Method of Concomitant Variations, which states:

"Whatever phenomenon varies in any manner whenever another phenomenon varies in some particular manner, is either a cause or an effect of that phenomenon, or is connected with it through some fact of causation" (Mill 1851, **1,** p. 409).

The correlational type of non-experimental design is an application of this method. It should be made clear that if A and B have been found to vary concomitantly, it does not follow that A causes B or that B causes A, for there are two other possibilities. Firstly, A and

B may be functionally interdependent, i.e. they may form a system within which they mutually influence each other. This possibility has been emphasised by the sociologists Weber and Pareto. Secondly, A and B may be common effects of C. These possibilities can be investigated by examination of the causal process, or by experimental investigations proper.

It is important to notice that with each of these methods of scientific inference it is necessary to consider a whole series of events before a causal relation can be demonstrated. In the Method of Concomitant Variations it is obvious that a number of pairs of measurements must be taken, representing the values of the two variables whose functional relation is being studied. In the Method of Difference it is necessary to use statistical methods, since in a science where there are uncontrolled variables it is impossible to find two instances differing in only one respect. All that can be done is to use two batches[1] of events which are equated or randomised with respect to other variables. A calculation may then be made of whether the average difference between the two batches could have occurred by chance alone. Strictly speaking, a similar calculation of 'significance' has to be made with correlational studies, to see if the correlation obtained could have occurred by chance, so that with this design there are two reasons for studying a plurality of events.

The Study of Single Cases

A case-study was defined above as an investigation of an individual or group in which the variables which are measured and whose empirical relation is explored are characteristics of the individual or group and not of a sub-unit of it. For example, a study of a single community which relates the family organisation to the level of economic development of that community is a case-study; a study of a single community which is concerned with the relation of size and leadership of small groups within it (e.g. Hemphill 1950*a*) is a valid non-experimental study of certain sub-groups in that community. Again, consider the Bank Wiring Observation Room study in the final phase of the Hawthorne studies (Roethlisberger and Dickson 1939, Part IV). In this group there was cohesiveness and a norm of output restriction: these phenomena are characteristics of the group and therefore, as an investigation of the relation between them, this must be regarded as a case-study. On the other hand, there was also

[1] The term 'batch' is used in order to avoid using 'group' in any sense other than 'social group'.

in this group a relation between the output and status of the men in it: these are characteristics of the members, i.e. sub-units, of the group, and the study of the relation between them constitutes a valid non-experimental study, albeit of somewhat limited generality. To study the relation between characteristics of personality it is necessary to study a number of individuals, and the same applies to groups and to communities. On the other hand it is perfectly possible to carry out a valid investigation of a single case, by statistical comparisons between different groups of measures. Thus Baldwin (1946) located trait-groupings in individual subjects by discovering which response-tendencies co-varied with time; Heron (1956) found the statistical difference between a series of response measures before and after an experimental change. The results are, of course, only valid for the case in question.

In addition to case-studies there are in the literature many reports of bad experiments, from which no valid conclusions can be drawn. A prominent example of this is the famous Relay Assembly Test Room experiment, also one of the Hawthorne studies. This has been examined in detail elsewhere (Argyle 1953*a*), and it is instructive to see how impossible it is to assess the weight of uncontrolled and fortuitous variables in such an investigation. While no scientific conclusions can be drawn from such bad experiments, they may often be suggestive of fruitful hypotheses.

It is now necessary to examine the claim that it is possible to draw valid inferences from the results of case-studies. It should be clear that case-studies as defined in this section do not satisfy the conditions for valid scientific inference as set out in the previous section, so that the supporters of the case-study method must use another type of scientific inference.

The first type of argument has been put forward by various psychiatrists and anthropologists, and is often associated with Allport (1937). This is to the effect that since each personality (or society, in the case of the equivalent anthropological argument) is unique, it is no good looking for general laws common to all. The error in this argument is that the uniqueness of each personality resides not in its laws, but in the constants which have to be inserted in the general laws. As Eysenck points out, each personality is certainly unique in that it differs quantitatively from others on many variables; the unique event is not an object of science, which seeks general laws about different events (1952, p. 18 f.). In any case it is curious to say that general laws should not be looked for when so many have been found. In the field of personality there are laws about the influence of various kinds of experience upon subsequent development, and of the regular correlation of certain attributes in developed personalities. The general laws about groups will be reviewed in Chapter V, and although there are fewer general laws about whole societies, a number have been found (cf. Sorokin 1928; Murdoch 1949).

The second argument in favour of the case-study method is that provided by psychoanalysts and functional anthropologists who practise the 'clinical method'. In psychoanalysis the position is admirably stated by T. M. French (1944, p. 257):

"It [the psychoanalytic interpretation] must find in the life history and present circumstances of the patient the proper emotional context for his apparently irrational behaviour so that his behaviour becomes 'natural' and 'understandable' to us."

The psychoanalyst explains the patient's behaviour by postulating unconscious motivations which, had they been conscious, would have made the patient's behaviour seem quite reasonable. There are further tests for validating such an interpretation—whether the patient is cured, whether he ultimately accepts it, and whether further behaviour or symptoms can be predicted from it. It is important to notice that no causal relationship is being inferred here at all, though it may sometimes seem to be implied in statements about childhood experiences. As stated above, causal laws cannot possibly be inferred from case-studies, but interpretations of the motivational state of an individual *can* be so inferred along the lines indicated above. The anthropologist, seeking to give a functional interpretation of the institutions of a society which he has studied, proceeds in a similar way to the psychoanalyst. Again the interpretation may be supported by the citation of evidence, and similarly it is not a causal law which is established: for this the comparative method is required.

Snygg and Combs (1949) and others using the phenomenal field approach claim that the causal explanation of any piece of behaviour can be arrived at by introspection. This claim is criticised at length in Chapter III (p. 84 ff.), so it will not be pursued here.

There are however certain points which have been made in connection with case-studies which may be admitted. As Lewin (1931) points out, it may be misleading to use statistical methods until the cases which are combined into groups for numerical treatment have been shown to be comparable. An example of this is that the comparative method in anthropology runs into difficulties about what constitutes a society in different cases, i.e. what is the appropriate unit for analysis. A second point which may be admitted is that in order to understand or to predict the behaviour of an individual or group, diagnosis must be made so that the values of the constants to be inserted in the empirical laws may be found. Although certain laws have been discovered, and certain empirical variables measured, social science has not yet reached the stage at which this can be done accurately. Thirdly, it is certainly true that the detailed study of a single case can be the source of valuable insights into possible mechanisms, so that fruitful hypotheses may be formulated. This is probably the most important use of case-studies. Lastly, while a single case cannot confirm a general law, it is sufficient to refute one, though not with very great force, since other uncontrolled variables may have been responsible.

What is the proper procedure for accounting for single instances of a phenomenon, or of the activities of single individuals or groups? Unfortunately, it is far more elaborate than the shorter methods advocated by certain clinical and phenomenological psychologists. Firstly, the independent variables which may be causally related to the behaviour must be located and the generalisations established which give the relevant causal relationships. Then the values of the independent variables and of the behaviour to be explained must be determined by measurement at the time in question, and the phenomenon shown to be an instance of the generalisations previously established. Finally, theories can be postulated to explain the generalisations, and therefore all instances of them.

Valid Non-experimental Designs

There are no experiments in astronomy, but the astronomer has the advantage that he can rely on each of his readings without fear of their being influenced by random uncontrolled variables. The social scientist suffers from a dual difficulty—the great difficulty of performing satisfactory experiments and the operation of uncontrolled influences. The second difficulty denies him the use of single instances, as argued above, so that valid non-experimental investigations must be statistical studies of a number of cases. There is one way of finding simultaneous functional relations, and there are two ways of finding causal sequences in time.

The first consists simply of finding correlations between two measures—each taken over a number of cases. An example (when the units are whole societies) is the correlation found by Hobhouse and others (1915) between economic conditions and other social institutions. At the group level there is the study by Katz and his co-workers (1951) of the productivity and manner of supervision of railway gangs. At the individual level there is the study by Festinger and others (1950) of the relations of geographical position, attitudes, and popularity in a group. Factorial studies of individuals (e.g. Eysenck 1952) or groups (Cattell 1948) could be included in this category, though the series of tests entailed in a factorial study makes it resemble an experiment. To establish a correlation of this kind does not of course show that any causal relation exists between the variables. Further investigation is needed to show if there is causation and if so in which direction, or if both variables are effects of a common cause, or if they are interdependent.

Of the two methods of cause-effect investigation, the so-called *ex post facto* method developed by Chapin (1947) is the most interesting. It is a modification of the after-only experiment with a matched control batch, in which the control batch is equated after the event with the group which has been exposed to the experimental variable. The two groups are matched in some way and their difference on the dependent variables assessed. There are two major difficulties with the method. Firstly, matching after the event results in the loss of up to 80% of the experimental population. Greenwood (1945) has discussed ways of reducing this. Second, there may be self-selection by the subjects for exposure to the experimental variable: if leaflets are distributed, those who agree with the content are more likely to read them. In some cases it is possible to discover if this has happened (Jahoda et al. 1951, pp. 286-93), but *ex post facto* results must always be analysed with care because of this possibility. In a genuine experiment the investigator allocates subjects to experimental or control batches at random.

A second way of establishing cause-effect relations is by means of so-called 'natural experiments'. Methodologically it makes no difference whether the manipulation of conditions necessary for an experiment is performed by the experimenter, by an administrator, or by chance. It is usual to call it a natural experiment in the last two cases, but obviously the calculation of results is not affected. While it is possible to perform experiments proper on individuals and on small social groups without undue difficulty, it is not possible to do experiments on whole societies. In addition there are areas of individual and small group research where humanitarian considerations prohibit the experimental method proper. Unfortunately most cases quoted of natural experiments do not come up to the required standards. The study by Leighton and Kluckhohn (1947), for instance, of three communities which differed in their exposure to certain variables, can only be regarded as a bad experiment since insufficient numbers were present. Such studies may however be even more suggestive than single case-studies, and if the three communities had been very similar in other relevant respects, tentative support for an hypothesis might have been obtained. A few valid natural experiments have however been performed which included over a hundred subjects in both experimental and control groups. The problems of design are the same as for experiments proper.

A third method which has been used for finding causal sequences makes the assumption that the culture of a society remains constant. The relation between childhood experiences and subsequent adult personality can then be investigated by the study of contemporary child-rearing methods and contemporary adult personality—the general approach of the Culture and Personality school of Kardiner, Du Bois and others. One of the few such studies which seems to measure up to the criteria for valid non-experimental methods is that of Whiting and Child (1953), who compared seventy-five societies. However, a causal interpretation cannot be attached to this investigation since child-rearing methods generally harmonise with other cultural influences and it is not possible to say that adult personality is related specifically to childhood experiences; in addition inheritance may be a common causal factor. When there is a discontinuity of experiences the later ones are often the more important, as Orlansky (1949) has pointed out. It may be concluded that this method is quite invalid, and that the only way to study this particular problem is by experiments or *ex post facto* studies, of which many have been carried out (cf. Orlansky, op. cit., and Child 1954).

It may be concluded that while the last method discussed is invalid, the three preceding ones are perfectly legitimate. In addition they have the advantage over experiments proper of not being artificial. These designs are of great importance and have often been overlooked by social scientists.

Experiments

There has been a great deal of argument as to whether experimentation is possible in the social sciences. Part of this has turned on the definition of 'experiment': the term will be confined here to investigations in which the investigator himself manipulates the conditions and makes observations in order to test an hypothesis. It has been objected that when the experimental approach is adopted, investigations tend to become 'artificial and trivial'—though this is, of course, better than being 'realistic, large, important, woolly and totally inconclusive' (Madge 1953, p. 261). In the field of experimental psychology, the experimental method has been used with great success over a very wide range of situations and types of behaviour. As will be seen in later chapters the experimental method has been extended to quite a variety of social phenomena, particularly in the field of small groups and interaction within pairs of people. While certainly not trivial, many of these experiments could be said to be artificial, so that the findings may not be true of naturally occurring behaviour. In the study of social organisations and communities there have been a few heroic attempts at experimentation, though never with a sufficient number of units for statistical tests to be applied (cf. Madge, op. cit.). The only successful scientific studies of such large sections of society have been where one of the valid non-experimental approaches has been used.

In the type of social research with which we are primarily concerned here there are three broad strategies. Firstly, every possible device can be used to conceal from the subjects that an experiment is in progress and that measurements are being made. Examples of this are Lippitt's experiment (1940) on boys' clubs where apparently deception was complete, and various industrial field studies such as those on group decision where the investigator was able to persuade administrators to make the necessary experimental changes (French 1953). Secondly, all pretence at naturalism may be abandoned, and subjects may communicate with message slips instead of talking, or wear oxygen masks or blood-pressure apparatus. It may be argued that behaviour taking place under such conditions is just as genuine and just as legitimate an object of study as any other, and that it is thus possible to answer questions that could not otherwise be tackled. As long as a more natural type of investigation is also being carried out on similar issues this seems a very desirable kind of research. In fact many experiments in our field fall somewhere between the first and the second kinds we have considered. The third strategy is not strictly experimental at all and comprises the valid non-experimental methods. These supplement proper experiments in that behaviour is studied in its normal setting.

The classical illustration of the disturbing effect of the experiment upon the phenomena under investigation is the experiment in the Relay Assembly Test Room of the Hawthorne plant of the Western Electric Company. Five girls were moved into a test room and kept under observation for five years, during which time a number of changes were made in the conditions of work, such as introducing rest periods and shorter hours. There was a steady increase in output up to 30% which was largely unrelated to the experimental variables, for when there was a return to the original conditions output was still higher than it was initially. It seems likely that the experimental variables were ineffective, but that some of the other changes brought about in order to do the experiment were the causes of increased output (Roethlisberger and Dickson 1939). The principal factor responsible is generally thought to have been the changed character of supervision, but the constant presence of an audience, and the desire of the girls to do well may also have been important, in addition to a number of other causes discussed elsewhere (Argyle 1953*a*).

What are the advantages of the experimental method where it can be applied? Given that the proper procedures are used in each case, experiments have no greater validity than the non-experimental designs—the conclusions follow just as rigorously in each case. However, since the experimenter is able to manipulate the variables, the direction of causation can be discovered—which is not the case with the correlational kind of investigation. Further, since subjects are allocated to experimental conditions at random, the batches can be equated properly and the dangers of self-selection as in the *ex post facto* design are removed. If conditions are held constant throughout, the variation in response within the various experimental batches is reduced and smaller differences between the means will be significant; if the conditions are systematically varied on the other hand, it is possible to find the range for which a given effect occurs, and the generality of the findings can be explored. Lastly, an experiment can be carried out when the experimenter wishes to do so, and there is no need to wait for the requisite conditions to occur naturally in the field.

In an experiment, a hypothesis is tested about the relationship between one or more independent variables (causes, experimental conditions) and one or more dependent variables (effects, behaviour measured). The independent variables are manipulated by varying the experimental conditions; the question is then whether these produce a variation in behaviour between the conditions in relation to the variation within the conditions due to other causes: the statistical tests for difference of means provide the appropriate criterion.

(1) *The Simple Successive-conditions Design*

In this type of experiment a single batch of individuals or of groups is exposed successively to two successive experimental conditions. For example, a number of groups may experience two different kinds of leadership in turn. Alternatively the batch may be measured on some variable before and after it has received some experimental treatment, such as exposure to propaganda. The independent variable is the variable situation or the presence or absence of the experience which is introduced. The essence of this design is that the same batch is exposed to both situations or both measurements, while in the after-only method, different batches are used for each. The great advantage of the successive-conditions design is that it avoids matching two batches, which is a matter of some difficulty. It is, in addition, possible to follow up individual members of the batch and see which are affected by the experimental variable, whereas this is impossible when only a single measure is taken for each. There is also greater statistical sensitivity when the same individuals appear for each measurement, as Thouless points out (1951, pp. 321–6).

The great disadvantage of this design is that the first condition or measurement may influence the second, particularly in social experiments; there may be unwanted learning effects such as primary-group formation in a small-group experiment, and the subjects may resist changing their behaviour to the tune of the experimental variable, or may deliberately alter it. Probably the avoidance of change is the greatest single factor, and its effect is to reduce the influence of the experimental variable. This would be expected in experiments on the effect of propaganda when the same attitude scale is given before and after: the way out is either to use equivalent forms of the scale or to use a different experimental design. Again, in Berenda's experiment (1950) on the effect of the group on children's judgments, the same effect can be seen: each child first judged the length of lines alone before judging again in the second condition in the presence of a group of misjudging confederates; the memory of their previous judgments made them more resistant to change from social pressure. Lippitt (1940) however used successive conditions in his experiment on the effect of autocratic and democratic atmospheres in small groups, and furthermore was able to observe interesting transfer effects at the change-over. The boys were unaware that an experiment was in progress and it may be that the successive-conditions design is practicable only when this is the case, or when the attention of the subjects is successfully directed elsewhere. A second drawback of this design is that other changes may have taken place with time, in addition to those intended by the experimenter. This is especially the case with long-drawn-out industrial experiments, where economic and organisational changes are liable to occur. The solution is to use a control batch either in the after-only design, or in the combination of that design with successive conditions. These alternatives will be discussed in the following two sections.

(2) *The After-only Design*

In this kind of experiment quite different batches of individuals or groups are allocated to the different experimental conditions. Alternatively, one batch may be exposed to some experimental treatment, such as suggestion, while another batch is not. It is essential in this design for the various experimental batches to be equated in some way, otherwise any differences found afterwards may be due to initial differences of the subjects rather than to the experimental variable.

The independent variable consists of changes in the situation, or the presence or absence of the antecedent experience, respectively. This design clearly avoids the two disadvantages of the previous design—the possibility of unwanted transfer effects and of unknown changes with time. These considerations are sufficiently important to make this design preferable in the majority of social experiments.

Its disadvantage, on the other hand, is the great difficulty of making the batches equivalent. This can be done either by matching or by randomisation. The same kind of calculation of the significance of difference of means must be made in each case, and though the method of matching is of no superior validity to that of randomisation, there is a gain in sensitivity if individuals are matched in pairs, as mentioned above. There will, of course, be doubts about the results if the matching or randomisation are not properly carried out, leaving initial differences between the batches. Randomised batches need to be larger for the same level of significance, owing to the reduced sensitivity; although troublesome, these are generally used.

To match two batches, either the individual members can be matched, or the frequency distribution of one or more characteristics can be equated in the two batches. In each case it must be decided what criteria shall be used. In experimental psychology a task is usually chosen as criterion such that performance at it correlates with the behaviour chosen as independent variable: thus in an experiment on the conditions of learning, intelligence test scores may be used for matching, since these correlate with rate of learning and the two batches would be expected to learn equally fast under the same conditions. In social psychology, on the other hand, such correlations are as yet almost unknown, so that it is difficult to know what criteria to use. In the case of individuals it would be possible to use general personality factors such as found by Eysenck (1952), since these account for much of the variance between individuals over a wide range of performances.

(3) *The Use of Extra Control Batches*

It is possible to combine the last two designs, using control batches in addition to before-and-after measurements. The chief virtue in this practice is that unwanted changes with time are eliminated. On the other hand, it suffers from both of the disadvantages of requiring equated batches and of there being transfer effects between successive conditions. Solomon (1949) has suggested the use of a second control batch which is exposed to the experimental variable[1] but not to the pre-test, in order to avoid sensitisation of the subjects to the experimental variable by the first measurement.

(4) *The Study of Individual Differences*

The independent variable may be an aspect of the subjects or groups rather than of the situation into which they are put. The batch may be divided into contrasted sub-batches and the significance of difference of their means found; if a numerical measure is available expressing the individual differences, a correlation can be found between these numbers (actual or ranked) and the dependent variable scores. One can also find which subjects or groups are most affected by an experimental variable. The personality dimension is of great importance in the study of social behaviour, and is of course a field of its own.

To conduct this kind of study it is important that the sub-batches should differ only in respect of the variable studied, otherwise the results obtained may be misleading. J. R. P. French (1944), for ex-

---

[1] This applies only to the type of experiment where subjects are exposed to some experience, such as propaganda, between successive measurements.

ample, compared the effect of frustration and danger on primary and temporary groups. However, he failed to equate his sub-batches for psychological sophistication—the temporary groups being composed of psychology students. This may explain why the temporary groups showed less fear and aggression than the others in the experimental situations.

(5) *More Complex Designs*

More complex designs are sometimes used when several independent variables are being studied simultaneously. The basis of these designs is the analysis of variance. The *variance* of a set of measurements is a statistic[1] representing the amount of scatter. When several independent variables are operating it is possible to break down the variance into parts attributable to each variable. Not only is this an economical method of working out a number of differences between means quickly; it also shows the relative importance of the different variables, in relation to each other and to the variation within the batches. The various experimental designs using analysis of variance are described by Edwards (1950).

The Generality of Empirical Results

As stated above, an experiment in social psychology is regarded as demonstrating an hypothesis if it is sufficiently unlikely that the variation in the dependent variable could have occurred by chance alone. If it would have occurred by chance only once in twenty times the result is regarded as 'significant', though a result occurring by chance once in a hundred times is obviously preferable. This level of acceptance is arbitrary and can be misleading. For a result which is contrary to theory and to other results, a higher level of probability is commonly demanded. This is the problem of significance, and it is clear that only by experiments and the varieties of statistical field study mentioned above can significant results be obtained. By these means it can be shown that the relation of two variables is not fortuitous but due to some causal process.

The problem of generality is quite distinct: it is the question of how far an observed empirical relation is true for wider ranges of subjects and conditions. Three aspects of this problem may be discussed: how far results obtained under the conditions of investigation *per se* can be regarded as true of other conditions: how far

[1] The variance is the mean of the squares of the differences from the mean of the measurement. See Guilford, op. cit., Chapter X.

behaviour under the particular conditions of a given design is general: how far the subjects or groups of the investigations form a representative sample of a population.

(i) *Generalisation from the Conditions of Investigation* per se

As has already been pointed out, experiments range from the highly artificial to the completely naturalistic. Non-experimental investigations, of course, entail no manipulation of conditions, and measurements are made of behaviour in its usual setting. Therefore with all non-experimental investigations and with some experiments it looks as if it is safe to suppose that the results apply when the investigation is not in progress. There is however the further point, also raised previously, that the investigator in the very act of observing or interviewing may change the values of the variables being measured. This must obviously be avoided in the ways suggested, otherwise the results may be misleading.

(ii) *Generalisation from the Limited Conditions of a Given Investigation*

While the purpose of a scientific investigation is to isolate causal sequences, the design may encourage unusual forms of behaviour which will attract undue attention. This criticism can be made of Sherif's studies of the formation of social norms in a totally unstructured situation (1935*a*). Such situations are rare, but other investigators have found the same results in situations with strong reality components present. In experimental psychology there are familiar instances when experiments have been designed from the point of view of a particular theory and emphasised appropriate processes. These difficulties can be avoided by restricting the generality of the results to the precise conditions of the investigation, until they have been found to hold under more varied conditions (Underwood 1949, pp. 378-9). Obtaining greater generality for results, and taking care that a freak process has not been discovered, are part of the same process. If several independent variables are manipulated in the experiment more information about generality will be obtained, as well as disclosing interaction between the variables (Fisher 1949).

(iii) *The Representativeness of the Sample*

The individuals, groups, or societies which are the units in an investigation will be only a limited selection out of all possible subjects. It is desirable to know how far the results would be true of other subjects. In the first place it can be hoped that they will be true of the limited population of similar subjects or groups. If the characteristics of subjects or groups are varied, some knowledge of the range for which the results are true will be obtained. From the size of the sample, the probability of the results holding for the rest of the population can be calculated, provided it is a truly random sample.

When groups or societies are the subjects, aspects of these will be the dimensions defining the population represented. In the case of individual subjects the most important variable is the sub-culture from which they are drawn. The subjects may, for example, be second-year students of a faculty of some university: it is interesting to consider the problem of generalisation outside such a sub-culture.

Social behaviour depends on the culture more than does the behaviour usually studied in experimental psychology laboratories, and if a psychological explanation of this is given, that in turn makes use of the cultural conditions. These can be considered in two sections: the influence of child training and the influence of present social norms.

Child training probably leads to general personality traits such as competitiveness and co-operativeness, which may be general for the culture. It is impossible to reproduce such childhood experiences in the laboratory, and experiments would have to be repeated in other cultures to obtain more general results. Strodtbeck (1951) treated the culture as the major variable in his study of husband-wife interaction, but it has never been treated as a subsidiary variable for exploring the generality of some other experimental result. It is however possible to reproduce specific motivating conditions, as was done by Deutsch in his study of co-operation and competition (1949a). This can be held to reproduce variations along one dimension in which cultures differ.

The influence of present social norms has been studied by Sherif (1935a) and Merei (1949), who allowed them to be set up experimentally. It could also be done by conducting field experiments against different institutional backgrounds, though this has not so far been done. As a result of this kind of investigation a distinction could be made between universal laws of social behaviour and those dependent on certain cultural conditions.

CHAPTER III

THE EXPLANATION OF SOCIAL BEHAVIOUR

INTRODUCTION

THE CONTENTS OF the last chapter are not likely to meet with much disagreement from social scientists: developments in this sphere of methodology are largely in matters of detail, of improving techniques in familiar ways. Accordingly it is possible to report in Part Two a considerable number of investigations whose findings can be accepted with a fair measure of confidence. Furthermore, such is the energy with which research is being pursued in this field that soon there will be a substantial body of empirical laws of social behaviour. On the other hand, the development of any systematic understanding of social behaviour is being delayed by the somewhat random and chaotic way in which research is being carried out; isolated teams of researchers seem to be oblivious of each other's work. It is hoped that the general picture given in Part Two of the results attained so far will be of service in this respect.

A more deep-rooted cause of the present dislocation of research is the widespread disagreement concerning theory and explanation. Theory is supposed to co-ordinate results and to direct research: at the moment a multitude of theor*ies* is dividing up the field into hostile factions. The differences between theorists are on three quite different levels: primarily philosophical disagreements about the nature of explanation, differences of opinion about the most useful *type* of social theory within the conventional tradition, and different theories of the same type about the same facts. There is a further complication, that these theories may be at the level of the individual, the group, or society.

Only one of the philosophical issues which can be raised about explanation in the social sciences will be discussed at length—viz. whether conscious processes can usefully be said to explain behaviour. This is important to-day in view of the number of social psychologists who have championed what to this author (and to many contemporary philosophers) seems to be the wrong answer to it. It will be discussed in the final section of the chapter. Other purely philosophical matters will not be dealt with here, partly since this is not the place and they are outside the competence of the present writer, partly since philosophers have clarified them enough for social scientists to be able to adopt a common point of view with confidence. Two such methodological assumptions should perhaps be stated, without any attempt to defend them (cf. Stevens 1939). The first assumption is what has been called 'operationism', 'physicalism', or 'logical behaviourism'. This is the doctrine that all statements in a science must be verifiable by means of observations made by the investigator, or must enable verifiable predictions to be made from them. Hence remarks about the experiences of subjects, for example, must be transformed into verbal statements of the subjects, recorded by the observer. The second assumption is what may be called 'scientific determinism'. It is necessary to suppose that human behaviour is predictable—an assumption justified to some extent by the discoveries of laws of human behaviour. If human behaviour were not predictable, the social sciences would not be a possible branch of knowledge. This is not of course to deny that people have the experience of deciding what to do, or that they are often free from environmental pressures when they do so: it is simply to say that the decision that is made can in principle (and sometimes in fact) be predicted.

These questions belong to the sphere of the professional philosopher: there is another which belongs to the philosopher of science. The problem is: what constitutes a scientific explanation and how does it work? The basis for the discussion of this is two-fold. In the first place there is a body of knowledge called 'The Philosophy of Science' built up by philosophers who have examined the activity of scientists—usually of physicists. This enables us to point to the general features common to all scientific activity, outside which a person simply is not doing science—and therefore cannot hope to gather the rewards of the scientific quest, i.e. the accumulation of an integrated body of verified knowledge. The philosophy of science also enables us to draw certain distinctions—for example between classifications and theories. The second basis for our critique is the debate about theory which has gone on inside experimental psychology during the last two decades. The philosophy of science does not apply directly to the social sciences, since it is based largely on the activities of physicists. In addition there is even controversy about what physicists are doing. In any case it could be argued that since the social sciences have a unique subject-matter, therefore a unique variety of explanation might be necessary. It is therefore extremely helpful to see what has been happening in experimental psychology, since this is one of the behavioural sciences, and one which is more highly developed than the others. In addition, as will be shown, the best way of explaining generalisations about individual social behaviour is to relate them to the laws of experimental psychology, while reductive explanations are also useful at the group and society levels.

From this background it is possible to state certain principles which may be held to characterise the *scientific* explanation of events. Firstly, single events are explained by the demonstration that they are instances of generalisations about the relations between two or more variables. As was shown earlier, it is possible to establish functional relations between two variables only by studying a number of cases; the 'phenomenal field'[1] and 'clinical'[2] types of explanation are ruled out by this principle. No distinction is drawn here between the notion of 'empirical law' and 'generalisation'. Some philosophers of science, speaking of physics, distinguish these on the grounds that laws are taken as true for a certain range of data over and above their established probabilities. Exceptions from laws then need explanation, and it is possible to use concepts whose use depends on the truth of the law[3] (Toulmin 1953). This distinction is not commonly drawn in the social sciences, largely because few generalisations have reached a high enough level of acceptance, so that this hierarchical development of concepts has not taken place.

The second feature of a scientific theory is that one or more generalisations are explained by deduction from further postulates, and in such a way that the prediction of new results follows. This will be regarded as the definition of a scientific theory, and will be used to distinguish theories from generalisations, and from classifications. These last will be discussed in the next section.

A second source of differences between theorists is in the type of theory which they deem desirable. Satisfying the criteria introduced above, there are several logically distinct forms of theory which may cover the same empirical facts. While many arguments have been brought forward for and against each type, these arguments are merely strategical, claiming that the sort of theory in question is likely to be more useful or convenient in some way. There seems to

---

[1] See p. 84 f.   [2] See p. 42.

[3] For example, the refractive index depends on the truth of Snell's law, otherwise it would not be a constant property of optical media (Toulmin, op. cit., Chapter III).

be no conclusive way of deciding which is best. Different theorists will prefer one kind or another, and we must simply wait to see which makes the most progress.

In the third section of the chapter, the main types of theory will be presented, and their pros and cons stated. A standard manner of presentation will be employed, both for schematic representation of the logical form, and for illustration of particular examples of theories. In each case the following will be indicated: (1) The generalisations to be explained; (2) the postulates from which they are deduced; (3) the logical status of the postulates; and (4) the predictions made.

It is only when the discussion has been limited to the scientific tradition and to one particular type of theory that differences arising from the *contents* of theories can be considered. The conventional doctrine is that two differing theories must be tested by crucial experiments for which the theories predict different results, but the position is actually more complicated than that. In the first place, when there is more than one theory for the same set of facts there is a job of 'intertranslation and differential analysis' to be done, to find the areas over which the theories predict the same results (and are therefore empirically equivalent), and the regions where they differ (and can be tested by crucial experiments) (Koch 1951). Unless theories are stated with precision this last is difficult, for their implications are ambiguous. Secondly, if a prediction is refuted, a theory will often not be abandoned by its exponents. It may, like Newtonian mechanics, be retained as a theory true for a limited realm of data. Scientists are however compelled to accept a new theory which explains all the facts explained by an old one together with others which that cannot explain. Successive theories thus cover wider ranges of data. Some psychologists favour 'miniature theories' which cover small fields with precision: it is important, on the other hand, that these should be seen as preliminary to wider theories, and some contemporary methodologists prefer 'theories of the middle range' (Merton 1949; Koch op. cit.). Another reaction to the failure of predictions from a theory is to modify the theory by the introduction of *ad hoc* hypotheses which enable it to accommodate the unexpected results. Such changes must however be tested by the examination of further predictions implied by the alterations. A third reaction is to question the interpretation of the experimental results, to say that they do not contradict the theory if certain complications of the situation are taken into account. This leads to a tedious and irritating kind of controversy. To avoid it, experiments should be as far as possible of a simple and straightforward design, in which all the variables are clearly identifiable and where only one process is taking place.

Later in this chapter, theories at various levels of empirical analysis will be discussed. The first level is that of individual behaviour. Most theories of individual behaviour do not refer to social behaviour, and so the possible inclusion of laws of social behaviour in theories of non-social behaviour is one issue that must be discussed. The second level is of the behaviour of small social groups, and the third of sociological generalisations about whole societies: several instances of laws at each of these levels were given in the last chapter. An example will be given of theories from each level whenever this is possible.

TWO PRELIMINARY STAGES TO THEORY-CONSTRUCTION

Generalisation

For practical purposes the most important part of a science consists of its empirical laws, summarising the functional relationships of variables as found in many investigations. Indeed, the first level of explanation of individual events is through their being shown to be instances of established generalisations. In this section the view that explanation need go no further will be examined, and the positive case for theorising expounded.

Firstly, some terminological issues must be tidied up, and the usage in this book indicated. By *explanation* is meant any formulation which makes an event or law more comprehensible pyschologically. This includes subsuming an event under a law, derivation of laws from postulates, and explanation of events by reference to conscious or unconscious processes. Only the second of these is called a *theory*, as explained above. Generalisations are thus an essential stage in the explanation of events. The reason that individual events are not related directly to theories is that in the social sciences it is possible to establish functional relationships only over a series of events, as explained in Chapter II.

Many social scientists have described their generalisations as theories, thus creating verbal confusion, and causing people to search for postulates when there were none to be found. 'Psychoanalytic theory' for instance turns out to comprise a set of weakly confirmed empirical statements. There are also analogies, about trap-doors, little men, and hydraulics, but these are of no predictive significance and were not regarded by Freud as being of any importance. Again, most of the classical 'sociological theories' turn out to be rather vague and weakly verified generalisations about the geographical, racial, or economic determinants of social phenomena (cf. Sorokin 1928).

Perhaps the simplest way to discuss the anti-theoretical approach is to state the positive case for theorising and see what objections have been made to it. A theory from which generalisations can be deduced does three things. It integrates different laws into a coherent body of knowledge, it enables further predictions to be made, and it gives a further feeling of explanation.

In connection with the first point, it is true that several generalisations can often be combined mathematically, as in the case of the Gas laws ($PV = RT$). On the other hand, a far greater diversity of laws can be accommodated by a theory. The inclusion of all facts under a single generalisation has sometimes been held to be an aim of science. While it is obviously valuable to discover far-reaching laws, it is surely hopeless to try to combine them at the level of generalisations. Some philosophers of science, following Ernst Mach, hold the view that the postulates of axiomatic theories are themselves simply high-level generalisations. This is a mistake, since these are usually only empirically meaningful via deductions made from them in combination, though in the case of lower-level models they may be directly meaningful at that level of empirical analysis.

The second argument in favour of theorising is that further predictions are made, so that there is a systematic extension of research which may lead to new discoveries. Skinner (1950) has objected that theories do not lead to fruitful research at all, since every theory is refuted in the end, whereupon the research conducted in its defence ceases to be important. In fact the crucial experiment strategy leads to successive theories of wider and wider scope, and therefore may be regarded as an efficient procedure. This is not to deny that there are other criteria of 'fruitfulness' besides that of sheer range of prediction: practical considerations as well as theory should be a guide in planning research. Often, however, a theory will have a large number of implications, and it is then possible to select for further study those of greatest interest on other grounds.

A number of experimental psychologists, such as Woodworth (1937), exemplify the anti-theoretical attitude. They adopt the *dimensional principle* by which the functional relations between all discriminable aspects of the dependent and independent variables are studied. The results are a series of curves showing these relations two at a time. Some psychologists fit mathematical equations to these curves and express the results in algebraic form: this is an important step in Hull's method, to be discussed later.

The third reason for theorising is that it explains the generalisations psychologically. This argument is on quite a different level from the two others, since it refers only to the motivation of the scientist, and not to methodological reasons for his actions. As F. V. Smith (1951) has pointed out, what is felt to be a satisfying explanation depends on the individual: Piaget (1926) showed for example that quite different sorts of explanation would satisfy children of different ages. This explains why some scientists are satisfied with generalisations while others are not. It cannot be correct to regard such satisfaction as a *criterion* for a type of theory, if it is a relative matter.

It is hoped that the above account brings out the main differences between those who stop at generalisations and those who require further explanation. There is one final reason for not theorising: this is lack of faith in the existing laws, and desire for better material before attempting to explain it further. While this is a healthy empiricist attitude, it can lead to indefinite postponement of the fatal day. Results are accumulating fast in the social sciences, and many of them are of a high standard. Correspondingly the functional relationships are becoming more closely circumscribed. In terms of sheer bulk there is a definite hierarchy of the disciplines: investigations in experimental psychology number by the thousand, in social psychology by the hundred, while in sociology acceptable data are much rarer. Only in sociology can it be true to say that it is early to theorise: elsewhere theory can act as a valuable guide to empirical research, and as an integrator of the results obtained.

Classification

Another important procedure which is sometimes confused with theory-construction is classification. In this section only the classification of responses will be considered—that of processes will be dealt with later. The classification of responses comprises the discovery of empirical variables, and the division of these into suitable categories or units of measurement. Earlier (p. 29) this was called the demonstration that concepts had functional unity. Guttman's method of attitude scaling (Stouffer et al. 1950) is a way of establishing dimensions of attitudes: before any measurements are made it is shown that there *is* an attitude continuum in the sense defined by him. Similarly the factor analysis of personality measurements or of mental-test scores establishes the dimensions which are the most powerful for prediction and which represent stable aspects of individuals.

The categorisation, or measurement, of a dimension may follow from the research establishing it. This is the case with the Guttman scale and the factor analysis of ability. In other cases there is only one step, which yields categories at once. Thus systems of categories for interaction recording can be set up simply by finding a series of divisions which can be used with high reliability.

This all entails empirical research. On the other hand, what is discovered is not a number of empirical laws but a set of usable dimensions and categories. Later research will use these as variables in empirical generalisation. The classification of responses, far from being a theoretical device, is actually prior to the discovery of empirical laws. At the same time it is often felt that categorisation does afford some explanation, and this feeling is enhanced by the tendency for research to be non-quantitative, merely to show that A depends on B, and not how much in relation to the effects of C or D, or what form the functional relation takes. Thus to know the results of empirical research may add little to knowledge of the dimensions of the variables. Although categorisation is certainly an important stage of research and may be regarded as explanatory, it must be emphasised that it is quite distinct from generalisation.

Theories may introduce new concepts or categories which abstract from events in a new way. Thus Freud brought in the developmental stages of the sexual instinct in childhood, making quite new divisions of the early years of life. Lewin (1952) in his 'life-space' language produced a novel means for describing psychological situations, in terms of goals, barriers, routes, and regions of activity. Information theory has introduced the notion of 'information', together with the ideas of 'source', 'channel', 'noise', etc. (Wiener 1948). These languages are each extremely convenient for talking about certain data, but it must be noticed that in all of these 'theories' not a single generalisation appears.[1] Schlick and Ramsey describe scientific theories as directions for the investigator to find his way about in reality, and Toulmin as 'maps for representing phenomena' (Toulmin 1953, p. 98 f., 103 f.). These descriptions refer primarily to the representation of phenomena by means of a language suited to

[1] For the mathematical side of such theories, see pp. 78–80.

the data. The theory proper is the axiomatic construction from which the generalisations couched in terms of this language can be deduced.

Some categorisers have thought that they were theorising. Parsons and Shils (1951), while admitting that theirs is a theory of the categorial variety (p. 50), claim to be using deductive techniques (p. 49), though clearly they cannot be doing so in the usual sense of deduction. There are no empirical statements in the book at all; in addition, their categorisation must be regarded as useless since their concepts and categories were created regardless of the possibilities of measurement. It may be that they have no functional unity: they may conceal more important distinctions or alternatively not be discriminable. This was found to be the case with the first stages of all the measuring instruments which have been properly developed, so that it scarcely seems worth pursuing the Parsons and Shils distinctions to the degree of elaboration to which they have been carried.

Eysenck (1952) also claims to be using the hypothetico-deductive method when he postulates the existence of a factor of neuroticism. This is misleading in that the existence of *any* dimension of personality could presumably be demonstrated by the selection and intercorrelation of a suitable battery of tests; furthermore rotation of the axes can generate a variety of equally good factors from the same tests. On the other hand neuroticism does have more functional unity than, for example, suggestibility (Krech & Crutchfield 1948, pp. 335–7). It is not so much a matter of asserting or denying the hypothesis that a given trait exists, as finding that certain traits are more useful classifications of responses than others.

This completes the discussion of the classification of *responses*. It must now be distinguished from the classification of *processes*, which will be taken up in the following section. The classification of responses is entirely concerned with the conceptualisation of responses regardless of the circumstances in which they are made—it is the measurement of a dependent variable. The classification of processes deals with the 'chapter-headings' of psychology, the areas into which sequences of events are grouped. It is supposed that once a process has been correctly placed in one of these areas all the generalisations in that area will apply to it. Thus the chapter-heading 'learning' may be defined as "a change in performance as a function of practice . . . [with] a direction which satisfies the current motivating conditions of the individual" (McGeoch 1942, pp. 3–4). In this case the changes of behaviour which take place in patients during psychotherapy may be classified as learning, and hence it is possible that the laws of learning may apply to them. Whether they do or not, clearly such laws cannot be applied to these changes until they have first been classified as learning and the variables identified appropriately.

DIFFERENT TYPES OF THEORY

Intervening Variable Theories

One of the most widely acclaimed forms of theorising in American psychology makes use of 'intervening variables'. It has been championed by two major theorists, Hull and Tolman, together with a number of methodologists. Its attraction seems to be that it appears to embody the 'hypothetico-deductive method', while at the same time there are no hypothetical terms at all. In the following account of the technique the original usage of Tolman (1936) will be followed, this being also that of MacCorquodale and Meehl (1948).

To express it schematically, let R be a function of two independent variables V_1 and V_2. Then $R = f_1(V_1)$, $R = f_2(V_2)$. In order to consider R simultaneously as a function of V_1 and V_2, let the influence of V_1 on R be represented by its influence on an intervening variable I_1, so that $I_1 = f_1(V_1)$. Thus the influence of V_1 on R is represented by its effect on I_1, an intervening variable. Similarly $I_2 = f_2(V_2)$. The combined effect of V_1 and V_2 when both are varied is represented by the equation $R = I_1 \times I_2$. To establish this final equation one of several steps may be taken: (a) It may be assumed that the influence of V_1 has the same form when V_2 is held constant at different values. (b) The influence of V_1 may actually be investigated at different values of V_2. (c) The influence of some combination of the independent variables may be explored as in (b), while assumption (a) is made for other combinations. Tolman (1936) describes procedure (a), while Hull's practice (e.g. 1951) is procedure (c).

The intervening variable simply represents that part of the variation in the dependent variable which may be supposed to be due to the independent variable in question. The combined influence of two or more causal variables is found by multiplying together the appropriate intervening variables. This can just as well be achieved by multiplying together the functional equations, i.e. by assuming that all the causal variables are independent and do not affect the form of each other's influence. An example of the method taken from Hull's *Essentials of Behavior* (1951) is given in an Appendix to this chapter, p. 93.

It should now be clear that the intervening variable technique makes possible the combination of two or more empirical generalisations concerning the influence of two or more independent variables. We may now assess the method according to the three functions of theories. Firstly, it certainly co-ordinates empirical laws, in the sense that it shows how they operate simultaneously. On the other hand, it does not relate generalisations deductively. As a matter of fact, the sense in which intervening variables employ deduction at all is rather bizarre. It may be argued that the final statement of the simultaneous operation of several independent variables is deduced from 'postulates', as Hull calls them. On the other hand, these postulates are themselves empirical generalisations, so that this is not an instance of the 'hypothetico-deductive method' or axiomatic procedure, described in a later section (Bergmann and Spence 1941). Koch (1941) has accordingly called Hull's technique 'telescopic', since it omits the stage of postulating primary axioms and interpreting theorems, essential to the hypothetico-deductive method proper. Intervening variable theories are commonly confused with axiomatic theories, and it is important to note this difference.

The second function of a theory is to predict new results, and many predictions have been made and verified by the use of Hull's formulations. It must be realised however that most of these predictions concern the value of the response for combinations of values of the independent variables other than those originally used. It is more natural to call such a process 'interpolation' or 'extrapolation' than prediction proper, which concerns entirely new situations. Other kinds of prediction are made by Hull, involving new situations—for example problem-solving (1953, Chapter X). These, however, consist of the classification of processes followed by same-level explanation predictions.[1] It may be concluded that the theory proper can predict only in a limited sense of prediction.

The third function of a theory is to explain psychologically. It is a good example of the relativity of satisfactory explanations to note that while many American psychologists seem to be entirely satisfied by intervening-variable theories, the majority of British psychologists are not.

Two misunderstandings of intervening variables are current, in addition to their confusion with axiomatic theories. In the first place intervening variables have sometimes been supposed to have some physiological reference, an idea which is reinforced by the nomen-

[1] See p. 66 ff.

clature of some of Hull's terms like 'afferent neural interaction'. MacCorquodale and Meehl (1948) have distinguished them from 'hypothetical constructs' which are not wholly reducible to empirical terms, and which have some kind of surplus meaning, usually in terms of physiology. Bergmann (1953) has claimed that there is no real distinction here, but in the view of the present writer there is a real difference between theoretical postulates whose meaning is exhausted by empirical statements of psychology, and those which in addition have physiological implications, so that their verification can proceed at two different levels of empirical analysis. Intervening variables simply represent, one at a time, the components of the response which depend on particular independent variables. There is a logical chain but no causal chain. Nothing would be lost by replacing the intervening variables by the equations which define them, and if this had been done in the first place misunderstanding of the valuable basic method could have been avoided.

A second misinterpretation of intervening variables is the supposition that the influence of one independent variable is expressed by its breakdown into two stages, with an intervening variable in the middle. Thus $R = f_1(I)$, and $I = f_2(S)$. Schachter (1951) for example combines this with the proper method: two intervening variables are related by graphs to three independent variables, and the dependent variables algebraically to the intervening variables. A number of complicated predictions are made, using the graphs, but one suspects that the graphs were drawn after the experimental results were obtained, since they have no adequate intuitive basis.

It is now possible to indicate the prospects for intervening variables in social psychology. Since there are just as many variables here as in experimental psychology, if not more, it may be thought that the method would be extremely useful for showing the manner of their simultaneous operation. However, apart from Schachter's theory, criticised above, the method has not yet been used, although many investigators have studied the joint effect of two or more variables.

The great advantage of the intervening-variable approach is that the independence of causal variables is not assumed; it encourages experiments designed to find out if one variable affects the form of the functional relations of another—to discover the 'interaction terms'.

The fitting of mathematical equations to curves is a separate issue. In the restricted fields of experimentation for which Hull's theories hold, it is possible not only to find whether one thing influences another, but also to find the form of the mathematical equation or curve expressing that influence, as well as the relative effect of other causal variables. By the combination of the intervening-variable method with curve-fitting, Hull has achieved the most exact means of prediction so far attained in psychology. Only at one or two points has any comparable degree of exactitude been reached in the sphere of social behaviour.

'Same-level' Theories

The next kind of theory to be considered is also the simplest: in fact it is so simple that it has often not been recognised as a specific kind of theory at all, and no name has previously been given to it. Nevertheless it is of some importance for the student of social behaviour, and it is necessary to examine some of the mistakes that may occur in its use. The method consists simply in explaining one generalisation by showing it to be an example of a previously established one.

To express it schematically, let $R_2 = f_2(S)_2$ be the generalisation to be explained, and let $R_1 = f_1(S_1)$ be an established law. The process $S_2 - R_2$ is first classified with S_1-R_1, so that S_2 can be measured along a similar dimension to S_1, and R_2 as R_1. f_2 is then shown to be the same as, or a special case of, f_1.

An example of this procedure is the explanation of the development of imitation given by Miller and Dollard (1941). The emergence of imitative behaviour as a result of experience is first classified as learning. Particular generalisations such as "rats and children learn to imitate if rewarded for doing so, and will learn to discriminate or generalise among leaders and situations" are then explained as instances of the law of effect and the principle of generalisation-discrimination respectively. This kind of theory will be called a 'same-level' explanation. It is often not recognised as a distinct form of theory, but clearly it satisfies the definition of a theory as a formulation from which the generalisation to be explained can be derived, together with other predictions. Its adequacy as a form of theory can be assessed by an examination of it in relation to the three functions of theories.

In the first place, the chief importance of same-level explanations is their capacity for co-ordinating generalisations prior to further explanation. By relating a new generalisation to an old one, the labour of explaining each separately is avoided, while the procedure in itself may be regarded as sufficient explanation for a first stage.

Secondly, although same-level explanations do not lead to predictions in the usual way, prediction is possible at the classificatory stage: once one process has been classified with a second process, all the laws that apply to the second can be predicted to apply to the first. If the predictions prove to be wrong, either the first process must be reclassified, or the laws true within the existing category must be said to be of limited generality. On the third criterion, it is undeniable that same-level explanation gives considerable cognitive satisfaction, since new results are reduced to old and familiar ones. This is of course particularly the case when the results are in a new and strange field of research.

Certain fallacies in the use of same-level explanations will now be examined, with reference to the writings of Miller, Dollard, and others of the Yale group. Firstly, it is necessary that the laws used to make explanations should be of sufficient validity to justify their use in this way. It is obviously useless to attempt to co-ordinate laws to one which is false, or is not known to be true. Dollard and others (1939) seek to explain a large number of data by means of the generalisation that 'frustration leads to aggression'. This generalisation was only very weakly confirmed at the time of their book, and is now known to be true only under very limited conditions, since there are many other responses to frustration (cf. Himmelweit 1950). Secondly, and for the same reason, there is no point in trying to explain generalisations before they are established. Dollard and Miller (1950) explain a series of psychoanalytic propositions, none of which can be regarded as representing any demonstrated empirical relationship. Thirdly, same-level explanation must be distinguished from the classification of processes. Miller and Dollard (1941) 'explain' various sociological phenomena, such as lynchings and the class system, in terms of imitation. This is classification of processes, from which it would be possible to proceed to compare laws about crowd behaviour and about imitation, and perform a same-level explanation. This is not done—it is only the conceptual form of the processes that is compared.

We may now consider the possibilities of giving same-level explanations of social behaviour. It is clearly not yet possible to explain generalisations about groups and societies, since there are insufficient established laws to which they can be related. On the other hand, generalisations about individual social behaviour could be co-ordinated to corresponding psychological laws of individual non-social behaviour which are better established. This involves for example classifying social learning with non-social learning, i.e. the learning of social behaviour with the learning of mazes and nonsense syllables. It has been claimed however that social behaviour is different in kind from non-social behaviour, so that such classifications should not be made. It is supposed that social behaviour involves unique elements. If this were so the generalisations would not fit and the explanations not succeed. It would be exactly comparable to attempts to explain problem-solving in terms of conditioning—the former involves an order of complexity which probably is not reducible to the latter, so that an alternative strategy of explanation must be sought. It seems, therefore, as if the justification of classifying social with non-social behaviour can be decided empirically. In Chapter IV some experiments on the perception of other people are reviewed, and it is shown that the results can be summarised quite naturally under the generalisations found for the perception of non-social objects. Miller and Dollard, as quoted above, showed that the learning of imitation followed laws familiar in experimental psychology. In each of these cases the classification of social with the corresponding non-social behaviour seems to be justified, and the same is probably true for most areas of social behaviour. It is of course quite possible that some complex forms of social behaviour may exhibit functional relations which have no counterpart in experimental psychology, in which case, as perhaps with problem-solving, the result must be explained directly without recourse to an intermediate stage of same-level explanation. As for the results which *can* be explained in this way however it seems the simplest policy to co-ordinate them with laws of experimental psychology, and leave further explanation to others. It has the advantage of providing the social psychologist with ready-made explanations, and of giving the experimental psychologist a broader testing-ground for his theories. In many cases the laws of experimental psychology will already be explained themselves by other theoretical formulations, in which case same-level explanations lead at once to further explanation.

Axiomatic Theories

None of the other kinds of theory discussed in this section involves anything but generalisations arranged in various ways. 'Same-level' theories show that one generalisation can be included in another, intervening-variable theories combine laws describing the simultaneous effects of more than one independent variable, and reductive theories (discussed later) show that generalisations can be deduced from others at another level of empirical analysis. The contemporary philosophical climate emphasises operational definitions of concepts, so that many psychologists have thought that psychology should consist solely of empirical generalisations about the relations of operationally defined variables. On the other hand, many of the traditional theories in physics *did* postulate unobservables, like the atomic hypothesis put forward to explain the Gas laws. Philosophers of science and logicians have described the technique of what will here be called the 'axiomatic theory' (Cohen and Nagel 1939; Braithwaite 1953).

The procedure involves the following four stages: (1) axioms or postulates are stated, giving the relations between a number of previously undefined terms, these being *implicitly* defined by the axioms; (2) theorems are deduced from the axioms according to stated rules; (3) the terms are related to empirical variables by means of co-ordinating definitions; (4) empirical laws can be obtained not containing undefined terms, together with further laws, whose verification is used to test the theory. This is demonstrated schematically by Braithwaite (op. cit., Chapter II), and discussed in relation to psychology by Koch (1941). Not only is this type of theory rare, but it is recognised that theories are thought of in the reverse of the order set out above. Euclidean geometry, though not a science, is the most familiar embodiment of some of the above features.

Some methodologists distinguish between theories with formal calculi, as above, and theories employing models (e.g. Cohen and Nagel, op. cit., p. 234). The present writer thinks that this is misleading, and follows Braithwaite in his very illuminating account of the relations of models to theories (op. cit., Chapter IV). A theory is commonly stated as a series of propositions arranged in deductive order; the first propositions contain theoretical terms, the later ones are empirical laws, and are deduced logically from the earlier. Such a theory can be expressed with greater precision by means of a calculus or mathematical representation which simply consists of the bare logical relations necessary for the deductions. The later propositions of the theory, together with the corresponding ones in the calculus, are meaningful as empirical laws. The earlier propositions are given meaning through their deductive relationship to the later ones. While the axioms are *logically* prior, they are *epistemologically* posterior (loc. cit., pp. 89–90). The theory and the laws explained are one interpretation of the mathematical system, which is deductively valid apart from any physical interpretations. The mathematics may also be interpreted in a second way, however: it may be interpreted in terms of a mechanical or other physical system to which it applies. In this case the axioms are physically meaningful and therefore epistemologically as well as logically prior to the conclusions. Such an interpretation is a *model* for the theory. Each is expressed by the same mathematics, but epistemological priority is reversed in the two cases: the propositions of the theory are given meaning from the bottom upwards, while the propositions of the model are given meaning from the top downwards (loc. cit., p. 88 f.).

It does not affect the theory in essence, therefore, whether a model is provided or not; theories stated only in terms of a model may be restated without the model. The main advantage of the model is that it is easier to handle. On the other hand, irrelevant properties may be attributed to it, as by those who thought of electrons as hard billiard balls (op. cit., p. 92 f.).

In the case of the social sciences another problem arises if they are regarded as being arranged hierarchically. Thus physiology is commonly said to be at a 'lower level of empirical analysis' than psychology. All that is meant is that psychological generalisations can in some cases be deduced from physiological findings, and that this is a satisfactory form of explanation. (Further problems concerning 'reductionism' will be taken up in a later section.) Some psychological theories are couched in terms of postulated neurophysiological processes, so that they are really speculations about the mechanism underlying behaviour. Physical theories about 'electrons' are quite different, since these ultimate particles are not directly observable. This kind of psychological theory is unlike true axiomatic theories as described above in that here the axioms are meaningful in terms of possible observations at a lower level. It is unlike a model as described above, in that the theory is a speculation about the mechanism that is actually there.

It is possible, on the basis of the foregoing discussion, to distinguish three kinds of axiomatic theory in psychology. The first kind has just been described, and consists of speculation about the mechanisms underlying behaviour. These are usually called *hypothetical construct* theories. In the second kind there is a model of the sort described by Braithwaite, sharing only formal properties with possible neurophysiological facts. These will be called *mechanism* theories. In the third kind of theory, there is no model at all, and the theory consists only of the mathematical calculus. These will be called *formal postulate* theories. In the cases of the first and third types of theory, it is of course possible to devise models in the Braithwaite sense, but this would not affect the content of the theory, as shown above. Similarly it is possible to re-state theories of the first and second kinds in purely formal terms. The remainder of this section will be devoted to a discussion of these three varieties of axiomatic theory. In each case an example from experimental psychology will be given, followed by a statement of the advantages of the sort of theory in question, and a discussion of the possible application of the method to the explanation of social behaviour, with examples where possible.

(1) *Hypothetical Construct Theories*

An example of a hypothetical construct theory is the following explanation of conditioning due to Pavlov, as stated by Hilgard and Marquis (1940, p. 328 f.). Referring to the diagram in Figure 1, impulses from the conditioned stimulus CS at first excite the original response to the conditioned stimulus. During conditioning CS is excited simultaneously with UncS, the unconditioned stimulus. CS is later able to excite RUncS, the original response to the unconditioned stimulus. It is supposed that simultaneous excitation of the fibre a at X changes the excitability of the synapses, so that eventually CS alone is able to excite a and so elicit RUncS.

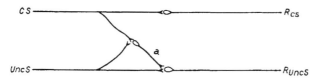

FIG. 1—PAVLOV'S THEORY OF CONDITIONING
(From p. 329 of Hilgard and Marquis 1940. *By permission of Appleton-Century-Crofts*)

This is not a very good example, since probably the only prediction that follows from it is that the conditioned response will be weaker than the unconditioned—because of the presence of two synapses instead of one. Better hypothetical construct theories are however too complex to be reported here.

The term 'hypothetical construct' is due to MacCorquodale and Meehl (1948), who distinguished them from intervening variables, though the sense in which the term is used here may be somewhat narrower than theirs. A hypothetical construct in psychology is an entity of a neuro-physiological type. The axioms of this kind of theory define the properties of the constructs, and from these psychological laws can be deduced, usually together with additional predictions. The unique feature of this kind of theory is that it can be verified in two quite distinct ways. In addition to the usual verification of psychological predictions, neurological research can confirm or refute the existence of entities as postulated in the theory. It is important, therefore, that such theories should be consistent with existing physiological knowledge. If the theory is confirmed neurologically, the status of the axioms is changed and they become laws of physiology, so that the theory becomes a reductive theory. If the reductive kind of theory is regarded as the ideal form of explanation, there is much to be said for the present kind as a half-way stage. On the other hand, such detailed speculation is likely to be wrong, since we know so little about neuro-physiology. Other kinds of axiomatic theory are able to afford predictions without detailed speculation of this kind.

How do hypothetical construct theories fare when assessed on our three criteria? In the first place, they often succeed in co-ordinating generalisations of quite different kinds; Hebb (1949) explains perceptual learning, various phenomena of motivation, and the functions of the frontal lobes, in a single theory, though this particular theory is unsatisfactory owing to the vagueness of the concepts. Secondly, they are more powerful predictively than any of the non-axiomatic formulations considered so far: they are able to predict results seemingly unrelated to the original laws. Lastly, many people find this kind of theory very satisfying as a form of explanation, though they usually regard the completed reductive form as superior.

Of what value are hypothetical construct theories to explain social behaviour? To explain generalisations about individual social behaviour the best policy is to relate them by same-level explanation to laws of experimental psychology. The latter may in turn be explained by hypothetical constructs. It is inadvisable to attempt direct hypothetical construct explanations for laws of individual social behaviour without this intermediate stage, since the laws of experimental psychology are well established, and the procedure suggested here avoids multiplication of theories. On the other hand, in the event of same-level explanation being impossible for some complex kinds of social behaviour, direct axiomatic explanation is the only course left open.

THE EXPLANATION OF SOCIAL BEHAVIOUR

To explain generalisations about groups and societies, hypothetical construct explanation of a sort is possible.[1] The lower-level elements are of course not at all hypothetical, since they can be none other than individual human beings. On the other hand, the psychological laws postulated may well be hypothetical.

As an example of the explanation of group behaviour in this way, the author's explanation of norm-formation may be instanced (see p. 157 f.). A number of generalisations about small social groups were explained by means of postulates about individual social behaviour. Further predictions were made, some of which have been confirmed experimentally.

We are not primarily concerned with sociological theory, but it is worth mentioning that generalisations about societies can in some cases be explained in the same way. An example is Horton's theory (1943) to account for some cross-cultural findings concerning alcoholism in primitive society. The following speculative psychological postulates are stated: (1) drinking alcohol reduces anxiety; (2) anxiety is caused by anticipation of punishment; (3) society punishes sexual and aggressive behaviour; (4) acts which reduce anxiety are learnt. From these postulates, certain deductions are made which can be tested cross-culturally: (*a*) The drinking of alcohol tends to be accompanied by release of sexual and aggressive impulses (from (3), (2), and (1)); (*b*) the strength of the drinking response in any society tends to vary directly with the level of anxiety in the society (from (4) and (1)); (c) the strength of the drinking response tends to vary inversely with the strength of the counter-anxiety elicited by painful experiences during and after drinking (from (*a*) and (3) and (2)).[2] (The theory has been re-cast into a deductive mould for convenience of exposition.) All of these deductions were tested in various ways with cross-cultural data obtained from the Yale Cross-cultural Index.

It is of importance to enquire how many sociological results can be explained by means of this kind of theory. It may be expected that sociological findings where individual behaviour is the dependent variable may in principle be explained in this way—generalisations about the development and change of personality, including beliefs and attitudes, and about rates of suicide and mental disorder. On the other hand, generalisations about social organisation or

---

[1] For further discussion of this cf. Argyle (1955).
[2] Mr. Colin Lees has pointed out that the reverse could also be predicted, since punishment increases the level of anxiety ((*b*), (2)).

other aspects of society as a whole could not be explained so easily. It is possible however that development of psychological knowledge about the working of social organisations (cf. Chapter VI) may bring these two within reach of speculative and reductive psychological explanation.

This concludes the discussion of the hypothetical construct type of axiomatic theory. It is suggested that as a method of explanation it is very useful for generalisations about small groups and for laws about societies where the dependent variable is in terms of individual behaviour. The important asset of the technique is that lower-level verification is possible, which if successful converts the theory into the reductive form, to be described later.

An important point is raised by the discovery that two contradictory deductions can be made from Horton's theory. Some theorists recommend the use of a strict mathematical notation throughout with all the symbols carefully defined. However, much can be gained by careful statement of the propositions as above and attention to the definition of terms. If this is done it is possible to achieve rigorous deduction while retaining the use of ordinary language with its advantages of comprehensibility. When social research acquires mathematical precision it will be time to abandon ordinary language.

(2) Mechanism Theories

In the second kind of axiomatic theory, a model is suggested whose presence in the organisation would account for the laws to be explained. It is not supposed however that this particular mechanism is actually present, but simply that the model bears a formal similarity to the neurological apparatus. Given certain functional relations between stimulus and response it is often possible to devise some machine which would be able to produce it, while having no idea of what neuro-physiological structures in detail are responsible. Many psychologists have invented machines which can reproduce some kinds of human or animal behaviour. The important thing is not merely to produce machinery which will ape human behaviour, but to think of models which will explain existing results and predict new ones.

The example which will be given of a mechanism theory is Lorenz's model for instinctive behaviour (1950, p. 255 f.). In Figure 2, the tap T supplies a constant flow of liquid corresponding to the continuous accumulation of energy specific to an instinctive response, and the body of liquid represents the internal state of motivation. The cone-valve, V, represents the releasing mechanism, and is operated by the weights Sp standing for the influence of appropriate stimuli, and opposed by a spring S, representing the inhibitory influence of the higher centres. Another feature is the variation in response R for different speeds of squirting out of the exit. The

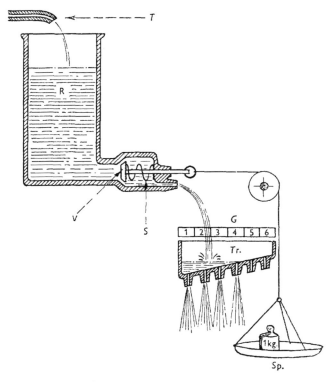

FIG. 2—LORENZ'S MODEL FOR INSTINCTIVE BEHAVIOUR
(From p. 256 of Lorenz, 1950. *By permission of Professor K. Z. Lorenz*)

generalisations explained by this model are: the energy of instinctive responses increases (*a*) with the period of internal accumulation, and (*b*) with the suitability of the stimulus. It also shows (*c*) how the nature of the response varies with intensity of stimulation. It has been pointed out by Deutsch that certain predictions made by the theory are opposed by the facts. (See p. 78.)

How are theories of this sort to be assessed on the three criteria?

As with hypothetical construct theories, they co-ordinate generalisations and make predictions. Whether they are felt to explain is a personal matter. It may be felt that these theories are unsatisfactory until the precise physiological nature of the mechanism has been identified: there may after all be many machines which can do the same things. The mechanism inside a clock could be a spring, an alternating current, or drops of water. While some scientists may be satisfied with a mechanism which shares the formal properties of the underlying physiology, and from which predictions can be made, others will not be satisfied until an actual or hypothetical identification of the mechanism has been made.

Hypothetical construct theories are verifiable at the neurophysiological level; is this also true of mechanism theories? While it is not possible to prove the applicability of these models, they should at least be consistent with existing knowledge at the lower level. The reason for this is that if the model is ultimately to be identified physiologically it must possess the right sorts of properties. Mechanism theories can be regarded as a stage towards hypothetical construct and reductive theories that is particularly useful when lower-level knowledge is lacking.

We can now consider the prospects for mechanism theories of social behaviour. Again, laws of individual social behaviour are best explained by co-ordination to laws in experimental psychology, which in turn may be explained by mechanism theories. It is possible that small group generalisations could be explained in an analogous manner. Homans (1951) hints at models for explaining small group equilibria. The references to equilibria in physical chemistry are unfortunately not developed to a stage at which any actual predictions can be made. This seems to be a possible way of dealing with small group laws, though the hypothetical construct method enables more use to be made of established psychological knowledge. When there is a lot of available knowledge about the lower-level data, the hypothetical construct method would be expected to be strategically more profitable than the mechanism approach. Accordingly, while the latter is suitable at the level of psychology, the former is more useful for groups.

Many of the old sociological theories were of the formal mechanism type, consisting as they did of analogies, comparing society to a machine, a growing organism, etc. These analogies were not however worked out sufficiently for any specific generalisation to be explained, or predictions made. It may be concluded that while mechanism theories are valuable in experimental psychology and hence for laws of individual social behaviour, the hypothetical construct method is preferable for generalisations about small groups and societies.

(3) *Theories with Formal Postulates*

The third kind of axiomatic theory is really another version of the second. It is the 'theory' as opposed to the 'model' in Braithwaite's sense. A formal postulate theory may be identical in structure with a mechanism theory, so that each will explain the same laws and afford the same predictions. Hence any theory of either kind can be converted into one of the other without change of empirical content. The mechanism can be regarded as one possible physical interpretation of the formal theory, and of course a whole family of models may possess the same structure. They will also have the same structure as the underlying physiological apparatus.

There are very few examples of theories presented in this way in psychology, and the one that will be given as an example has also been demonstrated as a model, in that a machine has been made (Deutsch 1954) embodying the structure of the theory, and behaving in the predicted way. The example is that part of Deutsch's theory (1953) which deals with instinctive behaviour.

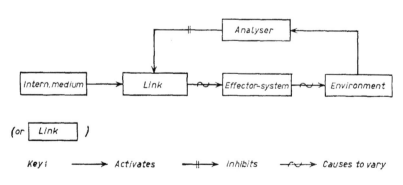

FIG. 3—DEUTSCH'S THEORY OF MOTIVATION
(From p. 305 of Deutsch, 1953. *By permission of Dr. J. A. Deutsch*)

The theory is presented as the specification for a generalised family of mechanisms, which work as described by the postulates. As shown in the diagram, there are five elements: (*a*) An analyser;

(*b*) a link; (*c*) an effector system; (*d*) an environment; and (*e*) an internal medium. The elements can be related in three ways, either by activating, switching off, or causing to vary.

The phenomena of instinctive behaviour can be deduced from five postulates:

(1) When the link is active, the motor organisation is made to vary.
(2) The variations in the motor organisation cause the environment to vary.
(3) A particular variation of the environment activates the receptor system.
(4) The activated receptor system switches off the link.
(5) The change in the internal medium irritates the link in proportion to the magnitude of this change.

If the theory is interpreted psychologically, it states that instinctive activity is brought about by an internal physiological state which initiates behaviour until environmental changes enable the animal to receive certain stimuli, which switch off the 'link' (an unidentified physiological element), which connects the bodily state to the motor system.

Although this field is rather thoroughly explored experimentally, certain predictions from the theory have been confirmed since it was first formulated: Kohn found that rats cease lever-pressing if a nutrient solution is injected into their stomachs, while Hull and Livingstone found that if food which an animal swallows is not allowed to enter the stomach, it will eat indefinitely. The receptors whose stimulation terminates eating turn out to be in the stomach. Both of these results oppose the Lorenz theory outlined previously, according to which behaviour should cease when the animal has worked off a certain amount of activity. It should be mentioned that experiments on thirst arrive at rather different results from the hunger experiments, since the switching-off receptors for thirst lie in the throat and mouth.

Since theories presented as postulates differ only in presentation from mechanism theories, they must obviously have the same strategical advantages and disadvantages. This form of presentation however has the asset that there is no danger of being misled by irrelevant features of the model, and that the systematic implications of the postulates may be deduced more rigorously. On the other hand, most people find it easier to think about models, and there is great resistance to the postulational approach.

It is not intended to discuss further the application of formal postulate theorising to social behaviour, but there are two theories in this field which deserve some consideration on their own account—Lewin's 'topological and vector psychology', and von Neumann and Morgenstern's 'Theory of Games and Economic Behaviour'. In each of these theories, mathematics plays an important role, so that perhaps a word is needed on the normal role of mathematics in an axiomatic theory. The axioms of a theory are pure assumptions: if the theory is a good one, certain propositions which are consequences of the axioms may be interpreted as empirical laws. Mathematics, on the other hand, is purely tautologous: given certain assumptions, the systematic implications of these can be worked out. The role of mathematics in an axiomatic theory is clear: established mathematical devices can be used for working out the implications of the axioms of the theory. It can also be used for predicting detailed empirical results in new and complex cases, as in geometrical optics. Sometimes the appropriate kind of mathematics does not yet exist, in which case scientists must either wait for the mathematicians, or develop the mathematics themselves.

It is probable that Lewin (1936, 1938, 1952) intended to use topology and 'hodology' as auxiliary mathematical tools for drawing inferences from the basic scientific axioms. Some commentators (e.g. Koch 1941) have thought that geometry was to comprise the *whole* of the axiomatic system, the theorems being co-ordinated to psychological laws; a more likely interpretation is that the 'dynamic' principles of substitution, satiation, and the rest are the ultimate scientific axioms from which consequences are to be drawn. Since the geometric deductive system was not developed, this was never actually done: in the most detailed piece of deduction to be worked out—the Zeigarnik theory (Lewin 1952, Chapter 1) no geometrical axioms are used. The test of whether a given mathematical system is applicable is either to see if the consequences drawn in this way are empirically correct or to examine the assumptions made—in this case, whether the behaviour-possibilities of a situation can be represented in two-dimensional space.

Even without the detailed theorems, such a mathematical system can be useful. It abstracts from the welter of possibilities those aspects of a situation which are relevant for a given purpose—in this case goals, barriers, and routes. It may suggest new concepts—such as psychological distance and direction here—which can be measured, and make new kinds of empirical law possible. It may enable important distinctions to be drawn—Lewin was able to distinguish between different kinds of conflict situation and force—thus clarifying the basic concepts.

Supposing that Lewin's theory was developed along the lines indicated, what kind of theory would it be? In many ways it looks like a model—the Person is like a ball pushed and pulled by quasi-electrical forces over a finite number of paths and between a number of barriers; *but it does not work on any familiar mechanical principles*, and the actual principles are not yet disclosed. Stated in formal postulates, the axioms would be psychological laws stated in terms of topological concepts; thus it would be a formal postulate system with the axioms at the same level as the laws, though stated differently.

Von Neumann and Morgenstern (1944) in their *Theory of Games and Economic Behaviour* have developed a mathematical deductive system which enables deductions to be made and problems solved which could not have been done before. As a mathematical system it is not empirically testable—its correctness is a purely logical matter. In order to predict behaviour, scientific axioms must be included—such as that people try to reach a 'minimax', together with assumptions such as that people have a fixed hierarchy of preferences and that certain behaviour will always have certain results in terms of gains and losses. It seems quite likely that these conditions hold in social situations, so that the *Theory of Games* may be of use here. Alternatively this may be regarded as a model, where the game is used as a model for economic and social situations.

(4) *Conclusion*

It is now possible to gather together the conclusions of this discussion of axiomatic theories under the different levels of generalisation to be explained.

The axiomatic explanation of individual behaviour may be accomplished by hypothetical constructs or by the mechanism/postulate approach. While the latter avoids dubious neuro-physiological speculation, the former enables use to be made of lower-level knowledge, and leads towards the development of reductive 'theories'; it is furthermore verifiable at two levels. It would be expected that as neuro-physiological knowledge increases, the hypothetical construct theory will become more feasible, and give way in turn to reductive theories. As for the mechanism or postulate modes of presentation, while models are easier to think about, postulates are less misleading and are essential if mathematics is to be used in the deduction. No distinction is drawn here between generalisations about social and non-social behaviour. As argued in an earlier section, laws of social behaviour should if possible be co-ordinated to laws of non-social behaviour. If they cannot be so classified, due to the emergence of phenomena unique to social behaviour, they must be explained directly by one of the axiomatic methods.

The explanation of generalisations about groups and societies is best conducted by a form of hypothetical construct theory, i.e. in terms of individual psychological processes. As more knowledge of individual social behaviour is acquired this theory, too, becomes of the reductive type. This approach has the great advantage here over the mechanism/postulate technique, that a great deal is known about the lower level and that there is an obvious unit for reduction.

Reductive Theories

In a 'reductive' theory, generalisations at one level are explained by deduction from laws at a lower level. This procedure is similar to that in axiomatic theories of the hypothetical construct variety, save that in this case the lower-level propositions are established laws instead of being speculative postulates. An hypothetical construct theory becomes a reductive theory when it has received lower-level verification. In experimental psychology, reductive theories are explanations in terms of known physiological data. One example of this is the explanation of the value of reaction times for different distances between the points of stimulation and response. The relevant physiological knowledge is (i) the intervening mechanism is transmission of an electro-chemical impulse through the nerves, and (ii) the speed of conduction of such impulses is a certain quantity. A more complex example is the explanation of the visual phenomenon of dark-adaptation in terms of the photo-chemistry of the retina.

Such explanations are rare in psychology since the relevant physiological knowledge is not yet available. However, many psychologists regard this as the furthest point that explanation in psychology can be expected to reach. Obviously further reductive explanations could be effected into the fields of biochemistry, etc., and ultimately to atomic physics, but there is a division of labour amongst scientists so that each is content with one stage of this process. Thus physiologists would be interested in the electrical and chemical explanation of why nerve fibres conduct impulses at the speed they do.

The reductive kind of theory may be examined in relation to the three functions of theories. Clearly this sort of theory is just as powerful in co-ordinating diverse generalisations as the axiomatic type, and it also co-ordinates laws at two different levels by bringing them into deductive relations. With regard to prediction, the situation is similar to that with same-level explanation: the theory itself provides no predictions, but these arise at the previous stage when the relevance of the lower-order data is being explored. In other words, as soon as the implications of the lower-order data are realised, predictions follow. If such predictions are not confirmed, either the lower-level law is at fault, or the experiment is inadequate, or there are other facets to the lower-order mechanism which had not been realised. On the third criterion—the extent to which a satisfying explanation is afforded—it seems to be widely felt that this form of explanation is ideal.

We may now examine the possibilities of reductive explanation for social behaviour. Again individual social behaviour may be explained by co-ordination to laws of psychology, which then receive reductive explanation. Generalisations about groups can be explained in principle by derivation from laws of individual social behaviour.[1] The author's theory of norm-formation described later (p. 157 f.) is partly of the reductive kind, since it contains the generalisation that people have a need for acceptance in groups: as will be shown, there is good evidence for this statement. Hypothetical construct theories, and the reductive theories they eventually become, seem the most convenient kind of explanation for small-group results.

The objection is sometimes made that groups surely contain 'something more' than individuals. For example, it is said, groups have 'atmospheres' over and above the behaviour of any individual, and norms may persist regardless of particular people belonging to the group. Two points need to be made to clarify this position. In the first place, the 'group' consists entirely, and without residue, of individuals, their interaction and shared activity. There are admittedly group customs and so forth, but these are composed of the members interacting in a co-ordinated manner. Secondly, although every member may behave differently in the group from outside it, this is not because of the influence of 'the group' or its 'atmosphere', but is a result of interaction with the other members according to the laws of social behaviour. There is, therefore, in principle no reason for supposing that group phenomena are not reducible to laws of

[1] In some cases this is the same as analysing group behaviour into individual behaviour and then explaining this.

individual social behaviour. As with all reductive explanations, the process awaits the discovery of sufficient lower-level laws; as yet laws of individual social behaviour are rather few. Meanwhile, explanations must be of the hypothetical construct variety.

Finally, the possibility of explaining sociological generalisations in this way may be considered. As with groups, the appropriate lower-level laws are those of individual social behaviour. The examples of hypothetical construct explanations of sociological generalisations could also serve as examples here if it is supposed that the psychological postulates have been confirmed. Some of the theories of Rashevsky (1951) are put forward as reductive explanations of sociology. However, Rashevsky's procedure is curious in that he does not start from any very definite sociological findings to be explained, though some predictions are made and have been confirmed; in addition, the psychological laws used would not be accepted by any psychologist, though it is of interest to note that these laws are themselves given hypothetical construct explanations earlier in the book. In his previous book (1947) the psychological assumptions were regarded as speculative, making the theory an axiomatic one, but later they are regarded as established.

It is necessary at this point to consider the objections made by Durkheim (1895) to the psychological explanation of sociological findings. Durkheim maintained (op. cit., Chapter V) that sociology constituted a valid and autonomous field of study that was irreducible to simpler sciences like psychology. 'Social facts' were distinguished from individual states of consciousness by the criteria of exteriority and constraint—as with law and morals. Quite apart from this notion of social facts implying mystical entities independent of individuals, it is obvious that modern psychology is not concerned with states of consciousness, but with behaviour, and that modern sociology is interested in phenomena which are either reducible to aggregates of individual behaviours (like suicide rates), or to combinations of individual behaviours (like social structures). Whatever may have been the position in 1895, the sociology of to-day is not concerned with a subject-matter that is irreducibly different from that of the psychology of to-day. Durkheim's second point is that social facts can be explained only in terms of causal relations to other social facts—in other words, sociologists should find laws at the level of societies as a whole. With this we are entirely in agreement: the point here however is, how shall such sociological laws themselves be explained? A third argument of Durkheim's is that while people in a society do similar things, they do so for very different motives, so that the study of individuals is bound to be misleading. In answer to this it must be noted that individual differences and deviations are of great sociological interest in relation to problems of delinquency, leadership, and innovation, and that part of psychology —the psychology of personality—is particularly concerned with individual differences. On the other hand, psychology can handle not only such individual differences but also the general trends in response to different situations. Some modern sociologists would relegate psychology to the role of accounting for individual differences, and fail to recognise that it can also account for the general effect of other factors. A further reply to Durkheim's claim that people do the same things for different reasons is that social psychologists have of late been particularly interested in the process of social control, whereby social pressures produce conformity in behaviour. A fourth argument of Durkheim's (1897, p. 318) is to the effect that the existence of regular statistical trends in, for instance, suicide rates proves the existence of collective tendencies exterior to the individual. This point is entirely fallacious: in any society, personalities are distributed in a constant manner which depends on racial composition and the social influences that Durkheim has described. Suicide occurs in those towards one end of the distribution.

To conclude this section, it has been argued that the reductive type of theory represents the final form towards which other kinds of theory move. This is true not only of the explanation of individual behaviour, but also of laws about groups and societies: objections raised in these cases have been shown to be invalid.

TWO ALTERNATIVE APPROACHES

The previous sections have discussed the approaches to explanation which are in line with orthodox procedure in experimental psychology. It remains to deal with two theories of social behaviour which deviate from the usual practice, but which have been very influential in social psychology. These are explanation by means of the 'phenomenal field' by Snygg and others, and Lewin's use of the 'life space', or psychological field.

The 'Phenomenal Field'[1]

The phenomenal field is "the entire universe, including himself, as it is experienced by the individual at the moment of action" (Snygg

[1] I am indebted to Mr. Alan Watson for his valuable comments on this section, though the final responsibility is mine.

and Combs 1949, p. 15). It is recognised that the agent is not conscious of everything all the time, but only of those aspects which are selected to be 'figured' in the centre of attention, the remainder being relatively unconscious 'ground'. The way in which needs and stimuli are represented in consciousness is partly known to us as the result of experiments on perception. It is supposed that behaviour is determined by the state of the phenomenal field at the moment of action, and that behaviour is explainable and predictable through this association. An example of the procedure is as follows:

"One of the authors was driving a car at dusk along a western road. A globular mass about two feet in diameter appeared directly in the path of the car. A passenger in the front seat screamed and grasped the wheel, attempting to steer the car round the object. The driver tightened his grip and drove directly into it. In each case the behaviour of the individual was determined by his own phenomenal field. The passenger, an Easterner, saw the object in the highway as a boulder and fought desperately to steer the car round it. The driver, a native of the vicinity, saw it as a tumbleweed and devoted his efforts to keeping his passenger from overturning the car." (Snygg and Combs 1949, p. 14.)

Note that while there is a direct relationship between the perceptions and the behaviour of each of the characters in this incident, the stimulus is the same for both. The advantages claimed for the phenomenological approach are: (i) it makes use of the fact that while behaviour is often closely related to perceptions, it is not so closely related to the stimulus conditions; (ii) it is possible to make use of the already established determinants of perceptions to account for the state of the phenomenal field; (iii) the 'private access' of introspection provides a method for explaining single cases without the bother of going through the usual experimental and statistical procedures. The principal exponents of this approach are Snygg and Combs (1949, 1950); Krech and Crutchfield (1948) claim to be following Lewin, but proceed throughout in the Snygg manner; many social psychologists maintain that it is necessary to consider not the physical environment, but the environment as perceived and interpreted by the individual—this is often called the 'perceptual approach' and thought to be rather a good thing.

The first general comment on this approach concerns the philosophical position which it assumes. It is supposed that conscious events cause the behaviour which they accompany. This is no place for metaphysical arguments, but it may be said that many philosophers would be in disagreement with this position, on the grounds that, *whatever conscious events are,* they are not the sort of things which can be regarded as causing behaviour—they fall into the wrong logical category.

The second general comment concerns the new technique of scientific inference proposed. For example, there may be direct introspective awareness that an act was performed for such-and-such a motive; or as a result of a certain perception. Although this does not encroach directly on the field of orthodox generalisations, it does point beyond conscious experiences to causes in the stimulus conditions or the hormones. It would only however be permissible to accept the direct experience of causality as veridical if it could be shown to tally with the use of the traditional experimental and statistical methods—which embody the accepted criteria for the inference of causation. It will be demonstrated in the following section that the two methods do not tally, and that in cases of 'rationalisation', 'suppression', and the rest, verbal reports fail to give an accurate picture of the causes of behaviour.

The third remark which may be made is that the approach derives some plausibility from a confusion between perception in the senses of phenomenal field and physiological stimulation. Obviously the second can be regarded as an intermediary cause, though a partial one, whereas the first cannot.

In Figure 4 an alternative (A) to the phenomenological (B) position is indicated. In each case physiological stimulation appears as a part-cause. In B the phenomenal field is shown as containing all of the causes of behaviour, while in A it is shown as a parallel response.

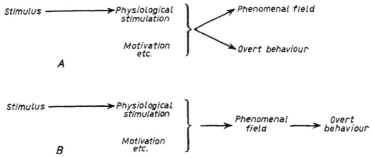

FIG. 4—THE PHENOMENAL FIELD AND BEHAVIOUR

It is now necessary to examine the empirical assumption that the phenomenal field at the moment of action contains all the determinants of behaviour. Instead of 'determinants' we must now speak of 'correlates', and the 'phenomenal field' is regarded as operationally defined by verbal reports. The evidence will be reviewed here briefly.

(1) *Present Stimuli.* It is widely true that we behave towards things as we perceive them, particularly in cases of perceptual illusion and constancy. This is not universal, however, and in the following three instances the correlation breaks down: (i) in a number of experiments on what Lazarus and McCleary call 'subception' (1951), subjects can give a differential response to sub-threshold stimuli; (ii) Gunter (1951) found that if red and green lights are presented binocularly, subjects see red-green rivalry but give the PGR conditioned to yellow; (iii) Maier (1931) found that hints given during problem-solving were effective, but that subjects were unable to remember them afterwards. The time interval was too short for this to be put down to forgetting, and it must be concluded that the hints made no conscious impression.

(2) *Present Motivation.* Verbal reports may indicate states of motivation by indicating perceptual distortion, the endowment of objects with 'demand-value', or the presence of desires. Whatever the semantic status of these qua conscious events, all may be found in verbal reports, though as 'measurements' the last two are as yet not established. Thus the positive form of the proposition that verbal and overt behaviour are correlated cannot yet be demonstrated. It might however be thought that the cumulative evidence for 'unconscious' motivation provided by psychoanalysis constituted a clear disproof (M. B. Smith 1950). Snygg and Combs claim however (1950) that although the motivational determinants of the phenomenal field in these cases lie outside it, they nevertheless influence it at the moment of action. Their example is as follows:

"A young man had an extraordinary phobia for flying birds . . . in his perceptual field a bird was an extraordinarily threatening object" (1950, p. 524).

On the other hand, examples can be found in which patients do not have such phenomenal experiences, as with epileptic fits and hysterical tics. Further, even when phenomenal experiences are present, they are often incomplete—the patient does not know which stimuli in a series of total situations are the relevant ones, and a stimulus is often quite meaningless to him until sufficient material has 'become conscious'. Under post-hypnotic suggestion a person will engage in behaviour and have no conscious understanding of why he does it. He may rationalise, inventing reasons for his actions. Similarly, in cases of sleep-walking, the person has no conscious experiences sufficient to account for his behaviour.

(3) *Past Learning.* The influence of past experience on behaviour is represented in the phenomenal field by what Snygg and Combs call 'differentiation', and Krech and Crutchfield call 'reorganisation'. It is an empirical matter whether such changes are perfectly correlated with changes in performance, and there is very little evidence on it.

There are however two kinds of learning where they do not seem to be. Experiments on concept-formation by Heidbreder and Bouthilet (Leeper 1951, pp. 731–2) show that concepts can be learnt and used without the subject being able to verbalise the cues. Again, as was first pointed out by William James, it seems that in a highly developed skill the performer is scarcely aware of the stimuli to which he is responding.

To conclude this brief examination it may be concluded that (i) it is an empirical, not an *a priori*, matter whether "the phenomenal field at the moment of action contains all the determinants of behaviour"; (ii) it is very difficult to demonstrate this; and (iii) there is considerable evidence that it does not.

The next step is to enquire whether behaviour can be predicted by means of the phenomenal field. Clearly it is impossible to predict behaviour from the field *at* the moment of action: it is necessary in turn to be able to predict what the field *will* be, or how some past state is likely to be modified by future events. Krech and Crutchfield (op. cit.) make use of established results concerning perception to predict perceptions from stimuli, motivation, etc. This is satisfactory as long as behaviour can be predicted from the phenomenal field, but it is not always clear how this can be done. Although this second stage in the two-step process from stimuli to response is satisfying to common sense, it is extremely puzzling to the psychologist. Asch (1952) tried to generalise about this curious relationship by saying that behaviour is always 'rational' in relation to what is perceived: however, in most senses of rational this is clearly false—consider, for example, the experiments on the effect of 'atmosphere' on syllogistic reasoning (Woodworth 1937, pp. 815–17), in which it was found that most people were taken in by certain invalid arguments.

Finally, it may be asked whether behaviour can be explained by the use of the phenomenal field. Previously an explanation was defined as any procedure which makes behaviour seem more comprehensible. Other sections have discussed the special techniques of theory construction which satisfy scientists in this respect. While it is undoubtedly the case that phenomenal-field explanations are commonly accepted in everyday life, it is also clear that they bear no relation to scientific theory. Can the phenomenal field—that is to say verbal reports about perceptions and motivations—play any useful part in understanding behaviour? Apart from the exceptional cases just mentioned, they provide a useful clue to perceptions and motivations. However, they do not give a 'private access' to the

THE EXPLANATION OF SOCIAL BEHAVIOUR 89

causal mechanism at work: they are simply another set of data to be explained. It is of course an important aim of psychology to explain verbal responses as well as others: the point here is that verbal behaviour cannot be used as a way of explaining non-verbal behaviour.

Lewin's 'Life Space'

The postulational aspect of Lewin's theorising has been discussed earlier in the chapter. Like Snygg, Lewin proclaims an interest in explaining single cases (1931), but in practice does not carry this out, so this part of Lewin's thought will not be discussed here. What will be considered here is Lewin's use of the 'life space' in explanation, this being somewhat similar to the phenomenal field approach and differing from the usual procedure.

Lewin's life space (1943a) is a rather similar entity to the phenomenal field, in that both are realms where all the causes of behaviour are supposed to be represented. However, the life space differs from the phenomenal field in that it is a purely theoretical device introduced to explain behaviour; it is not observable in any way. Lewin states that "what is real is what has effects", i.e. the life space is to include all the determinants of behaviour. Hence there is no question about whether the life space contains all the determinants of behaviour as there was with the phenomenal field. Lewin (loc. cit.) and others write as if the life space differed from the phenomenal field simply in being more inclusive, by including unconscious factors and the rest. This however is misleading, since the two concepts are quite distinct in other ways. Whereas the phenomenal field is known via verbal reports (in fact must be so defined), the life space cannot be known in this way if it is to include all determinants of behaviour. Lewin does suggest the use of verbal reports, but these are clearly inadequate. The alternative way of assessing the life space is to infer it from the behaviour which takes place. This also is impossible however, since the laws in which Lewin is interested relate the life space to behaviour, and the whole procedure is clearly circular if the life space has to be deduced from behaviour in the first instance.

Even were it possible to obtain satisfactory operational criteria for the life space, it would still be very difficult to obtain predictions of behaviour when the empirical laws were known. As Spence (1944) has pointed out, Lewin's is an R–R theory, not an S–R theory. This is because the laws in which Lewin is interested relate states of the life space to behaviour, while it has been seen that, however the life space is to be defined, it must be in terms of subsequent behaviour, verbal or not. There are three ways in which this objection might be met, so that behaviour could be related to antecedent conditions. (i) If laws similar to those of perception were found which related the life space to antecedent conditions, behaviour would be predictable by means of a two-stage process. At best this derives an S–R law from the combination of S–R' and R'–R laws, which seems an unnecessarily involved procedure: it would be easier to abandon the life space and relate behaviour directly to its antecedents. (ii) If it is assumed that there is a 'closed system', i.e. that for a period of time there are no external influences, it is possible to predict the life space at t_2 from its state at t_1 (Lewin, op. cit.). This is impossible, however, since the life space at t_2 must be different or else nothing would happen, as at t_1. (iii) If certain assumptions are made about the effects of e.g. motivation on the life space, predictions can be made, as in Zeigarnik's theory (Lewin 1940). Such assumptions must obviously be replaced by empirical generalisations about the effect of motivation, which leads to the same position as (i). Spence's criticism may be upheld, then, that use of the life space does not make the prediction of behaviour possible. All that can be done is to note with satisfaction after the event that an R–R law has been fulfilled. Furthermore, on one definition of the life space, both R's are the same, while the other definition is open to all the objections to the phenomenal field.

It must be concluded that Lewin's use of the life space is unsuccessful, because this cannot be satisfactorily defined save in terms of behaviour—making the whole process circular. Furthermore, prediction is impossible without anchorage in the antecedent conditions of behaviour—which is best achieved without the life space.

Several psychologists have drawn attention to the similarity of Lewin's technique to the psychology of personality, in that both deal with R–R laws. In fact there is no parallel here at all, since R–R laws of quite different types are involved. Lewin's generalisations at best relate two aspects of responses for the same situation. The findings of personality psychology, on the other hand, consist of correlations between the responses of a number of people over a series of different situations. While experimental psychologists seek to predict behaviour in different situations regardless of individual differences, personality psychologists seek regularities in the individual differences.

Lewin attempted to extend his life-space approach to groups, the equivalent concept being called the 'social field'. In so far as it resembles the life space the considerations of the previous section apply, but in so far as it is a group version of this, several other problems arise which will be considered here. As used by J. F. Brown (1936), the social field represents the relevant common elements in the life spaces of the group members, and is used to account for their joint, parallel behaviour. It would presumably be found in practice by averaging the life spaces of the individual members. It is true that members of a group come to share ways of behaving, and that presence in a common situation will also make for similar life spaces. It is however quite out of the question that these should be identical in view of individual differences in personality and informal status. The use of the concept seems to imply identity of the life spaces of the group members, and hence its use is restricted to the explanation of behaviour which is identical for all the members.

A further point is that Brown's diagrams always show the group members responding to common situations or objects which are external to the group, but they never indicate any interaction between the group members. The social field used in this way can show parallel behaviour, but not interaction. Lewin (1947, pp. 10–13) however makes an interesting attempt to use the social field to account for interaction between two people. The life spaces of two people are first drawn up at time t_1; they each show intended behaviour of ego and expected behaviour of alter. He then constructs the social field at t_1, by mixing up the individual life spaces in a quite arbitrary manner. He derives from this the separate life spaces at t_2, though it is by no means clear how this is carried out.

It is unfortunate that Lewin's attempt to provide a means of handling serial interaction has failed, because as yet there is no satisfactory means of dealing with this problem.

APPENDIX

AN EXAMPLE OF THE INTERVENING-VARIABLE TECHNIQUE

(Hull 1951)

(1) A learning experiment was carried out on rats in a Skinner box. In this the effect of number of trials (N) on reaction latency ($_sE_R$) was found. A curve was plotted showing the functional relation and an equation was fitted to the curve:

$$_sE_R = 3\cdot55(1-10^{-\cdot0305N}) \qquad \text{(p. 31)}$$

This represents the quantitative influence of the independent variable N on the dependent variable $_sE_R$. N is supposed to act, not on $_sE_R$ directly, but upon $_sH_R$, an intervening variable named 'habit strength'.

Thus $_sH_R = 1-10^{-\cdot0305N}$ (omitting the constant factor 3·55)
(p. 31)

(2) A second experiment found the effect of another independent variable, stimulus intensity (S), on $_sE_R$. The equation representing this influence is:

$$_sE_R = 1\cdot328(1-10^{-\cdot440\log S}) \qquad \text{(p. 44)}$$

Again S is supposed to act on an intervening variable, V, so that—

$V = 1-10^{-\cdot440\log S}$ (omitting the constant 1·328) (p. 44)

(3) A third experiment studied the effect of N on $_sE_R$ under different conditions of S. Here N is replaced by D, the number of days of training. For two values of S two equations were found for the relation of $_sE_R$ and N.

(a) $_sE_R = \cdot87\,(1-10^{-\cdot10\,D}) - \cdot130$
(b) $_sE_R = \cdot14\,(1-10^{-\cdot12\,D}) - \cdot024$ (p. 42)

Clearly the functional relation between $_sE_R$ and N holds for both values of S. Increasing S influences the coefficients (·87 and ·14), not the powers (·10 and ·12), which can be assumed to be equivalent. Thus it is deduced that $_sE_R$ is a multiplicative function of $_sH_R$ and V, i.e.

$$_sE_R = {_sH_R} \times V,$$

where V and $_sH_R$ are defined in terms of S and N respectively. This last step shows that the form of the functional relation between $_sE_R$ and N is unchanged for different values of S, and that the influence of S is to multiply the value of $_sE_R$ by a certain factor. The second experiment showed how this factor was related to S.

Part II

GENERALISATIONS AND THEORIES

CHAPTER IV

INTERACTION BETWEEN TWO PEOPLE

THE PERCEPTION OF OTHER PEOPLE

THERE ARE SEVERAL purposes for which the perception of other people is important—the assessing of personality in selection interviewing, the recording of social behaviour by observers in small-group experiments, the judging of emotional states by psychotherapists and others, and the perceiving of the attitudes of others to oneself in many practical situations. It will be noticed that the object of 'perception' in all these cases is rather different from that in the traditional experimental psychology of perception: instead of judging sizes, colours, and shapes the observer is assessing more complex qualities like personality traits and emotions which must be inferred from directly observed cues. In addition, it is not simply visual perception that is involved, since auditory cues of speech are often part of the total pattern of stimuli. Again, in many experiments the observer is able to watch a whole sequence of behaviour, while in some of the researches included here the observer is also an interviewer.

In other respects the problems of studying the perception of other people are similar to those in the perception of simpler physical stimuli. The stimulus conditions or the state of the observer are varied systematically and the perceptual responses compared. These responses are usually recorded by asking the observers to rate the quality under observation on a five- or seven-point scale, though matching and phenomenological descriptions can also be used. Great interest has been taken in the *accuracy* of these judgments, and the perceptions may be compared with objective test scores, in the case of intelligence for instance, or with the consensus of other people's judgments for personality traits; the latter is a rather different kind of criterion so far as measurement of accuracy is concerned.

To the question 'How accurate are judgments of other people?' no direct answer can be given, since it depends on the personality of the observer and the amount of information. The interview provides better opportunities for observation than most other situations, but even the interview has come under heavy criticism of late.

There are two grounds for criticism. Firstly, in selection schemes in which an interview has followed objective tests and group discussions (the interviewers knowing the results), the validity of the interview rating has not been significantly higher, and has occasionally been lower, than the results of the tests alone. In Kelly and Fiske's study of the selection of clinical psychologists (1951), the first interview lowered the validity from ·17 to ·15, and the second raised it from ·19 to ·27, if the validities of the successive stages of testing are compared. In the Civil Service Selection Boards the interview increased validity only from ·44 to ·47 (Vernon 1953, p. 29). In answer to this criticism it may be pointed out that the interview *alone* might have had a good validity here; further, in some cases the interview has been able to increase the validity of objective tests—as with *some* Personnel Selection Officers during the war. (Vernon and Parry 1949, pp. 157-9.) The second criticism of the interview is that when used alone it sometimes has a very low validity. Himmelweit and Summerfield (1951) found a correlation of only ·067 between interview ratings of incoming students at the London School of Economics and their final results. However, Handyside and Duncan (1954) found validities of ·17 to ·66 for different interviewers in supervisor selection, and Estes (1937) found that ratings of personality in an interview had correlations of ·24 to ·61 with objective tests.

The truth of the matter is that the *validity* of the interview depends on the skill of the interviewer (which can be increased by training), as well as on the nature of the trait being rated and the opportunities for observing the candidate. Consequently the validity is unpredictable, and the reliability low: Vernon and Parry (1949, pp. 152-5) report *reliabilities* of ·5 to ·6. This defect can be reduced by the use of several interviews. While the value of the interview has been overestimated in the past, it is a mistake to suppose that it is completely useless.

The accuracy of judgments when less information is provided is naturally rather lower. Brunswik (1945), for example, found that judgments of I.Q. from photographs correlated ·10 with test intelligence. In general, correlation of judgments with a criterion vary between ·10 and ·65, depending on the various conditions to be discussed below.

The Personality of the Judge

The evidence on this factor has been reviewed recently by Bruner and Tagiuri (1954) and Taft (1955), so only a brief account will be given here. *Similarity* between observer and judged in respect of age, sex, social background, and personality characteristics improves the accuracy of judgments, though the advantage of similarity for the perception of personality may be due to projection, which usually distorts: this does not matter when the other person is like oneself. *Intelligence* is closely related to ability to judge emotions, but probably only slightly to ability for judging personality traits, and some investigators have found no relationship. *Introversion* has been found by several investigators to characterise the good judge of personality, and with it other traits such as being cautious, reserved, and unemotional. These may well be summarised by Allport's term 'detachment' (1937, p. 515). *Emotional adjustment* has been shown to bear a relation to accuracy of judgment, while of course psychotics suffer from gross distortion of perception as a result of motivational factors. Sears's finding (1936) that undesirable traits may be projected on to others, so that they are judged as too high on those traits, has not been confirmed. Authoritarian judges suffer more from halo effect (Frenkel-Brunswik 1951). *Aesthetic sensitivity* was suggested by Allport as a characteristic of the good judge (loc. cit.), and subsequent research has confirmed this. Psychologists, women, and older people (for adults not children) have no superiority of judgment.

The Motivation of the Judge

Experimental psychologists have found in the perception of simple physical stimuli; that motivation of the percipient can have the effect of lowering the threshold for recognition under short exposure, of distorting in a wish-fulfilling direction when the stimuli are vague and ambiguous, and of causing the sizes of desired objects to be overestimated (cf. M. D. Vernon 1952, pp. 231–47). In the study of the perception of other people, research has centred on the second of these three effects—the 'distortion' of the perception in relation to the actual stimuli.

The best demonstration of the distorting influence of motivation in social perception is Pepitone's experiment (1950) in which boys with a greater incentive to be accepted by a committee tended to perceive that they had in fact been accepted, though the committee-members behaved in a standard way for all the subjects. McClelland and his associates (1953) have developed a measure of the achievement motive based on responses to the vague situations portrayed in the T.A.T.

Emotional states also affect perceptions of others. The classic experiment here is the one in which Murray (1933) found that in the anxious state following a game of 'murder', a number of girls judged portraits to be more malicious than they had done before. Leuba and Lucas (1945) induced by hypnosis the three moods happy, critical, and anxious in three subjects, each subject experiencing the three moods in turn. The subjects gave descriptions of the same six pictures when in each mood, and it was found that the moods had a strong effect both on what was seen and on the story or explanation given.

The 'set' of the observer before he sees the person to be perceived is important. Kelley (1950) gave brief character sketches to his observers beforehand, half of these containing the word 'warm', half the word 'cold'. This experimental variable influenced ratings made of the people observed—those introduced as 'warm' were judged to be more considerate, sociable, humorous, etc. Similarly in a number of small-group experiments reported in Chapter V, the friendliness of groups was manipulated by experimental instructions, and the liking of the other members increased. It would be interesting to know how much genuine interaction is required to correct erroneous information given in advance. The problem is complicated by the fact that the observer will himself behave differently towards a person described as 'warm' and may thus tend to elicit warm behaviour.

Several investigators have found that the attitude of the percipient towards the subject may influence his perception. Fiedler (1949) showed that observers tend to regard people whom they like as more similar to themselves than they really are. Horowitz and his co-workers (1951) found similarly that members of discussion groups perceived their friends as agreeing with them more than in fact they did. An interesting study by Bieri (1953) showed that when a pair of strangers had interacted and come to a number of agreements they tended to perceive each other as more like themselves than beforehand. Lastly, Wittreich (1953) obtained some evidence that married couples, when looking at one another in the Ames distorting rooms at Princeton, did not have the usual size illusions. This result however could have been an effect of experience rather than of attitude.

The Amount of Information

It has been demonstrated in a number of experiments inspired by information theory that the recognition of letters and words is more accurate and quicker if more 'information' is supplied—that is to say, if no parts are omitted and the conditions for observation are adequate. Much the same is true of the perception of people, though 'information' is now being used in a much vaguer sense. For example, emotions can be judged more accurately if the context in which a person is perceived is known, and if a sequence of behaviour is shown, as opposed to a single static photograph. Overt personality traits like aggressiveness can be more easily judged than more covert ones (Wolf and Murray 1937). Again, some subjects are more easily judged than others: Estes (quoted by Bruner and Tagiuri 1954, p. 643) named such persons 'open' as opposed to 'concealed', though it is not known what the corresponding personality traits are. While a longer interview or period of observation is in general better than a shorter, and while observers who are better acquainted with the subject often do better, there is some evidence that intimate acquaintance leads to leniency and increased halo effect in ratings (cf. Vernon 1953, p. 117 f.).

Research on the cues used in the perception of other people has shown that quite small quantities of information may be used, with a certain amount of success. Thornton (1944), for instance, found that the same people were judged to be more intelligent when wearing spectacles, and that when subjects smiled this affected all the ratings they received in the favourable direction. Sarbin and Hardyck (1953) showed line diagrams of bodily postures and found a high degree of agreement on the gesture supposed to be portrayed ('resigned', 'suspicious', etc.). Sarbin and Williams (1953) similarly found agreement on the age, sex, and occupational roles of the speakers in a series of tape-recordings of single sentences such as "All right, boys, get in there and fight". In another auditory experiment, Ruesch and Prestwood (1949) found that anxiety could be transmitted via tape-recordings and that the relevant cues were certain properties of the pitch and frequency of the words used.

The cues which are used may not always be the right ones. Brunswik (1945) discovered, for example, that height of body and height of forehead were used as cues for intelligence. However, while judged I.Q. correlated with body height ·25, height correlates with I.Q. to only about ·10. In other words, the cue in this case is being relied upon to a greater extent than is warranted by the actual relation between the cue and the quantity rated. Presumably all these cues have to be learnt, and it would be of interest to know how they come to be overused in this way, if this result is at all general.

Systematic Errors of Judgment

The most common error of judgment is known as *halo effect*, and is the tendency to make a general response to a person and not rate him independently on a series of traits. When a number of people are assessed, halo effect appears as an unduly high correlation between the ratings for pairs of traits. For example, Brunswik (1945) found a correlation of ·84 between judgments of intelligence and energy, while objective test scores for these two qualities correlated only ·28. The point is not that the ratings correlate, but that they correlate too much. In practice, halo effect can be reduced by asking observers to rate all the subjects on a single trait before going on to the next: this is possible when marking exam papers, but not when interviewing candidates. Again, rating scales should be arranged so that the desirable end of the scales appears left and right at random. Vernon (1953, p. 116) suggests removing the halo response by averaging ratings in the favourable direction and eliminating it statistically: however, as he recognises, this presupposes that the underlying traits are all independent.

Experiments on the development of perceptions of personality from verbal material have given some information on how halo effect works. Asch (1946) presented judges with lists of qualities supposed to characterise some person and asked them to write a personality sketch. Half the lists contained the word 'warm', half had the word 'cold' instead.[1] The descriptions of the warm subjects differed very considerably from those of the cold, though the warm/cold variable did not affect all other dimensions equally. In a later experiment, Asch (1952) found that the polite/blunt variable did not have such a marked effect as warm/cold, showing that traits differ in their power to influence others by halo effect. It was also clear from these experiments that observers make an effort to integrate their perception into an organised whole, and this has been compared with Bartlett's "effort after meaning" and the *Gestalt* principles of configuration. Asch (1952) found, for example, that subjects asked to form impressions of two people characterised by three traits each, and then of a single person possessing all six, had greater difficulty in performing the latter task than those who did it straight off.

Frenkel-Brunswik (1951) has developed the personality dimension of 'rigidity', or intolerance of perceptual ambiguity. It was found that some children saw their parents as wholly good or bad,

[1] This is similar to Kelley's experiment, which was really a repetition of Asch's work using real subjects instead of the list of words.

while others saw both positive and negative features in them. Evidence was found to show that the former children were in fact ambivalent to their parents, as shown by less direct measures of their attitudes. There are thus individual differences in the extent of halo effect, and the authoritarian or prejudiced person has been found to show this most (Adorno et al. 1950).

Judges vary in the way they use rating scales, and the differences between them may be classified as *constant error* and *central tendency*. Constant error is the average difference between rating and objective measure in a number of ratings by the same judge. When no objective measure is available, this appears as differences between the average ratings of different judges. O'Comisky (1955), for example, found that one of his observers rated all subjects "below average" for every trait. If ratings by a number of judges are to be averaged this does not matter, but if different interviewers are used for different candidates, it would be necessary to make a correction for the different average rating of each judge. Central tendency is a common error of judgment—the use of only the central categories of rating scales, and avoidance of the extremes. When this occurs less information is being communicated than if the whole of the scale were used. More serious however is the fact that different observers have different degrees of central tendency. Vernon reports (1953, p. 140) that the percentage of extreme judgments on a five-point scale varied from 17% to 98% for a number of different observers. Clearly if such ratings are combined the judgments of the observer using a greater range will carry greater weight, so a correction needs to be applied.

The Effects of Experience

In experimental psychology two main problems about the influence of learning on perception are whether the recognition of squares, triangles, and other shapes is innate or acquired, and whether the way in which ambiguous figures are perceived can be influenced by reward. For social perception, interest has been taken in the problem of how stereotypes influence perception. The cues for social perception, which are presumably learnt, have been considered above.

It has long been known that people hold certain 'stereotypes' about the personalities of members of particular races (Katz and Braly 1935), and the same is probably true of members of certain social class, age-sex, and occupational groups. Krech and Crutchfield (1948, p. 94 f.) maintain that we perceive first the social group to which a person belongs, and then either assimilate him to the stereotype for that group or contrast him with it—in both cases maintaining the belief that most group members conform to the stereotype. This could be regarded as a special case of halo effect between judgments of race, class, etc., on the one hand, and of intelligence, personality, etc., on the other. There are probably individual differences in the dimensions of others which are most salient—the dimensions of class and occupation might be more or less salient for some people than those of intelligence and personality. The finding that prejudiced people can recognise members of the disliked race more accurately than can non-prejudiced people could have been predicted from this (e.g. Allport and Kramer 1946). Similarly, prejudiced persons are less accurate in perceiving traits and attitudes (Scodel and Mussen 1953).

Self-perception

The perception of oneself deserves a separate section, although there are similarities to the perception of others. There are two experimental situations which may be classified as self-perception. The first is that of the personality questionnaire, such as the Bernreuter Personality Inventory and the Minnesota Multiphasic Inventory: the questions ask not so much for self-ratings on personality traits as for reports of behaviour in a variety of different situations, such as "Do you day-dream frequently?" Secondly, there is the level of aspiration situation where subjects estimate their future score at a task or test, their past performance being known to them.

The 'accuracy' of self-perception has a rather different significance for each situation. Personality inventories have been validated against ratings by other people, and by comparing the scores of contrasted groups of neurotics or delinquents and normals—these in turn depending on diagnosis by psychiatrists and others. The evidence on the validity of these questionnaires has been extensively reviewed by Ellis (1946), who found that 124 investigations of group tests showed correlations of more than ·4 with the criterion, but that 135 showed correlations lower than this. On the other hand, individually administered tests such as the M.M.P.I. fared better, though they have not been so widely studied. These results give some support to the many *a priori* arguments for the invalidity of personality questionnaires, though it seems that certain questionnaires individually administered can achieve a reasonable validity. However, the best-known inventories—those devised by Bernreuter, Bell,

Thurstone, and Woodworth—are extremely unsatisfactory. 'Accuracy' in the level of aspiration situation has a rather different meaning—here it is a matter of making correct predictions about future scores. In fact, it is found that most people aim higher than their previous performance, and the difference between predicted score and past score is used as the measure of level of aspiration (usually expressed as a percentage of the past score).

A number of investigators have tried to discover what kind of personalities have most *insight*, that is to say are most accurate at self-perception. Several studies reviewed by Bruner and Tagiuri (op. cit.) show that the people good at judging others can also rate themselves in agreement with others' ratings. However, if the criterion of accuracy in self-perception is the judgment of psychiatrists a different kind of person proves to be the most insightful: Vernon (1933) found that the two criteria correlated only to the extent of ·39. It is not very clear what are the personality characteristics associated with insight in this second sense.

Most investigators agree that level of aspiration correlates fairly highly (about ·6) between different experimental situations. Himmelweit (1947) found a higher level of aspiration among dysthymic than hysteric neurotic patients, suggesting that it indicates introversion, though other investigators have obtained less definite results here. P. S. Sears (1941) found that unsuccessful children and those lacking in confidence set themselves unrealistically high levels of aspiration. On the other hand, Gould (1939) found that some subjects lowered their *public* level of aspiration in order to avoid failure—a process familiar among groups of students awaiting examination results. Lewin and others (1944) summarise the situation by saying that the cognitive probability judgment is influenced both by the seeking of success and by the avoidance of failure; like the rest of Lewin's theories however this does not enable us to predict what is going to happen in a given case.

One of the central tenets of the school of non-directive therapy is that patients under treatment come to hold more favourable perceptions of themselves. (It is not clear whether this is to be regarded as a *cause* of the recovery.) Raimy (1943) and others have in fact confirmed this by investigations of patients. A further result obtained by Aidman (1951) is that patients come to have an increased congruence between the different aspects of their self-perceptions.

Self-perception is greatly influenced by *reference groups*. A reference group in this connection is a group or class of persons with which a person compares himself in respect of his success, personal qualities, good fortune, etc. In Chapter V (p. 154) a quite different sense of reference group is introduced—a group to which a person wishes to belong or by which he wants to be accepted. While the same group may serve both functions, these meanings are distinct (Kelley 1952). Self ratings on social status vary, depending on the groups with which a person habitually compares himself (Hyman 1942). This is similar to the way in which absolute judgments of weight depend on the previous range of stimuli to which a subject has been exposed. Another investigation of the perception of one's own status made use of two extreme reference groups—'tramps and gypsies' at one end, 'Lords, Bishops, and Judges' at the other (Jahoda 1953). There is a further question of why a person should choose one reference group rather than another, and the discovery that a person has a certain reference group does not explain anything until this origin is known.

Level of aspiration also depends on reference groups. Chapman and Volkmann (1939) and subsequent investigators found that subjects would adopt, or change towards, a level of aspiration that was in conformity with the announced scores of certain desirable groups, as opposed to those of groups in which the subjects were not interested. Rasmussen and Zander (1954) found that the ideal performances of a number of teachers were close to the perceived performances of attractive groups. It would be confusing to call such attractive groups 'reference groups', since the term was introduced to include all groups with which a person compared himself, both favourably and unfavourably. Furthermore, while they may be membership groups or would-be membership groups (the other sense of reference group) they need not be so, as in the case of such reference groups as 'young married women' or 'graduates'.

Self-perceptions are probably influenced by motivational factors. Sears (1936) found that people rated 'stingy' by others tended to underrate their own and overrate others' possession of this trait: a neat demonstration of the Freudian mechanism of 'projection'. However, later investigators have not been able to repeat this result. It has often been suggested that self-perceptions are learnt through discovering the attitudes of others to oneself: McIntyre (1952) and others have found that self-acceptance correlates with acceptance by others, though it would be expected that the relationship would hold only for groups whose acceptance is desired and whose norms are agreed to. However, perception of the attitudes of others to oneself is not wholly accurate and people overestimate the friendship of others when motivated to be accepted (Pepitone 1950), and when they like the other person themselves (Tagiuri et al. 1953).

The Explanation of these Results

Throughout this section on social perception an attempt has been made to indicate the continuity of the results with those more familiar ones obtained for the perception of physical objects. The effect of motivation and learning, the tendency to organise into wholes, the influence of the personality of the percipient and the conditions of observation, are much the same in both cases.

There is in addition a theory postulated in connection with certain aspects of self-perception. Merton and Kitt (1950) introduce the notion of reference group to account for the different degrees of resentment towards call-up and degrees of expectation of promotion among various categories of American soldiers. For example, married men were found to be more resentful of being called up than unmarried men: this is explained by saying that married men compare themselves with married men in civilian life or with unmarried men in the Army (who did not have to sacrifice so much). This explanation is unsatisfactory on several counts. Firstly, it is only a *post hoc* correlational interpretation of the Lewinian type, and of course no predictions follow. Secondly, there is no explanation of why these particular reference groups should be chosen, and thirdly, there is no independent evidence that they are.

THE EFFECT OF THE PRESENCE OF OTHER PEOPLE

The Influence of an Audience

One of the very simplest social situations is that of being watched by other people. It is, moreover, of some practical importance, since most people feel anxiety when first speaking or performing in public or appearing at a board interview, and it would be valuable to discover how to minimise this stage-fright. Most of the experimental work however has been concerned with the less ambitious problem of how task-performance is affected by the presence of an audience. In some cases a purely passive audience has been employed, in others it has been of a deliberately threatening character. This last condition used to be described as 'ego-involvement', though the term is generally replaced nowadays by 'stress'. This is perhaps fortunate, since 'ego involvement' was used in a variety of ways, for instance by Sherif and Cantril (1947). Holt (1945), reviewing early research, points out that it usually referred to a condition in which the subject's status was at stake. The experimental production of this condition can be achieved in various ways—instructions about the importance of the audience or of the 'test' being performed, or a critical, derisive attitude on the part of the audience. As a matter of fact most audiences have some ego-involving effect, so the experiments on passive and threatening audiences are grouped together here.

Most investigators have found that performance slows down when an audience is present. A translation task (Combs and Taylor 1952), block assembly (Ichheiser 1930), and psychophysical choice time (Wapner and Alper 1952) have all been found to take longer under audience conditions. In several cases more mistakes were made as well, and Cowen (1952) found an increased rigidity at problem-solving. However, it is usually found that certain subjects do better when they are being watched, and Dashiell (1930) found that word-association was faster—though Ekdahl (1929) found it slower.

The disturbing influence of emotional states has sometimes been held to be responsible for this retardation. Moore (1917) in fact found that induced states of anger, embarrassment, and sexual arousal all interfered with performance. However, not all emotions are disorganising, as Leeper (1948) has pointed out, and they may act as a kind of motivation.

Another important aspect of this question is concerned with the test scores of subjects when confronted with different behaviour on the part of the tester. Lord (1950) found that a cold manner produced more mistakes than a warm manner in a card-sorting test, and greater emotionality in the Rorschach. Sacks (1952) showed that greater rapport produced increased scores on an intelligent test. These experiments have important implications for the conduct of both laboratory experiments and mental testing—the conditions of each require to be more standardised than they sometimes are.

It has often been pointed out that in crowds people seem especially free from restraint—the very reverse of ego-involved. Festinger, Pepitone, and Newcomb (1952) set up an experimental situation in which subjects were encouraged to make hostile remarks about their parents. A positive correlation was found between making many hostile remarks and being unable to recall later who said what. This was interpreted to indicate that those subjects who became 'de-individuated', i.e. whose ego-involvement was minimised, were most free from restraint. It is also of interest to notice that these subjects were the most attracted to the group—suggesting that being freed from restraint is a satisfying state.

In Chapter V, evidence is quoted to indicate the effects of threat on group performance as such (p. 148 f.).

The Effect of Co-workers

The second topic to be discussed in this section is the effect on individual performance of introducing a co-worker. The performance of subjects working alone at a task is compared with their performance together—all are carrying out the same tasks and they are told that there is no competition. A number of laboratory experiments were conducted along these lines in the period 1920-35 using tasks such as multiplication and cancellation of numbers (cf. Dashiell 1935). None of these experiments was very satisfactory, since few subjects were used and no statistical tests were applied to the results. However, all showed rather similar results. The speed of performance of a variety of laboratory tasks is increased, but subjects also suffer from emotional excitement, as inferred from their reports and observed from their behaviour (e.g. F. H. Allport 1924; Moede 1920). The quality of work is poorer, performance at a reasoning task was found to be worse (Allport 1920), stutterers were slower to make associations (Travis 1925), and variability of performance with time increased (Mukerji 1940). Several investigators have found that this social facilitation provided by a co-worker wears off with time. The effects of a co-worker resemble competitive behaviour (see p. 128 ff.) both in the increased speed of work and in the emotional interference. It is clear that even with instructions to the contrary, the response in our society to a co-worker is to compete with him. It is interesting to note that in Dashiell's experiment (1930), subjects working alone at the same time worked faster than those working alone at different times, and as fast as those working together, presumably because competition was not ruled out in the first condition. Another effect of introducing a second person doing the same task however is that the two will work at much the same speed, i.e. 'output norms' are set up. Thus those who did best in the alone situation will gain least from having a co-worker (Allport 1924).

THE INFLUENCE OF ONE PERSON'S BEHAVIOUR ON ANOTHER

Emotional Contagion

The second group of problems to be considered about the interaction between two people is concerned with the effect of A's behaviour on B. To begin with, there is the case where A is simply in an emotional state. The recognition of emotional states has been considered earlier in this chapter, so it remains to discuss the effect of such states on the observer. It has been widely assumed that a process called 'emotional contagion' takes place, and that B will simply tend to share the emotion of A. In fact there is little exact evidence to support this. Mintz (1951) found that emotional facilitation failed to produce panic in small experimental groups. On the other hand, Ruesch and Prestwood (1949) found that anxiety was transmitted via tape-recordings of therapeutic sessions, and Escalona (1945) showed that babies of neurotic mothers would not feed properly with their mothers but would with nurses, suggesting that the anxiety of the mothers was producing the feeding disturbance. McDougall (1908) called this 'sympathy': he supposed there was a universal human tendency to feel the same emotions as other people. Nowadays psychologists want to know more about the detailed conditions under which behaviour takes place, and the question is when exactly do such sympathetic responses occur? Before the notion of sympathy can be used to explain crowd behaviour or reactions to mass media it is essential to know more about it. A certain amount of research has been carried out on sympathy in children; however, sympathy here has the slightly different meaning of 'concern with the affairs of others', though this may be closely related to the other meaning. L. B. Murphy (1937) found frequent sympathetic responses among fifty-four 2–4-year-old children; those children showing most sympathy also showed most aggression, a result confirmed by other investigators. Washburne (1935) found sympathy to be related to adjustment in adolescents, while Murphy found that insecurity increased sympathetic behaviour in some children and reduced it in others. It is common observation that sympathy is greatest towards people who are liked, but there are as yet no investigations of this.

Imitation

The overt behaviour of A may produce direct imitation on the part of B. The classic experiments here were those of Miller and

Dollard (1941) using children and rats. They found that if subjects were rewarded for imitating they would learn to imitate, and furthermore would learn to generalise and discriminate among different leaders and situations. These experiments have been repeated by Schein (1954) with adults. While learning to imitate by reward took place, there were considerable signs of interference by other motives, such as avoiding what was regarded as 'cheating' or 'copying'. This sort of experiment has been criticised by Asch (1952) on the grounds that it is designed in a way which excludes any understanding of the situation. He cites experiments by his students where the introspective reports show complex hypothesis-behaviour before correct 'imitation' behaviour occurred.

Interesting light is thrown on the subject of imitation in a field setting by the studies of Lippitt and Polansky (Lippitt et al. 1952; Polansky et al. 1950) in their studies of boys' summer camps. Amongst other things they found that the boys in a camp were arranged in an informal hierarchy, in which lower members followed the behaviour of senior ones. On the other hand, it seems that this was largely due to deliberate attempts at influence on the part of the high-status members, and that spontaneous imitation was actually more common among the senior than among the junior members. Grosser, Polansky, and Lippitt (1951) also carried out a laboratory experiment in which pairs of children were left alone and forbidden to do certain things. One child was a confederate of the experimenter in each case; if this child disobeyed the adult instructions, the genuine subject also was much more likely to do so.

There are many theories of imitation, and some of these are reviewed by Miller and Dollard (op. cit.). McDougall's theory of an instinct to imitate is nowadays discounted, since it has to presuppose such a large number of innate S-R connections—one for each act which can be imitated. Miller and Dollard's theory that imitation is learnt—a kind of 'learning set' or 'deutero-learning'—is supported by their experiments. However, as mentioned above, Asch has objected to these experiments on the ground that understanding of the situation is ruled out. He would prefer to classify imitation as a kind of problem-solving behaviour. It is possible to afford some reconciliation of these views by saying that some forms of imitation are no more than blind reinforcement learning, while others are more suitably regarded as cases of problem-solving. At the same time it should be stressed that an objective, behavioural, approach to the explanation of problem-solving is to be preferred to Asch's exclusively cognitive, phenomenological account.

Suggestion—the Influence of Communication on Behaviour

One of the most important uses of communication is to influence the behaviour of others. This may take place in a face-to-face situation or through the mass media of radio, television, etc. Some reference will be made to each of these in this section. The suggestion may be to change an opinion or belief, or to make some simple movement such as falling forwards while blind-folded. The latter type of 'ideo-motor suggestion' is often distinguished from the former or 'prestige suggestion'. An interesting difference which has been found is that subjects tend to be normally distributed for ideo-motor situations but bimodally for prestige suggestion (Aveling and Hargreaves 1921).

One controversy in connection with suggestibility is whether or not it can be regarded as a unitary personality trait. While several investigators are happy to speak of a general factor, others have found very small correlations between different tests and talk of different types of suggestibility (cf. Coffin 1941, p. 20 f.). Clearly there is *some* correlation between suggestibility in different situations, and clearly this correlation will be considerable if these situations are sufficiently similar. On the other hand, zero correlations have often been found between different situations, and as yet no agreed classification has been arrived at. However, a number of studies show that suggestibility is greater in children and in women (cf. Coffin, loc. cit.). It has often been thought that hysterics (extroverted neurotics) are very suggestible: a careful study by Eysenck (1947), using sixteen tests for suggestion, shows that suggestibility is closely correlated with neurosis, and is actually slightly greater in anxious and obsessional patients (introverted neurotics) than in hysterics. The experimental evidence is conflicting concerning the correlation with intelligence, though a slight inverse relation is indicated. Research on the effectiveness of advertising also shows that less intelligent people are influenced more (Burtt 1938).

Several investigators have shown that communications are believed if the subject is already favourable to the content of the communication. (This is a slightly different problem, concerning the *acceptance* of communications rather than any change of behaviour.) Coffin (1941), for example, found a high correlation between readiness to accept pro-Allied propaganda and favourable attitudes towards the Allies among American students at the beginning of the last war.

The prestige of the source of suggestions is an important factor in their effectiveness. To avoid the circularity of defining a prestigeful source as one whose suggestions are accepted, some investigators such as Sherif (1935*b*) first obtained preferences, in this case for different authors, before attaching their names to literary passages to be judged. Expert opinion is most effective on technical matters, while group or majority opinion is more potent for matters related to the affairs of the group. The respective position of source and subject in the social structure are also important. There is a certain amount of research on mass media concerning different techniques of persuasion. Conflicting results have been obtained on the relative merits of logical and emotional approaches (Hovland 1954). An interesting experiment by Janis and Feshbach (1953) investigated the effect of arousing anxiety in a talk on dental hygiene: they found, contrary to expectations, that most influence was produced by minimal fear arousal. Hovland and his associates (1949) found that it paid to present both sides of the argument to those initially opposed to it, and to the more intelligent.

The ambiguity of the stimulus or other object of influence is an important factor. It is a widely confirmed principle of perception that as the stimulus becomes less definite—conveys less information—other non-cognitive factors become more important. Coffin (1941) found that subjects were most easily influenced by suggestions for judgments of 'orthosonority' (a non-existent dimension of sounds), volume, and pitch in that order: evidence was produced to show that this is the order of ambiguity of these dimensions. He also found that suggestibility correlated negatively with knowledge about the subject of suggestion and positively with the difficulty of problem. More evidence on this question will be given in connection with the formation of norms in social groups (Chapter V).

The explanation of the effects of suggestion must now be considered. One widely held theory is to the effect that suggestions influence the way the object is perceived, so that a different evaluation or opinion is held about it (Asch 1952). This kind of theory was criticised on methodological grounds in Chapter III (p. 84 ff.), where it was argued that this two-stage process was philosophically untenable and had serious empirical difficulties. However, evidence has been brought forward thought to support it: Asch and his co-workers (1940) asked subjects to rank ten professions in order of social usefulness and intelligence. Different experimental batches were given various suggestions about how 'politics' should be rated and these suggestions brought about judgments differing from those of the control batch. Subsequent interviews revealed that the different batches of subjects were thinking of quite different kinds of politician, and that their ratings were quite appropriate for the type of politician in question. This experiment does *not* show however that a prior perceptual change brought about the change in judgment—merely that it accompanied that change. Both perception and response were influenced by suggestion, and in closely related ways. Other experiments have been reported concerning social influence in small groups where no perceptual change accompanied the response: Asch (1952) himself in an experiment on social influence on perception found by subsequent interview that only one subject out of thirty-one reported any change in perception of the stimulus—the remainder simply altered their judgments in order not to be ridiculed. A further and more subtle point is that perceptual changes may occur after the decision to change the judgment has been taken. Luchins (1945) discovered that his subjects definitely tried to see the object of the suggestions differently. It may be that in suggestion it is the verbal report which is affected: the perception may or may not change, but this is not a cause and may be more like an effect of the verbal change.

Another possible way of explaining the effects of suggestion is to classify it with imitation and to explain both as behaviour learnt via the satisfaction of various needs. A particular instance of this is satisfaction of the need to be accepted or approved of by the person making the suggestion. This would unify the explanation with that given for norm-formation (p. 157 f.), and would explain the importance of the prestige of the suggestor. The individual difference results are more difficult to account for: presumably it could be said that women and children have lower status (or are supposed to give way in our society). Unintelligent people (and children) have less knowledge and therefore problems will be more ambiguous, but this does not account for differences in ideo-motor suggestibility. Neurotics may have a greater need for acceptance (insecurity), and this would explain why they give way. Little useful can be said about the effect of different techniques except to point out that Janis and Feshbach's experiment (1953) throws doubt on the theory that propaganda works by arousing states of anxiety (or other needs) and then producing ways of reducing them.

CONTINUOUS INTERACTION BETWEEN TWO PEOPLE

The investigations which have been described so far in this chapter have been concerned with relatively isolated, one-way processes of interaction. In practice, of course, interaction takes place in both directions and is more continuous than this. When two people come together for some purpose they could be said to manoeuvre, or try out, various styles of behaviour, until they discover some mutually satisfactory social relationship. This process has often been described by novelists, but it presents unique difficulties to the investigator. For one thing, it cannot very easily be experimented upon; all that can be done is to observe such ongoing sequences of behaviour and try to analyse them afterwards. There is also a conceptual problem of how best to describe such a complex and developing 'social system', and what variables and types of generalisations should be studied. The problem has some parallels in the study of double stars in Astronomy, where each one is affecting the other and there is no simple one-way causal process.

In the first place, it may be useful to recapitulate the different possible methods of recording continuous interaction. Chapple (1940) proposed the study of purely temporal aspects of interaction —the length and frequency of verbal contributions, silences, interruptions, etc. A quite different approach is that of Bales (1950) used for small groups, and of Snyder (1945) for the study of psychotherapy, wherein each contribution a person makes is placed in one of a number of categories of response. Subsequent analysis can be carried out to find either the 'profile' of each person—i.e. their relative use of the different categories—or the sequences of interaction—i.e. the probability of behaviour of one type succeeding another. If mathematical methods such as analysis into stochastic processes should ever be used in this field, then analysis would have to be made of whole chains of responses. If, on the other hand, the Theory of Games is applied, then some measurement of the preferences, or motivations, of the two people will have to be attempted.

The next question which may be discussed is how far a person modifies his behaviour in response to the other person. Goldman-Eisler (1951), using Chapple's method, found that the frequency of long silences was quite characteristic of an individual no matter with whom he interacted: this was not true of the frequency of long speeches. Block (1953) used the rather different approach of asking members of a department to sort cards to show which best described their interactions with each other. She found individual differences in the extent to which people varied their behaviour with others, particularly in respect of the other's status. It is familiar that an individual's social behaviour varies with the position in the social structure of the person he is with—whether this is in industry, an extended primitive family, or the class system. In addition, since a person will occupy a position in a number of such social structures simultaneously, his behaviour may change dramatically as he moves between situations where different structures are relevant (cf. Argyle 1953*b*). It is also a familiar experience that a person's behaviour will change when he is with people of different personalities, though the extent and details of this have not yet been explored. Cameron (1947) suggests that paranoid personalities are unable to vary their behaviour or 'take different roles', and Gough (1948) predicts the same thing for psychopaths.

It is of interest to enquire what are the relative characteristics of two people which determine how well they will get on. There are several respects in which two people may fail to get on, some of which are in the area of styles of social behaviour. For example, two very dominant people, or people of very different speeds of interaction, would presumably not get on very well together: they may not be able to arrive at a joint social system or pattern of behaviour which is mutually satisfactory. Research on friendship has so far been concerned more with common values and background than with styles of interaction. However, Schutz (1953) has made an interesting start with an experiment on the productivity of compatible and incompatible groups: 'incompatible groups' contained, for example, a person who liked intimate, personal groupings, and another who did not. The whole question of which sorts of people are incompatible remains to be sorted out, but Schutz achieved some success in that his 'compatible groups' had a better performance than other groups on tasks requiring co-operation between the members.

A different approach to this problem is to examine those special interaction techniques which can be acquired through learning, such as those of the psychoanalyst, the non-directive interviewer, and the social case-worker. Such skills to a large extent suppress the natural personality, and furthermore the latter may be permanently affected if such 'acting' is continued. Research on non-directive therapy has produced objective evidence about this technique. Gump (1944), for example, showed by analysis of recordings of therapeutic sessions that non-directive therapists gave more reflections of feelings, while psychoanalysts gave more interpretations. Phillips and Agnew (1953) demonstrated that trained counsellors gave frequent reflections of feelings to hypothetical clinical situations, while untrained people offered interpretations, evaluations, etc. The techniques of non-directive therapy and psychoanalysis are good examples of narrowly defined techniques of serial behaviour, which can be learned. Other instances are the leadership methods adopted successively by the same leaders in Lippitt's experiment on boys' clubs (1940), quite different profiles of behaviour being obtained in the 'democratic' and 'authoritarian' phases.

Since in all of the special cases just mentioned the person whose behaviour was analysed was in a dominant or authoritative position, it is probable that the behaviour of the other person was considerably affected. Research on sequences of interactions confirms this expectation, though no one as yet has properly investigated, for example, the influence of the patient on the analyst. Snyder (1945) showed that acceptance and reflection of feelings on the part of a therapist leads to insight on the part of the patient, whereas interpretation creates resistance. This result has been confirmed by a number of other investigators from the non-directive school (cf. Seeman and Raskin 1953), but E. J. Murray (1954) found that interpretation led to the disappearance of the symptom in question (though this was usually replaced by another), and Gillespie (1953) found no relation between resistance and non-directiveness.

In the field of social case-work, P. V. Young (1935) gives some very interesting extracts from interviews with difficult clients, showing the kinds of technique used by skilled workers. Oldfield (1941) gives examples of tactics used by interviewers—such as earnestness to make the subject take things more seriously. Many of these things are used by everybody, though they could not necessarily be verbalised, and may be below the conscious level. The recent books by Stephen Potter (e.g. 1952) give lists of ways for making the other person look silly or feel uncomfortable: the fact that many people find this very amusing may be because the books make conscious certain facts about social interaction which previously were unconscious, besides providing some defence against the use of these methods by others.

What kind of explanation can be given of these findings about serial interaction? Since so little is known in the way of generalisations it is perhaps premature to ask for a theory. The problem is perhaps more one of providing a new set of concepts, and a reformulation of the problem, which will give a direction to research. A deductive theory is not required at this stage: what is wanted is a set of concepts which will enable useful questions to be put. There are several possible lines of attack here, and they will be outlined briefly.

Ruesch (1949a) has suggested that social behaviour should be analysed into 'social techniques', and that is perhaps a convenient unit of analysis here. By social techniques Ruesch means such patterns of behaviour as maintaining prestige, stressing identity with the other, keeping at a distance, being dependent, etc. These have not been developed into a set of empirical categories yet, and this would obviously be the next step. Personalities can be classified according to the techniques which are most often used. A finer analysis is also suggested by Ruesch (1949b): short-term techniques such as joking, flattering, bribing, teasing, etc., serve the longer-term ones. Ruesch suggests that each variety of mental abnormality can be analysed into the overemphasis of one of these techniques. Some such higher-level or 'molar' analysis of individual interaction patterns seems a necessary conceptual and classificatory step as a preliminary to the discovery of generalisations.

A different set of concepts for describing interaction between two people is that centring round the notion of 'role'. As used by Sarbin (1954) and others, a role is a sequence of learned actions performed by a person in an interaction situation.[1] On the basis of the behaviour of the other person the latter is assigned to a 'position' or set of anticipated actions: this is simply a form of social perception.[2] Each person takes a role in response to his perception of the other, the latter confirming or correcting the expectations of the former. A person is said to be able to 'take the role of the other' if he can act their part or predict their behaviour correctly. This approach has led to a number of experiments on the perception of self and others, but has failed to open up the field under discussion.

It may be suggested that both of the above two approaches need supplementation by measures of the motivation of the subjects. Thus not only does each person anticipate certain behaviour on the part of the other, he also wants him to behave in certain ways—to be friendly, to go away, to reveal certain information, to get cured, etc. The particular role which will appear surely depends not only on the anticipated behaviour, but also on the desired behaviour of the other. If the first role adopted is unsuccessful in achieving this end, a whole variety of alternatives may well be tried out. The process of

---

[1] This is a different usage of the term 'role' from that introduced later in connection with behaviour in organisations (p. 175 ff.).

[2] It will be noticed that this approach is guilty of the perceptual fallacy discussed earlier.

interaction may be pictured then as a sequence (more or less rapid) of roles on the part of each person, depending on the state of motivation of each, and in response to the anticipated behaviour of the other. The state of motivation will change according to whether it is thwarted or frustrated by the behaviour of the other, and in the latter case another form of motivation may become salient. Anticipations of the other become corrected by experience, and different tactics (or roles) may be adopted accordingly.

Another conceptual approach to the two-person situation deals with the permanent changes as a result of the interaction, with particular reference to psychotherapy. Dollard and Miller (1950) and Butler (1952) have applied generalisations from studies of learning to account for such changes—by showing how the therapist rewards certain responses, and so on. As was indicated earlier, the defect of this approach at the present moment is that so very little is actually known about the conditions under which psychotherapy is effective. We do not even know whether it is more effective than leaving people alone (Eysenck 1952), and comparisons with such controls are not very encouraging so far, though an adequate controlled study has yet to be carried out. It would be most valuable to know the best techniques for curing each type of patient—and it seems likely that the same medicine will not suit all patients equally well, as many psychologists seem to have imagined in the past. When such information is forthcoming, the time will be ripe for explaining the results in terms of the interaction processes involved.

CHAPTER V

SMALL SOCIAL GROUPS

THE INFLUENCE OF CERTAIN GROUP DIMENSIONS ON GROUP BEHAVIOUR

THERE ARE MANY different kinds of small social group, and in this section the characteristics of the different kinds will be considered. The division could have been made according to the activity of the group—laboratory groups, industrial groups, friendship groups, committees, therapy groups, children's groups, etc. This however would conceal the common elements in the behaviour of these different sorts of group; accordingly three dimensions along which groups vary have been selected, and evidence has been collected from very varied sources concerning the behaviour associated with these dimensions. At the present stage of research it seems better to regard the activity of the group as a subsidiary variable, since groups of all kinds tend to behave in rather similar ways. In other words, it looks as if something approaching universal generalisations are emerging which are true for all groups.

Group Size

One of the most obvious ways in which groups vary is in size. The problem to be considered in this section is, "How does the behaviour of large groups differ from that of smaller groups?" A problem that is sometimes raised in this connection is, "How small is a small social group?" This is an irritating question, since there is no very satisfying way of answering it, save to say that a tradition has grown up for investigating groups of up to about fifteen or twenty in size. Obviously there is no sharp distinction between large groups and small, and in this chapter some of the ways in which they differ continuously will be described.

(a) *The Effect of Size of Group on Output*

The experiments comparing performance alone and together were discussed in Chapter IV. The general findings were that when working in the company of other people subjects tended to work faster, but the quality of their work was poorer and fluctuations increased; subjects placed together settled down to the same speed. The output of groups of different sizes has been the object of recent research. Marriott (1949), in an investigation of 251 groups in two motor-car factories paid on a group-bonus scheme, found a negative correlation between output and group size, groups of under ten producing 7% more per man than groups of over thirty. However, this may be due to the group-bonus scheme, which becomes ineffective for large groups. There is no direct evidence to show that smaller groups as such have higher output. On a quite different sort of task—a tug-of-war—Köhler (1927) found that the larger the group the less hard each man pulled. He found that up to twelve men there was a logarithmic decrease, every man pulling 10% less hard for each person added. He also reports the curious finding for teams of two that the best total pull, in relation to performance alone, was obtained when the weaker man had 65% to 75% the pull of the stronger.

(b) *The Accuracy of Judgment of Individuals and of Groups*

All the experiments here are concerned with groups versus individuals, and not strictly with size of group. One kind of result which has been obtained is that the collective judgment of a group is superior to the judgments of most of the individuals. However, two distinct processes are involved—firstly, discussion leads to the improvement of individual judgments, and secondly, the combination of individual judgments is advantageous. As an example of the first process, Thorndike (1938) presented a variety of problems with graded alternative solutions, to a total of one thousand two hundred subjects in groups of four, five, and six. Ten minutes' discussion led to an improvement in the number of correct solutions. Munsterberg (1914, p. 266-71) found that the number of subjects out of a class of four hundred who correctly guessed the number of dots exposed on cards increased from 51% to 78% after an initial show of hands for different judgments. Other experiments show a tendency to change towards the average of the group judgments where there is an objectively correct solution (F. H. Allport 1924, pp. 274-8).

The other process was thought to be illustrated by Gorden (1924), who found that by combining individual judgments in aggregates and averaging them, an increased accuracy of judgment was obtained which improved with the size of the group. However, as Stroop (1932) pointed out, this was the result of statistical combination, not of social interaction. Such a result will always be found when individual judgments are scattered on both sides of the correct answer. Timmons (1942) designed an experiment to find out if the group product as a result of discussion is simply an average of the individual judgments. The group judgments of sixty-seven groups of four were closer to the solution of experts than were the average judgments of matched batches of control subjects. In addition to this effect, different members of the group will have differing amounts of influence by virtue of their positions in the informal status hierarchy of the group. This will be discussed later.

(c) *The Effect of Group Size on Problem-solving*

When a number of subjects combine in a group to carry out simple problem-solving they generally do better than any individual alone. Klugman (1944) found that children doing problems from intelligence tests together solved more problems correctly but took a longer time; Shaw (1932) obtained the same result in an investigation of groups of four on a series of elaborate problems. (*N.B.* This is the opposite result from that obtained for *individual* task performance alone and together.) Watson (1928) found groups of all sizes from three to ten considerably better than individuals in accuracy of solution, and also slightly faster. This was true for nine different types of problem, though the degree of superiority was greater for more complex problems. McCurdy and Lambert (1952), however, found that groups were inferior to individuals in a temporal maze problem, in which the weaker members could spoil the group performance. This is the opposite situation from the others, in that here individual shortcomings rather than talents determine the group result.

The jury has inspired several experiments on the supposed superiority of group problem-solving. The usual form of these experiments is to arrange for an unexpected dramatic event, or to show a film, in front of several witnesses, who are either cross-examined or write down their accounts of what took place. Members of a 'jury' then discuss the witnesses' reports and come to a conclusion. Dashiell (1935) found that each of his eight experimental juries improved their average score for correctly reported items about a critical event as a result of discussion, that the jury as a whole gave a more complete and accurate account than the individual jurors, but that 13% of the individual jurymen did better than the jury as a whole.

SMALL SOCIAL GROUPS

Several experiments have compared the efficiency of problem-solving groups of different sizes. J. R. Gibb (1951) compared groups of many sizes up to ninety-six and found the number of ideas produced increased with size though not in proportion to the number of members. Other studies however show that increased size is not necessarily an advantage for solving particular problems. Taylor and Faust (1952) compared individuals with groups of two and four at the parlour game of 'Twenty Questions', and found that groups of two reached the solution with a smaller average number of questions, but that groups of four had fewer failures (i.e. not finding the right answer in twenty questions). South (1927) compared groups of three and six on several kinds of problem; groups of three were faster and equally accurate in judging emotions and marking English compositions, while groups of six did better at multiple-choice problems. South concludes that larger groups are superior at problems which cannot be solved immediately but which require the rejection of wrong hypotheses. He also found mixed groups less efficient than groups of subjects of the same sex. Watson (1928), however, found no significant relation between efficiency and size for nine kinds of problem. It can be concluded that there is usually no advantage in problem-solving groups having more than two or three members, and that for certain kinds of problem it is a positive disadvantage for them to be larger.

(d) *Individual Satisfaction with Group Membership*

There are no direct studies of the comparative satisfaction of people working alone and together, but surveys have shown that industrial workers prefer to work in small groups (Viteles 1954, p. 138 f.). Research by the Acton Society (1953) showed a positive correlation between absenteeism and span of control down to a limiting span of fifteen workers per foreman. Hewitt and Parfitt (1953) similarly found in a large factory that the percentage of absenteeism due to 'other causes' (i.e. voluntary absenteeism) in groups of four was a third of that in groups of thirty-six, and a quarter of that in groups of 128. Voluntary absenteeism is related to low job satisfaction (see p. 173), so that it may be deduced that satisfaction is higher in smaller groups. H. Campbell (1952) found that dissatisfaction with an incentive scheme was greater in larger groups *amongst those with no knowledge of the scheme*—suggesting a general dissatisfaction among members of large groups.

(e) *Social Interaction in Groups of Varying Size*

Several studies indicate that larger groups have a more hierarchical nature. Hemphill (1950*a*) gave a questionnaire enquiring about the size and leadership of one group with which each subject was acquainted. He found that leader-centred direction was tolerated to a greater extent in groups with more than thirty members. Similarly, Carter and his co-workers (1951*b*) found a greater correlation between authoritarianism and leadership in larger groups. Bales and his associates (1951) discovered that with larger groups the distribution of quantity of participation becomes increasingly unequal for groups of all sizes from four to twelve (see Figure 5, p. 141).

In a study of 228 work-groups in an American engineering factory, Seashore (1954) found that smaller groups tended *on the average* to be more cohesive from a size of four to twenty-two. A more striking result of the same study however was that smaller groups tended towards either extremely high or extremely low cohesiveness when compared with larger groups.

There is some evidence that norm-formation proceeds more rapidly in smaller groups: Hare (1952) found that discussion among troops of scouts had more effect on their opinions in groups of five than in groups of twelve. This would be expected if cohesiveness is greater in smaller groups, as norm-formation is greater in cohesive groups (cf. p. 127 f.).

(f) *The Explanation of these Results*

There is no clear evidence about the influence of size of group on output. Group discussion however leads to the improvement of individual judgments. This is an instance of norm-formation: when there is variation between members in some matter of importance to the group, convergence towards the group average takes place. In addition, as Kelley and Thibaut (1954) point out, the overt judgments which form the basis for group discussion may differ from the private opinions of the members, being in general cautious and less extreme. When judgments are involved, and when as is usual the judgments spread on both sides of the 'correct' one, convergence involves the improvement of individual scores. The explanation of the finding that discussion leads to a group judgment which is better than the average of the individual scores is less simple. Group members of higher status have more influence over the group judgment: possibly these people also have the ability to make more correct judgments. Since status in the group is correlated with intelligence, this is quite likely.

Groups are superior to individuals at problem-solving, except in such artificial situations as that created by McCurdy and Lambert (1952), in which the progress of the group depends on its slowest member. On the other hand, large groups are no more effective than small ones, and the evidence on the whole suggests that they are less so. It is easy to think of reasons why groups should be better than individuals, but all these explanations also entail the superiority of larger groups. Thus it may be suggested that in a group (*a*) there is a greater chance of at least one able person being present, (*b*) different members may be able to deal with different aspects of a problem in line with their special abilities, (*c*) more suggestions are put forward, as found by J. R. Gibb (1951), (*d*) people will consider and formulate their suggestions more carefully if they have to be placed before others, as was indicated by Bos's findings (1937), (*e*) incorrect suggestions are rejected or modified more quickly (Shaw 1932), and (*f*) fixed 'sets' can be avoided (Taylor and Faust 1952). All these suggestions are very reasonable, but all of them lead to the prediction that larger groups will be better than smaller ones. The failure to find this superiority means that in larger groups some opposing processes must be at work to offset the advantages. For example, in larger groups people are more likely to forget the previous contributions of other members (Taylor and Faust, loc. cit.), and they are less able to participate to the full.

Small groups show signs of greater satisfaction than larger ones. Findings about satisfaction may be regarded as basic data about human motivation. Hence there must be a common need which is satisfied better by membership of small than of large groups. The results on norm-formation and leadership will be discussed in the appropriate sections.

All these explanations are of the *post hoc* variety, and have not been tested by further predictions. The differences of performance alone and in groups of different sizes present a series of very interesting problems in social psychology, and the existence of a considerable amount of evidence makes it a field worthy of further study.

Group Cohesiveness

The cohesiveness of a group is the extent to which the members like one another: this is the operational definition which will be adopted here.[1] It can be measured therefore by the average score members give one another on a sociometric rating scale (Back 1951), or by the number of sociometric choices members give one another in relation to their total choices to a wider population (Festinger et al. 1950). In addition, some of the ways of producing cohesive groups are so clear-cut that they can be used to create different experimental conditions without need of further check. In this section the conditions that produce cohesiveness will be discussed first, followed by the influence of cohesiveness on satisfaction, output, and conformity.

(a) *The Causes of Cohesiveness*

The most obvious cause of cohesiveness is simply mutual compatibility of the group members. This may occur by chance, by natural mobility, or by deliberate arrangement. If people are allowed to be with those they like, or to choose which group to join, the groups will become more cohesive. Moreno (1953, pp. 500–27) was able to re-group 102 girls in a delinquent community according to their sociometric choices, increasing the average cohesiveness of the fifteen cottages concerned from 51% to 61%. Sociometric re-grouping can be regarded as a reliable way of manipulating cohesiveness experimentally.

Cohesiveness can also be increased without changing the composition of the group. Homans (1951) postulated that frequent interaction leads to increased liking between people, and vice versa. Since then, some limited evidence for this proposition has been obtained, and this is reviewed later in the section on the effects of spatial proximity in groups. Homans also maintains that liking (or cohesiveness) leads to more interaction. Back (1951) found that in cohesive groups there were more attempts to exert influence, in an experiment where the groups were trying to come to an agreement.

A third way in which cohesiveness can be influenced is through skilful handling of the group by its leaders or by one of the members. Fox and Scott (1943) claimed that absenteeism (which is probably related to low cohesiveness) was reduced as a result of training foremen in the art of induction of newcomers and promotion of cohesiveness, but this was unfortunately not the only factor varied,

---

[1] Festinger and his associates (1950, p. 164) define cohesiveness as "The force acting on the members to remain in the group", meaning to include the attractiveness of the group as a goal as well as the attractiveness of the other members. However, they only measure the second part of this.

so that no conclusions can be drawn from this widely quoted study. In the study of Basic Skill Training Groups, Lippitt (1949) distinguished that kind of behaviour which is directed towards building cohesiveness. It is likely that certain kinds of personality can promote or reduce group cohesiveness through their presence. It has sometimes been reported that psychopaths upset therapy groups, and Haythorn (1953) discovered an inverse relationship between the amount of striving for prominence of a person and the cohesiveness of the groups to which he belonged.

Fourthly, cohesiveness in laboratory groups can be affected by experimental instructions. Subjects can be informed that the other subjects have been selected on the basis of personality tests so that they will be found highly congenial (or uncongenial) (Back 1951). They can be told that the other subjects like (or dislike) them very much (Hutte 1953). Alternatively, they can be given different instructions about the prestige of the group, and instructions which make the task more or less pleasant. Back (op. cit.) found that the last two sorts of instructions had much the same effect as information about congeniality of companions, and it is probable that in real groups the attractiveness of the task or of membership *per se* leads to similar behavioural results.

In the experiments to be reported below, cohesiveness was manipulated in one of the ways described, and was generally confirmed by direct measurement. In the field studies which are discussed, natural groups were simply measured for cohesiveness and compared on other variables.

(b) *The Effect of Cohesiveness on Satisfaction*

Several investigations show, directly or indirectly, that members are more satisfied in cohesive groups. Van Zelst (1952*b*) re-grouped two work-teams of builders sociometrically and found a significant increase in job satisfaction, both as compared with two control groups and as compared with their initial state. Darley, Gross, and Martin (1951) found greater satisfaction with village life among the more cohesive of thirteen cottages on a university housing estate, and Marquis, Guetzkow, and Heyns (1950) found satisfaction to be related to cohesiveness in a field study of seventy-two committees. Chapin and his co-workers (1954) found that satisfaction correlated highly ($\cdot 74$) with amount of participation, in a study of forty groups of students and forty of firemen; this may be counted as indirect evidence for a relation between cohesiveness and satisfaction, if cohesiveness is related to extent of participation. Seashore (1954) found that insecurity and anxiety were lower in cohesive workgroups: the former variables may be regarded as components of job satisfaction.

There is indirect evidence from studies of absenteeism and turnover—if this is assumed to be related to satisfaction. The work of Mayo and Lombard (1944) and of Fox and Scott (1943) is often taken to show that low cohesiveness is related to high absenteeism and labour turnover, but as noted above this was inconclusive. Moreno (1953, p. 527) found that sociometric re-grouping in a reformatory reduced the number of girls who ran away.

It may be concluded that there is good direct evidence that satisfaction is higher in more cohesive teams, and there is some evidence that cohesiveness is related to absenteeism and labour turnover, which often accompany low satisfaction.

(c) *The Effect of Cohesiveness on Output*

It is often assumed that cohesive groups work harder, but the evidence on this point is rather conflicting. In two studies of groups of builders, Van Zelst (1952a, 1952b) found that output was increased and labour costs reduced as a result of sociometric reorganisation. On the other hand, it may be objected that the results might be due to 'Hawthorne effect',[1] though this would be expected to have diminished by eleven months after the experimental changes.

Goodacre (1951) found a correlation of ·77 between cohesiveness and ratings of efficiency in a field study of twelve Army reconnaissance teams of six. A carefully designed laboratory experiment by Schachter, Ellertson, and Gregory (1951) found that cohesiveness heightened the influence of the group over its members, and that the influence could be in the direction of either increasing or decreasing a member's output, depending on his relation to the norm: as a matter of fact, groups of high cohesion were able to exert most influence in the *downward* direction. There is an important difference between this investigation and the previous two, which may account for the conflicting results. Van Zelst's and Goodacre's subjects were members of teams who co-operated and were genuinely interdependent; Schachter's subjects, on the other hand, were working alone at individual tasks, believing themselves to be members of a group. It may be suggested that cohesiveness increases output in

[1] i.e. the fact that people often work harder when they are being investigated.

functionally interdependent groups only. This prediction was confirmed by Schutz (1953), who found increasing differences in output between cohesive and non-cohesive teams as the co-operative content of the task increased.

Seashore's survey (1954) of 228 work-teams in an engineering factory was designed to test a rather different hypothesis. He found that cohesive groups had higher output only if they also felt secure with regard to the company.

(d) *The Effect of Cohesiveness on Norm-formation*

Festinger, Schachter, and Back carried out several investigations of this relationship and it was shown that norm-formation is more extensive in cohesive groups. Back (1951) obtained this result for experimental groups of two, in which cohesiveness was manipulated by instructions as described above; he also found that there was more communication in cohesive groups. Schachter (1951) confirmed this in small groups proper into which a deviating confederate had been introduced: it was found that the deviate was rejected more strongly in the more cohesive groups. Schachter, Ellertson, and Gregory (1951), in the experiment referred to above, organised 'groups' of varying cohesiveness where the members worked alone and received a standard series of messages, ostensibly from the other members: members of cohesive groups were more influenced by the identical messages. It seems that conformity is greater in cohesive groups, and that this is partly due to a greater willingness to be influenced, but may also be due to the greater amount of communication and the greater rejection of deviates in these groups. All these experiments were conducted with great experimental rigour and sophistication, but on the other hand the nature of the actual group situations was highly artificial. In the Festinger, Schachter, and Back study (1950) of a housing estate at the Massachusetts Institute of Technology, however, a correlation between cohesiveness and conformity was again reported.

Finally, there is an interesting study by Steinor (1954), who gave a questionnaire to a large sample of people. He found that there was a smaller discrepancy between own attitude and the perceived attitudes of various groups when strong pressures from those groups were experienced. One determinant of such pressure is probably cohesiveness as indicated by Schachter's and Back's experiments.

It may be concluded that there is considerable evidence to show that cohesiveness leads to greater conformity.

(e) *The Explanation of these Results*

Satisfaction is high in cohesive groups. The interpretation of this is simply that in Western culture there are social needs which are satisfied by belonging to cohesive groups. This is no more than a scientific demonstration of the obvious fact that people want others to like them and prefer situations in which other people do like them.

There is some evidence that output is higher in cohesive workteams when there is interdependent work. There is a very simple explanation which may be offered for this: (1) There is a need to be liked by other people (see above); (2) this need is satisfied by interaction with people who like one; (3) interdependent work entails interaction with other members of the team; (4) therefore there will be more work in cohesive teams on interdependent work. The testing of this theory could be effected by testing (2) directly.

The explanation of the relation between cohesiveness and conformity will be discussed in the section on norm-formation.

Co-operation and Competition

By a co-operative group is meant a group in which the members help one another to reach some joint or group goal. In a competitive group the members are concerned with private and mutually exclusive goals: the goal is limited, so that if one member reaches it the others cannot.

(a) *The Measurement and Manipulation of the Co-operative/Competitive Dimension*

The earliest experiments in this field depended upon experimental instructions to bring about competitive or co-operative attitudes in different subjects. Whittemore, however (1924, 1925), found that his subjects had difficulty in maintaining these attitudes, although the significant results obtained in these and similar experiments indicate that the method did have some effect.

A more successful method, used in later work, is to manipulate the goal structure of the situation. In the competitive situation, one subject in a group is rewarded if he does better than other members; in the co-operative situation the group is rewarded. This method was first used by Morton Deutsch (1949*b*) in his experiment on group problem-solving. Similarly, Horwitz (1954) showed that when a group decision was taken by the members of a group they became motivated towards the goals of the group.

Probably some individuals tend more towards co-operative behaviour than others, and Mead (1935) has suggested that whole societies vary along the competitive/co-operative dimension; this last interesting suggestion requires to be followed up by the development of a method of measuring the co-operativeness of a whole society. Dreyer (1954) found that groups tend to be more competitive when the members are of about equal ability, otherwise the inequality of success is accepted more readily.

There have been a number of field studies in which existing or natural groups have been compared on this and other dimensions. Fouriezos, Hutt, and Guetzkow (1950) devised an eleven-point rating scale for the amount of self-oriented needs displayed in group behaviour. This may be regarded as a measure of competitiveness. A related study by Lewis (1944) showed that need-states of group members could be discharged by task-behaviour on the part of other members, in co-operative but not in competitive groups. She used the Zeigarnik effect (improved memory for uncompleted tasks) to measure needs in this experiment.

(b) *The Output of Competitive and Co-operative Groups*

Whittemore (1924, 1925) aroused alternate co-operative and competitive attitudes in twelve students copying newspaper material with rubber stamps. They worked 14% to 36% faster in the competitive condition, but the quality of work was inferior. This result, that competition increases speed but reduces quality, was also obtained by Triplett (1898) with children turning crank-handles, and by Moede (1920) in an experiment on boys at a dynamometer task.

Other experimenters compared the effect of inter-individual and inter-group competition: the latter may be regarded as intra-group co-operation. Maller (1929) compared the speed of carrying out additions of 1,538 children aged 8 to 17 under these different conditions of motivation. The speed of work under conditions of individual competition was 6% greater than with co-operation. Sims (1928) studied thirty-six students and found individual competition at a substitution test produced scores about 50% higher than under inter-group competition.

The conclusion of these and other results is that both individual competition and co-operation increase the speeds of subjects at individual laboratory tasks, but that individual competition has the greater effect.

Other investigations have been concerned with competition and co-operation in problem-solving groups of different kinds. Deutsch

(1949b) compared ten groups of five subjects, the groups being matched in pairs and placed in competitive and co-operative reward situations. The co-operative groups had a higher output as measured in each of several ways—e.g. the number of ideas agreed upon for action, problems solved, etc. On the other hand, ratings for individual productivity were not always greater for the co-operative groups. This experiment is noteworthy for its careful design and rigorous measurements. Marquis, Guetzkow, and Heyns (1950) found in their field study of a number of committees that those characterised by a lack of self-oriented needs among their members had the higher productivity. In a later phase of the same enquiry, Guetzkow and Gyr (1954) found that conflicts were resolved more readily in such committees.

It appears that while competition rather than co-operation speeds up individuals working at *separate* tasks, the reverse is the case where the group is working at a *joint* task.

(c) *The Effect of Co-operation and Competition on Satisfaction, Emotionality, and Norm-formation*

In Deutsch's experiment (1949b), interpersonal relations were better in the co-operative groups—the subjects were friendlier and rated each other higher. This is to say that the co-operative groups were more cohesive, and, it may be presumed, more satisfied. Co-operative groups tend to be cohesive, and vice versa, though these dimensions are operationally independent. Marquis and his collaborators (1950), in their study of committees, found greater satisfaction where self-oriented needs were weak. It seems that satisfaction is greater in co-operative groups, at any rate when these are engaged upon group tasks. The same may not be true of groups where the members are engaged upon individual activities, and Maller (1929) found that 74% of the children in his experiment preferred the competitive arrangement.

Competition may create emotional disturbance in different ways. Several of the experiments on individual task-performance revealed signs of emotional tenseness, in addition to diminished quality and greater variability of performance (Moede 1920). Triplett (1898) found that all of his forty children (aged 8 to 17) lost control of the crank-turning apparatus in the competitive condition. Grossack (1954) found that there was less tension in an artificial co-operative group situation, where all the subjects were alone and received messages ostensibly from other group members, showing that the co-operative situation may provide emotional support. A rather different kind of disturbance was brought about by Mintz (1951) in a very ingenious experiment. Forty-six groups of from fifteen to twenty-one subjects had to pull corks out of a bottle, each subject having a string attached to his cork. When an individual reward was given for extracting them quickly, the corks tended to get jammed in the neck. The presence of excited accomplices slowed down the co-operative groups, but did not cause a jam. Mintz concludes that panics, to escape from burning theatres for example, may be due not to emotional contagion, as has often been supposed, but to the competitive structure of the situation.

One prediction from a theory of the author's (to be described below) is that norm-formation will proceed more rapidly in co-operative groups. Some evidence can be found to verify this prediction. Whittemore (1924) found that the quality of work done in co-operative groups was more homogeneous in quality (though not in quantity) than in competitive groups. While there was no direct measurement of norm-formation in Deutsch's experiment (1949*b*), members of co-operative groups were more receptive to one another's ideas, co-ordinated their efforts more, and showed greater homogeneity of contributions. Grossack (1954) found more changes of opinion in co-operative groups, while Guetzkow and Gyr (1954) found conflicts resolved more easily. A student working at Oxford, V. P. Holloway, made a direct test of the hypothesis in a perceptual judgment situation. Pairs of subjects gave psychophysical judgments of a series of stimuli repeated in randomised order. Norm-formation was measured by the number of changes in the direction of the partner's estimate on later reappearance of a stimulus. Subjects in co-operative groups did change more frequently in the direction of their partner's judgment, though the level of significance of this result was low.

(d) *The Explanation of these Results*

The most important theory in the field of co-operation and competition is that put forward by Deutsch (1949*a*). This theory is expressed in the terminology of Lewinian 'field theory'—an approach which has been criticised earlier (p. 89 ff.). However, it may be suggested that the empirical content of the theory is independent of this terminology, and that it can be rephrased behaviouristically in such a way that all the predictions still follow from it. The postulates of the theory, together with those deductions which have been verified by Deutsch or others, are given below. It is an axiomatic theory of the hypothetical construct type, the postulates being unverified generalisations about individual behaviour.

Basic definition.—A co-operative group is one in which the needs of the members would be satisfied by the attainment of some joint goal; a competitive group is one in which the goals of the members are mutually exclusive, so that if the needs of one member are satisfied, those of the other members will not be. (This is a repetition of the opening statement of this section.)

Postulate 1[1] (substitutibility): in a co-operative group, if member A carries out an act there is no need for B also to do it, since this act has promoted the goals of each. This does not apply to competitive groups.

Postulate 2 (cathexis): in a co-operative group, A's actions will tend to satisfy B's needs, therefore B will approve of A's behaviour. The opposite applies to competitive groups.

Postulate 3 (inducibility): in a co-operative group, since A approves of B's actions he will be more open to suggestions from B than in a competitive group.

Postulate 4 (facilitation): in a co-operative group, A is likely to help B, since this will tend to promote the reduction of A's own needs. In a competitive group, A is likely to obstruct B, for complementary reasons.

Postulate 1 gives rise to several deductions, none of which have yet been significantly verified. However, the postulate itself was confirmed by H. B. Lewis (1944), using the Zeigarnik effect, as described above. From *Postulate* 2 it follows that co-operative group members will be more friendly, and that they will value the group's products more highly. Deutsch confirmed both these results. *Postulate* 3 was verified directly by Deutsch, together with a number of deductions from it. In co-operative groups there is greater co-ordination of efforts, more acceptance of other's ideas, more rapid agreement, and greater group productivity. Marquis and Guetzkow (see above) also obtained these results. It can be inferred from *Postulate* 4 that competitive group members will pay less attention to one another and hence have communication difficulties and will not have a shared orientation to their task, as compared with

---

[1] All the postulates save the third can be deduced from the basic definition, so that there are really only two ultimate postulates. *Postulate* 3 is said to be derivable from *Postulate* 2, but it does not in fact follow.

members of co-operative groups. These deductions were verified by Deutsch. From the derivations concerning the superior co-ordination and communication in co-operative groups it can be deduced that the quality of output will be better. From *Postulate* 3 and the derivation about communication it follows that members of co-operative groups learn more from one another. Both of these last deductions were confirmed by Deutsch.

The general findings on competition and co-operation reported in the earlier parts of the section will now be discussed in relation to this theory. The superior productivity of co-operative groups, when the members are working at a joint task, is explained by the theory. This does not apply to situations where the group members are engaged on entirely independent tasks, and the theory is unable to explain the greater productivity of competitive groups here. The latter finding may be regarded as a demonstration that motivation (in Western culture) is stronger for competition: in this case the superiority of co-operative groups at interdependent tasks is even more striking.

The greater satisfaction experienced in co-operative groups can be deduced from Deutsch's theory. It was predicted, and confirmed, that members of co-operative groups would like one another more than the members of corresponding competitive groups. That is to say, co-operative groups are more cohesive, and the members will be more satisfied, as was reported above.

The emotional disturbance found in competitive groups may be due to the hostile relations between the group members, as follows from Deutsch, or to over-motivation as suggested by Triplett (1898). The panic created by Mintz (1951) is due to a rather special kind of competitive situation: this is an unstable situation in which simultaneous striving leads to a blockage of progress which in turn heightens the state of motivation.

Two deductions about norm-formation can be made from Deutsch's theory. Firstly, *Postulate* 2 states that in a co-operative group there is no need for A to repeat B's action: therefore there should be less norm-formation with respect to the means of attaining the goal. On the other hand, *Postulate* 4 states that A will be more open to suggestions from B in a co-operative group: therefore, when for some reason the task of the group is agreement, this will take place more rapidly in co-operative groups. The relevant investigations have all been concerned with the second aspect of the case. The second prediction also follows as a deduction from the author's theory of norm-formation (see p. 157 f.).

The Factor Analysis of Group Measurements

The previous three sections have examined the effect on group behaviour of three group dimensions which are based largely on common sense—size, cohesiveness, and co-operativeness. Individuals as well as groups vary along many dimensions, and several personality psychologists have resorted to factor analysis as a means of discovering a small number of factors which will summarise conveniently the variation of individuals along many different measurable dimensions. It may be found that the dimensions known to common sense may not turn out to be the most important ones psychologically. However, Eysenck, an important exponent of the factor-analytic approach to personality, chooses measures that will probably relate to dimensions already in use (e.g. neuroticism, introversion–extroversion), and adjusts his factors to agree with clinical ratings (Eysenck 1952).

It is important to emphasise that the dimensions obtained by means of factor analysis are relative to the population and the set of measurements used, and in particular to the method of factor analysis. Furthermore, the factors can be converted into a large number of other factors by 'rotating the axes'. It follows that factor analysis is not a means of discovering the ultimate psychological structure of individuals (or groups), but is simply a convenient means of summarising a large number of measurements.

While it is useful to study the variation of groups in many directions at once, too much should not be expected from factor analysis. It would be of great interest to locate and define in terms of convenient measures those dimensions in which we are already interested. It is not so useful to obtain sets of fourteen or fifteen factors which do not make very much sense, and which would equally well be replaced by a quite different set.

Hemphill and Westie (1950) factor-analysed one hundred ratings made by judges on thirty-five clubs and extracted fourteen factors. The use of ratings here is not sufficiently objective, and the hundred ratings would doubtless suffer from halo effect. Cattell, Saunders, and Stice (1953) set up eighty experimental groups and obtained ninety-three objective measures of each. These measures included: (1) population variables, or averages of individual characteristics, such as I.Q.; (2) structure variables, or patterns of interaction within the group, for example the status gradient; and (3) performance measurements of the group acting as a whole, such as its pull at a tug-of-war, or its speed of voting. Fourteen dimensions were extracted from the matrix of correlations between all these measurements, some of which look fairly sensible, some of which do not. Enough has been said to indicate that such factors require validation against some external criterion to be really useful. Needless to say, the fourteen dimensions of Cattell and Hemphill are completely different from one another. It is possible that they are mutually convertible by rotation of the axes, but in view of the entirely different tests this seems unlikely.

INDIVIDUAL PERSONALITY AND GROUP BEHAVIOUR

The main problem of this section is the relation of individual differences to group leadership, for it is here that most research has been done. Leadership will be discussed first, followed by an account of some other effects of individual differences upon group behaviour.

Leadership

The quest for the particular personality characteristics which make people leaders was a preoccupation of many early social psychologists. The first studies produced contradictory and inconclusive results, and there is now a reaction in which exponents of the so-called "interactional theory of leadership" maintain that quite different kinds of people lead in different groups and situations (C. A. Gibb 1950). The evidence for each of these positions will be reviewed below, but before this can be done it is necessary to say something about what is meant by 'leadership'.

In this section we are only concerned with the leaders who emerge or are elected in initially leaderless groups. As is pointed out later, formal leaders may be appointed for a variety of reasons, and their personality may change through experience of the position (p. 175 f.). There are two principal operations by which the leaders of a group may be known—nomination by the members, and observation of the group in action. Nomination can take various forms. In some studies of student groups, leaders had been previously elected. In other investigations, members have been asked to say whom they would prefer as leaders. This is not the same as a sociometric questionnaire which measures popularity, though there is evidence that popular people also tend to be chosen as leaders (Jennings 1950; Stogdill 1948). For this reason, sociometric popularity and leadership will not be discussed separately here. Through the observation of behaviour it is possible either to rate the group members directly or to carry out interaction recording with emphasis on initiating, following, etc.

Carter and Nixon (1949) found that interaction recording did not correlate well with the other techniques for measuring leadership. Bales (1953) found that the popular person was rated lower on leadership by observers in later meetings of groups. Clearly the two methods are measuring slightly different variables. There is even more doubt with regard to some of the personality measurements used in these studies: while height, weight, and possibly intelligence are measured in similar ways by different researchers, the same is not true of personality traits.

A further difficulty is that the people who emerge as leaders of groups may behave quite differently: there are elaborate classifications of leadership types: the point is that 'leadership' is an impure notion, and requires further refinement before any exact work can be done. This is a task for the future.

However leadership is defined, in an informal group, there is never one leader and a set of followers: all lead to some extent. For example, Bass (1950) found that leadership is correlated with quantity of participation in discussion groups. Bales and his co-workers (1951) have shown that the distribution of participation in discussion groups is as shown in Figure 5 (p. 141). Even in groups with an appointed leader, the other members will participate in leadership activities: when the official leader is weak, it is more likely that informal leaders will take over his functions (Katz et al. 1951).

(a) *Personality Traits Associated with Leadership in General*

How much truth is there in the claim that there is one kind of person who always leads in any group or situation? Stogdill (1948) has reviewed 124 investigations of leadership in relation to twenty-nine aspects of personality. More than fifteen studies show that leaders have greater intelligence (average correlation ·28) and scholarship, social activity, socio-economic status, and 'dependability'. Over ten investigations demonstrate that leaders have greater sociability, 'initiative', persistence, knowledge of and insight into the situation, self-confidence, and verbal facility. On the other hand, the average correlations of these personality qualities with measures of leadership are small, and in the case of most traits some studies have shown a negative correlation. Furthermore, many of the investigations reported by Stogdill were concerned with groups of children or of students, which must be regarded as a rather narrow range of groups. Nevertheless, there does seem to be fairly strong support for the generalisation within this range, if the lack of comparability of personality measurements mentioned above is borne in mind. If the average correlations, in the region of ·2 to ·3, are accepted, and multiple correlations for a number of aspects of personality calculated, the success of prediction of leadership may be regarded as quite considerable.

It is not intended to discuss this matter further, in view of the admirable review by Stogdill. Before a final conclusion can be arrived at, it will be necessary to carry out a widespread investigation of many different kinds of groups, using a standard criterion of leadership and the same measurements of personality throughout.

(b) *Personality Traits Associated with Leadership in Different Situations and Groups*

Although the systematic study of leadership suggested above has not yet been carried out, there have been a number of studies of leadership in two or three different kinds of group. It has been shown, for instance, that delinquent leaders are more aggressive, impulsive, and excitable than other members of their groups, and that this is not true of the leaders of other kinds of group (cf. C. A. Gibb 1950). Similarly, it was found that leaders of athletic groups and of boys' gangs are superior in strength and physique rather than intelligence. In any particular kind of group there is probably a set of personality characteristics which is associated with leadership. Detailed research must be carried out in each particular context. Recent investigations into the kind of leader who is most acceptable in the U.S. Army disclosed a negative correlation of leadership with authoritarianism (Hollander 1954; Masling et al. 1953). This is obviously an important kind of result to know about in the context of a particular social organisation, and is supplementary to knowledge of the effectiveness of various kinds of leader (cf. p. 194 ff.).

Another series of researches is concerned with changes of leadership in the same groups engaged on different activities. Several studies of schoolchildren (e.g. Caldwell and Wellman 1926) show that the leaders of the same groups for athletic, social, and academic purposes were different. Carter and Nixon (1949) carried out an experiment in which groups of two had to solve different kinds of problem; they found that for intellectual and clerical tasks the leader was the same, but different from the leader in mechanical-assembly tasks. These authors put forward the notion of 'families of situations', the idea being that leadership will remain constant within each family. Similarly Gibb (1949) found an average correlation of ·67 for leadership at eight tasks in ten ten-men groups.

Leadership has also been studied in different groups of the same kind engaged on the same sort of tasks. Bell and French (1950) found a correlation of ·75 between leadership in six different experimental groups: i.e. the same person tended to lead in each group in which he was placed. This experiment indicates that the variation due to the composition of the group is small. However, Sanford (1950) found that authoritarians preferred authoritarian leadership, as shown by answers to a questionnaire.

Several investigators have studied the persistence of leadership in the same groups in successive years. Page (1935) found a correlation of ·67 between first- and fourth-year leadership rank among West Point cadets. Levi (1930) found various correlations between ·19 and ·52 for leadership in successive years at school.

Finally, Sterling and Rosenthal (1950) showed that in one discussion group the leadership alternated with the phases of discussion. They suggest a relation between personality traits and the phases of group behaviour when a person leads: for instance, an aggressive person would lead during aggressive phases.

To conclude this evidence for situational factors in leadership, it may be said that there is evidence that leadership depends on different personality qualities, varying with the type of group and the group task, and that it may also depend on the membership of the group.

(c) *The Explanation of these Results*

Again, there is little in the way of systematic theory to report. Several writers have put forward the somewhat vague theory that the leader is the person who is best able to contribute to group needs. This proposition is extremely difficult to test in the absence of independent criteria for what the group needs are. On the other hand, there is fairly wide evidence that the leader is the person with most knowledge of the situation (cf. Stogdill's review), or the person with the greatest ability at the task being performed (Carter and Nixon 1949). The other leadership qualities are general personality traits: while these may be related to the needs of the followers, it is more likely that the explanation lies in cultural conditioning towards liking certain kinds of person; this is supported by the finding that socio-economic status contributes to leadership. A third factor may be social skill at co-ordinating and harmonising the other group members: this is supported by the fact that leaders are found to be more sociable and co-operative than others, though they are not in general more extroverted.

Connected with the first theory is a group of experiments concerned with whether a leader has a more accurate perception of the attitudes of the other members. It is argued that a leader is more able to satisfy the needs of the others simply because he has a better idea of what their needs are. Chowdhry and Newcomb (1952) found that the leaders of four fraternities had the most accurate perception of the attitudes of the others on relevant issues. Greer (1954) found that the leaders and most popular members of sixty-nine infantry squads had a more accurate perception of the hierarchy than the others had; Bell and Hall (1954) showed that leaders of experimental groups scored higher on two tests of 'empathy', and Gage and Suci (1951) that teachers approved of by pupils had a more accurate idea of children's opinions. However, there is some opposing evidence: Hites and Campbell (1950) found no difference with fraternity leaders, and Talland (1954) with ten therapy groups. With the exception of Greer's investigation, none of these studies used more than a very few groups. It seems probable that the proposition is true within certain limits, but it is not yet clear what those limits are. It seems unlikely however if there is enough in the proposition to give much support for the theory that leaders can best meet the needs of their group members. Even if the proposition was true it still would not help the theory much, since leaders might gain their superior knowledge from being in a better position as leaders for observing and contacting the members, or from being able to influence the members towards their own views. (Gorden (1952) found a tendency to err in the direction of one's own opinion in judging the views of others).

A final question which may be raised is how far a leader must conform to the social norms. This will be discussed in the later section on the rejection of deviates—the reverse side of the same question.

Individual Differences in Personality in relation to Style of Group Behaviour

A number of experimenters have studied the relationship between various measures of personality and patterns of individual behaviour in groups, in addition to the influence of different individuals on the group's performance. It is difficult to come to any very clear-cut conclusions here, since the personality measures are all exceedingly diverse and of unequal value, apart from the fact that quite different aspects of group behaviour have been examined.

The first series of investigations is concerned with differences in personality between those who conform and those who deviate in pressure-to-conform situations.

One of the most interesting experiments was carried out by Barron (1952), who studied individual differences in a social pressure situation devised by Asch (1952). Subjects make a series of psychophysical judgments about which of three lines displayed is equal in length to a standard: this is repeated twelve times with different sets of lines. The three lines are quite unequal in length, so that the correct answer is obvious in each case; however, other 'subjects' are present, who in reality are confederates of the experimenter, and during certain trials in the series they are unanimous in naming one of the wrong lines. Some subjects yield to the majority in this situation: some do not. Barron gave a number of tests to forty-six subjects who yielded and to forty-four who did not. The two most interesting results which he found were that there was no difference in stability, as measured on one of Guilford's questionnaires, but that yielders had a perceptual preference for simple as opposed to complex designs. Eysenck (1954, p. 189) relates this to a previous finding of his own to the effect that extroverts prefer simpler pictures and other works of art, and deduces that yielders must be extroverted. It should be possible to obtain a more direct test of the hypothesis by a repetition of Barron's experiment, and making use of the tests for introversion which emerged from Eysenck's investigation of that trait (1947). Further evidence is provided by Hoffman's study (1953), in which it was found that those people who were most influenced by supposed majority views scored highly on parts of the F-scale (cf. Adorno et al. 1950): the dimension measured by the latter correlates with extroversion to some extent (Eysenck 1954). Hoffmann also found that yielders showed greater anxiety, and it will be recalled from the experiments on suggestion reviewed earlier (p. 110 f.) that neurotics were more suggestible than others. (According to Eysenck (1947) *introverted* neurotics are somewhat more suggestible than extroverted ones.) Later investigators might well study the relation between neuroticism and yielding to social pressure.

Bales and his collaborators (1951) at Harvard have obtained valuable material on the distribution of participations in discussion groups. A very large number of groups of different kinds and sizes has been observed and the behaviour recorded systematically. The results obtained were found to be much the same for quite different sorts of group, varying only with the size. As shown in Figure 5,

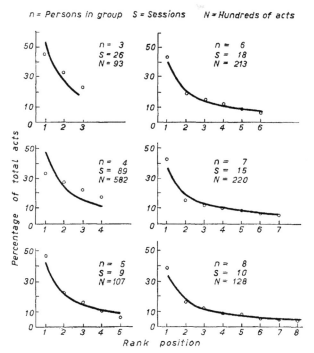

FIG. 5—THE DISTRIBUTION OF PARTICIPATION IN SMALL GROUPS

(From p. 467 of Bales et al. 1951. *By permission of Professor R. F. Bales*)

there is a J-shaped distribution, with a few of the members doing all the talking, and this effect becomes more pronounced with larger sized groups. All leaders of discussion groups are faced with this problem of unequal participation, and the best means of reducing it remains to be discovered. It is interesting to note that the result is quantitative and gives the mathematical *form* of the relationship concerned—a rare event in this field.

Several investigators have tried to find out the personality variables associated with high and low participation in groups. Bass (1950) found that high participation correlated with I.Q., and also that it was related to leadership, so that all the factors associated with leadership must presumably apply. As for personality traits, I. S. Brown (1950) showed that high participation correlated with the 'manic' sub-scale of the M.M.P.I. and the 'social' scale of the Allport-Vernon values questionnaire. Halmos (1952) found that isolates in society show a greater tendency to anxiety and depression symptoms.

Other aspects of the style of behaviour in groups have been studied in relation to psychiatric measures of personality. Swanson (1951) used the 'Blacky' projection test, Coffey and his co-workers (1950) made use of ideologies as inferred from autobiographies, and Thelen (1954) used predictions made by psychiatrists. While each of these investigations showed positive results, they are all expressed in terms of highly individual concepts, so that it is impossible to give any general findings.

It would not be expected that a person's behaviour in a group could be completely predicted from knowledge of his performance in individual situations like personality tests, because his behaviour will be affected by the other members and the group situation. Nevertheless, it is interesting to find that a person's behaviour can partly be predicted in this way. One importance of such prediction is in the selection of people to work in teams. The expense of group selection methods could be avoided if suitable tests could be found to do the same job.

Lastly, some experiments have been done which show the influence of individual members on the performance of groups as a whole. Rosenthal and Cofer (1948) found that the presence of a confederate of the experimenter with an "indifferent and neglectful attitude" had the effect of preventing agreement among the others and reducing their belief in the attainability of the group goals. Haythorn (1953) showed that certain individuals when present in groups were both popular and tended to facilitate group functioning: these people were high on a personality factor of co-operation, prestige, efficiency, and insight when assessed as individuals.

The Effect of Status Differences on Group Behaviour

Throughout this chapter it is the *informal* small group that is under consideration. By an informal group is meant one in which there are no differences of function prescribed for individual members. Groups are said to be either *informal* or *organised*: they are organised when there exist *positions* or *offices* which must be filled by one member or another—when, for example, there is an official leader or secretary. The consideration of organised groups is deferred until Chapter VI.

In the case of informal groups, status differences may still arise. In the first place, group members may occupy positions of differing status in the outside community or in the social organisation of which the informal group is part. For this and other reasons an informal hierarchy will be developed in the course of successive meetings, those at the top of the hierarchy being described as leaders. Experiments on status differences will be considered under these two headings.

(a) *Differences of Status due to Positions Occupied outside the Group*

This is a major independent variable determining individual behaviour in groups apart from personality differences—though the two may not be entirely independent. A number of studies of students and children reviewed by Stogdill (1948) show that leaders tend to be of higher socio-economic status than other members. Other investigators have studied the effects of different positions in a social organisation: Bass and Wurster (1953) found that leadership was associated with position in the hierarchy among groups of oil-refinery supervisors. This result is not surprising, but it would be of great interest to know if it was due to (a) differences of personality between status levels, (b) a generalisation of deferential social habits, or (c) leadership training and experience on the part of the higher-status members.

Hurwitz, Zander, and Hymovitch (1953) carried out an interesting field study of a one-day conference of forty-two social scientists who met in groups of six in four different combinations. It was found that the low-status members liked the high-status ones most, talked to them most though their total participation was small, and overestimated the extent to which the high-status members liked them. The latter, it was found, talked most, largely to each other, and did not overestimate their popularity.

Several experimenters have manipulated the status of group members by giving them preferential treatment. Thibaut (1950) divided groups of ten boys into high- and low-status sub-groups by giving half the group the more pleasant role in team games. During the course of the experiment, communication from lows to highs increased but became less aggressive. Kelley (1951) created differences of status within small groups by experimental instructions concerning the importance of each individual's part in the group task.

Again, there was more communication upwards in the hierarchy, especially on matters irrelevant to the task; there was restraint of critical communication, especially from low to high, as compared with control groups in which no hierarchy had been established. Finally, it has been found in a number of sociometric field studies that there is a tendency for people to name as friends those of slightly higher social status than themselves (e.g. Lundberg and Steele 1938). To summarise these findings, group members of high social status tend to be leaders, to be more popular, to participate more, and to receive more communication.

Kelley (1951) has put forward a theory to account for upward communication in hierarchies. High-status positions are valued; when their attainment is impossible, communication to high-status members acts as a substitute means of locomotion. The evidence for this is that upward communication is greater among those who are keen to rise in the hierarchy but have little chance of doing so. This theory is of the same-level type, bringing new facts under the old principle of substitution of goals. However no further predictions follow from it.

Lastly, it was found by Staton (1948) and Swanson (1951) that too great a range of status in a group prevents the formation of a cohesive or efficient group.

(b) *Behavioural Correlates of Informal Status*

The behavioural criteria of informal status are the same as those for leadership, and it too may be measured by mutual ratings. In this section, evidence will be quoted to show that this is a unitary phenomenon comprising several related aspects of interaction.

Bales and his colleagues (1951), as stated above, found a J-shaped distribution (see Figure 5) of quantity of participation over a wide range of different kinds of discussion groups, and discovered, furthermore, that the more a member said the more was said to him. For any pair of members communication tends to be upwards—for although the high member communicates more it tends to be to the group as a whole. Several unpublished studies quoted by Riecken and Homans (1954, p. 795) show that the number of interactions both initiated and received correlates with sociometric rank. When these findings are combined with those of the previous section it seems clear that informal status comprises popularity, as well as the initiation and reception of communications. The fourth variable considered in the last section was 'leadership': two studies have been concerned with the operation of informal leadership. Lippitt and Polansky carried out a series of studies[1] on summer camps for different kinds of boys, and found that leadership was related to status as measured by mutual ratings.

There is an interesting investigation of status consensus. Heinecke and Bales (1953) discovered that groups in which there is less consensus about the status order are less efficient: they suggest that the lack of consensus is the *cause* of the inefficiency, though of course this cannot be deduced from a non-experimental study.

Another aspect of informal status is concerned with alliances in groups. Mills (1953) arranged forty-eight groups of three to prepare joint stories based on T. A. T. cards. The commonest result was that the two most active members supported each other, forming an alliance: the third person disagreed with them and was rejected. Strodtbeck (1954) found rather different results, however, when the groups were composed of members of a family. Hoffman, Festinger, and Lawrence (1954) found that in a problem-solving situation a coalition tended to form against the person with an initial lead; the task here was a competitive one, but subjects stood to gain by combining resources with one other member.

THE INFLUENCE OF THE ENVIRONMENT ON SMALL GROUPS

Cultural Factors

The culture consists of the shared behaviour, beliefs, and material objects belonging to a society or part of a society. The culture is not therefore a determinant of behaviour, but summarises the behaviour common in a society in so far as it differs from that in other societies. *Culture* is a dispositional concept, like *personality*.

Far too little is known about cultural variations in group behaviour. Most of the research reported in this chapter was carried out in the U.S.A. during the last twenty years—a very small segment of the total range of societies known to sociologists and anthropologists. The generalisations stated here are thus largely laws of behaviour about present-day American groups, and may later prove to have no wider application. The next stage of research should be the repetition of the main experiments in a variety of different societies. By this means it should be possible to estimate how much is general to all societies and how much is dependent on particular

[1] Polansky, Lippitt, and Redl 1950; Lippitt, Polansky, and Rosen 1952.

cultural conditions. It may even be possible to relate the variable components to such factors as child training, inherited characteristics, and climatic conditions for different societies. This is looking a long way ahead, but it seems likely that the findings of social psychologists will be found to be even less universal than those of experimental psychologists: even there it is by no means certain how much is universal, and Gregory Bateson (1944), for example, has cast doubt on the universal applicability of so basic a finding as the Law of Effect.

There are one or two scattered findings concerning cultural variations in group behaviour. Strodtbeck (1951) found that in experimentally induced marital arguments the outcome was correlated with the relative power of the sexes in different societies. Gyr (1951) questioned nationals from several continents and found evidence of variation in committee behaviour, for example in the formality of meetings, the neutrality of the chairman. Neither of these results contradicts any generalisations stated elsewhere in this chapter, since they describe states of affairs rather than functional relationships. It would be a different matter if, for example, it was found that in some society large groups were preferred to small, or autocratic leadership produced more work than democratic. It is in fact quite likely that the second result is true in some societies (Germany, it has been suggested). The first example—preference for small groups—obviously defines the condition of satisfaction for a social need which is probably learned. It would be in no way surprising if such needs differed between societies, and there is clear evidence in the anthropological literature for, e.g. variations in the need for status, both in its strength and in the means of its satisfaction.

One of the most interesting theories of the effect of cultural variation on groups is due to Sherif and Cantril (1947). By means of an extensive documentation of the sociological literature they show that small group formation is extremely widespread among American adolescents, and is less so before and after this stage of life. They maintain that the reason for this is the fact that the American adolescent is in a stage of transition from childhood to adulthood society; he is insecure because he has no stable position in either world, and is confronted by conflicting attitudes towards himself on the part of others. In response, adolescents create their own peer-group society which gives them the security they need. Two comments may be made on this view. Firstly, it is not supported by evidence sufficient to establish a causal relation between occupying an ambiguous position in society and developing small groups; there are many other features of adolescence which could be responsible. Some support is perhaps given to the generalisation by Thrasher (1927) and other students of delinquency, who have shown that delinquent gangs form in areas which are "interstitial to the more settled, more stable and better organised portions of the city" (p. 22). However, delinquency is associated with such areas for other more patently obvious reasons, so that it would be expected that delinquent *gangs* would also be more common there. Another comment on the Sherif and Cantril position is that it entails the following theory. It postulates a need to have a stable and consistent perception of oneself, together with the notion that self-perceptions depend on the reactions of others. It would be necessary to make this theory rather more precise and to derive some new predictions from it. If Sherif and Cantril's view should prove correct, it would be a nice demonstration of cultural differences, since the circumstances of adolescence vary so much between different societies and different periods.

The Group Task and Other Group Experiences

(a) *The Nature of the Group Task*

We may begin by recapitulating some of the results from previous sections. In the discussion of leadership, evidence was quoted which showed that different leaders would emerge in the same group as the nature of the group task changed—the leader being the person most competent at the task. To this may be added a finding of Bales and his associates (1951) to the effect that the distribution of participation in discussion groups is most equal in groups dealing with problems for which there is no specific answer and in which none of the members possesses specialised information. A second problem reviewed above was that of the relative efficiency of individuals and groups at various kinds of problem-solving tasks. Small groups and individuals are superior to larger groups at tasks where the group score depends on the performance of the poorest member—who may spoil the score by making crucial errors. Small groups are also superior at tasks which depend essentially upon the group reaching agreement over some issue. On the other hand, larger groups are better at tasks for which the labour can be divided and in which the presence of a talented person or expert is important—for larger groups are more likely to contain such a person.

One interesting dimension of group tasks is the extent to which they entail interaction between the members. It was shown above that cohesive groups, and groups with mutually compatible members, are more efficient than other groups for tasks entailing interaction between the members, but not for tasks which the members could perform individually. Heise and Miller (1951) found that variations in communication channels (see p. 190) affected the group efficiency differently for different tasks: re-assembly of a list of standard words was best done when all channels were open, whereas the task of constructing a sentence from words scattered among the members was more efficiently performed with one member in a central position, the others being able to communicate with him only.

(b) *Frustration and Threat*

There is some evidence that one effect of frustration on small groups is to increase cohesiveness. This was shown by Wright (1943) in an experiment on pairs of young children, and by Thibaut (1950) in his experiment on underprivileged groups of boys. Shils (1950) interprets some of the researches on the American soldier as indicating that frustration increases cohesiveness, but the causal factor could just have well been shared experiences and enforced interaction. There is some opposing evidence from the Lippitt experiment (1940) on autocratic and democratic leadership in boys' clubs, discussed later (p. 194): the frustrations of autocratic leadership produced aggressive behaviour which in some groups sometimes took the form of scapegoating individual members. Possibly frustration tends to produce both aggression and increased cohesiveness, the resultant behaviour depending on other variables. There is a well-known experiment by J. R. P. French (1944), in which it was found that organised (and presumably cohesive) groups showed more aggression in a dangerous situation—the groups were locked in a room which appeared to be on fire. This result must be discounted however, since the non-organised groups were composed of psychology students, who were not so taken in by the experimental arrangements.

An individual (or group) is said to be exposed to 'threat' or 'ego-involvement' if he believes that he stands to gain or lose by his performance. Lanzetta and his associates (1954) found that several different kinds of threat all had the effect of making members more concerned with acceptance in groups, while the groups to which they belonged were less efficient, and the members displayed less leadership and task-oriented behaviour. J. R. Gibb (1951) found similarly that the number and quality of problem-solutions diminished under threat conditions. As reported in Chapter IV, one effect of threat on individuals is for task-performance to deteriorate (p. 105 f.).

Lanzetta's explanation is that threat creates anxiety, and that the support of others is needed to reduce the anxiety; therefore members are less aggressive, and waste time becoming accepted by the others instead of getting on with the job. While this is plausible, it fails to account for the appearance of aggressive behaviour under some conditions.

(c) *The Spatial Arrangement of Groups*

Several investigators have found that friendships are made and groups formed by people who live or work near one another. Festinger, Schachter and Back (1950) carried out an interesting study of a housing estate for ex-service students and their families at the Massachusetts Institute of Technology. Families of rather similar background had been allocated to the houses at random. It was found that sociometric choices were most often made to next-door neighbours and became less likely for people at greater distances. Furthermore, the most popular individuals were those whose front doors had to be passed by others, and who were therefore more likely to meet other people. The strength of the proximity factor is indicated by the fact that in the two parts of this estate, 60% and 76% of choices went to next-door neighbours. Kuper (1953) found a similar result in an English housing estate. It would be expected that the spatial factor would become less important, and personal compatibility more so, in less homogeneous communities. Furthermore, Loomis and Beegle (1950) found that although spatial proximity was an important determinant of friendship in a newly formed farming community, it became less important with the passage of time.

Further evidence on this point comes from research in the U.S. Army into the effects of mixing white and Negro soldiers. It was found that the prejudice of the white soldiers was diminished in proportion to the closeness of contact (Information and Education Division, 1945). The same thing has been found on inter-racial housing estates (Wilner and Walkley 1952). The greater racial prejudice of Southern as opposed to Northern whites in the U.S.A. would seem at first sight to conflict with these results, as contact is presumably more extensive in the South. Probably prejudice is diminished only under conditions of equal-status contact, or as a result of involvement in the same group.

There is a little experimental evidence on this general problem. Bovard (1951*b*) found that greater liking, as recorded on an eleven-point scale, was produced in group-centred classes where interaction amongst the class was encouraged. Sherif (1951) found that segregating boys together in huts at a camp produced great changes in the patterns of sociometric choices, in the direction of choosing the members of the same hut.

It seems safe to conclude, to a first degree of approximation, that spatial proximity and increased social contact make for increased liking and the formation of groups. It seems that this factor becomes less important as time proceeds, and probable that equal-status contact is necessary. Furthermore, it is common experience that increased contact with *some* people leads to a deterioration of relations, though the conditions for this can as yet only be guessed. As mentioned previously, Seashore (1954) found that smaller groups on the average tended to be more cohesive than larger ones—confirming that increased interaction leads to liking: however, further analysis showed that this relationship was really curvilinear and that smaller groups were either very high or very low in cohesiveness. Thus in a minority of cases increased interaction results in decreased liking.

One explanation for this result has been provided by Newcomb (1947). He maintains that hostilities grow and persist between individuals or groups as a result of barriers to communication. Under such conditions, inaccurate perception of the other person may develop and cannot be corrected. This may be restated in non-perceptual terms to say that when there is no interaction between people they are unable to correct false anticipations of the other's behaviour which are the basis of dislike. This as it stands will not explain the *growth* of hostile attitudes, since no explanation is given of why the inaccurate perceptions should err on the undesirable side; similarly, it will not explain why interaction between strangers leads to increased liking.

Another type of explanation which may be offered is in terms of changes in the behaviour of people as a result of interaction. It was suggested previously (p. 113 f.) that a pair of people will adjust their modes of interaction to one another: this will be in the direction of increasing harmony and mutual satisfaction, and hence the two will come to like one another more. Alternatively, there may be modification of other aspects of behaviour or belief: this does in fact occur, and the conditions and explanation of this are given later during the discussion of norm-formation. When this has happened, the people concerned like one another more, simply because we do like those who share the same behaviour and beliefs: the explanation of this is also considered later.

SPONTANEOUS CHANGES WITH TIME

Norm-formation

There is widespread sociological evidence for the fact that small groups, like larger ones, develop shared behaviour and beliefs, or *norms* (cf. Sherif and Cantril 1947). These are the small-group equivalents of what has been called above the *culture* of a larger society. There are three ways in which norms may be set up:

(a) People may join groups because they share the beliefs of existing members;

(b) deviating members may be rejected; or

(c) the behaviour or beliefs of members may converge over time.

While (a) certainly occurs with some kinds of group, it will not be discussed here since it is not a change over time. Experiments have also shown the operation of (b); this will be considered in the section on the process of norm-formation, where it will be treated as a sanction for deviance rather than as part of norm-formation in itself. While there have been several field studies of (c), this problem has been approached mainly through laboratory experiments, and it is largely these which will be considered here.

(a) *The Determinants of Norm-formation*

In the following paragraphs the influence of a number of specific determinants will be described. Nearly all the experiments cited have made use either of perceptual judgments or of opinions, with disclosure of the actual or supposed views of the other group members between successive judgments. If two people are counted as a group, the experiments on suggestion and social influence could have been included here; the findings are very similar, which indicate that this classification is justified.

The dimensions of groups have been discussed earlier in this chapter, so it will suffice to summarise briefly their relation to norm-formation. There is little evidence on the effect of group size, though there is some indication of more rapid norm-formation in smaller groups. However, it is clear that norms are formed more rapidly in cohesive and co-operative groups.

The relevance of the aspect of behaviour or belief about which a norm is being formed is an important determinant. On theoretical grounds it would be expected that norms would be formed only about things directly relevant to the group's purpose; sociological studies of output restriction in industrial groups and of delinquent gangs have been concerned with highly relevant aspects of group behaviour. There is however very little direct evidence for the proposition. Schachter (1951) found that there were more communications and greater efforts to influence others on topics relevant to the group's purposes. A major difficulty with the proposition concerning relevance is the difficulty of measuring it, although its manipulation is straightforward. It is of interest to note that Bovard and Guetzkow (1950) explain their finding of greater initial variation of perceptual judgments in established as opposed to temporary groups, by saying that in the course of time groups discover which aspects of behaviour are outside the area of norm-formation.

The perceptual ambiguity of the stimulus is probably a determinant of social influence and group convergence. It is a widely accepted principle of perception that as the stimulus becomes less definite, other factors become more important. Evidence was given in Chapter IV, during the discussion of suggestion, to show that a person is more easily influenced when the stimulus is ambiguous (p. 111). There is no direct evidence on this point for group situations, though a comparison of the results of different experiments is revealing. Sherif (1935*a*) obtained considerable influence with very little effort for the highly unstructured 'autokinetic effect': subjects judged how far a stationary light in a dark room had 'moved'. Asch (1952) was able to produce 32% errors for psychophysical judgments well above the threshold, but he applied the intense social pressure of a complete majority (of confederates) opposing the genuine subject in each case (cf. p. 140). Schonbar (1945), who used slighter pressures for similar judgments, failed to obtain significant results.

Whether the behaviour is public or private to the rest of the group is a variable of some theoretical interest. An experiment by the author was devised specifically to investigate this. Groups of two rated the merits of a modern picture and then discussed it under instructions to reach an agreement, communicating with message slips. One subject in each group was a confederate of the experimenter and always made a completely different judgment of the picture from the real subject, and sent a prearranged series of messages. After fifteen minutes' discussion the subjects were asked to give a final opinion about the picture: some of them did so anonymously, placing their rating in a sealed envelope, others told the confederate face-to-face. There was found to be no social influence at all in the first (private) situation, and a considerable amount in the second (public) situation.

Schank (1932) found a difference between publicly expressed views on card-playing, smoking, and drinking in a Methodist rural community, and privately expressed opinions. Gorden (1952) obtained a measure of attitudes to Russia of the thirty-six members of a co-operative living project; when later asked to state their opinion in the presence of the other group members they were found to change their judgments in the direction of what they thought was the group norm. In each of these three investigations the object of social influence was verbal behaviour—there is no evidence that the non-verbal behaviour was affected at all. Further research is needed to show if the public/private variable influences other kinds of behaviour. It is interesting to notice in connection with this point that Schachter and Hall (1952) obtained more volunteers for an experiment from classes of students when they could offer their services in private (the group norm being supposed to be *against* volunteering here), but no more students actually turned up. In the author's experiment, no social influence was found in the private situation. It must be emphasised that this result would not be expected in the case of non-experimental groups, where the process of 'internalisation' might be expected to occur.

The subject's perception of the norms appeared as an independent variable in Gorden's experiment quoted above. In accordance with the arguments produced against the 'cognitive' type of theory in Chapter III, it must be maintained that perceptions cannot be causes: all that was demonstrated in this experiment was that the perception of social norms and the direction of change under social influence are concordant. Each of the two aspects of behaviour is determined by much the same set of causes, hence their apparent relation. Gorden's results could be interpreted as convergence to an actual norm of group opinion. The same is true of Steinor's findings (1954): in this investigation it was found from answers to a questionnaire that those people who experienced strong pressures to conform tended to agree with perceived norms, but there was no independent measure of the real norms. McKeachie (1954), however, found more convergence towards actual norms than to perceived ones. It is important to separate these issues, since distorting processes are liable to influence perception; Gorden (1952) and several others found that people tended to perceive the group norm as being nearer to their own opinion than it actually was. This may be a kind of perceptual defence, and its effect would be, according to the cognitive theory, to reduce norm-formation.

The pressure to uniformity in a group is an interesting determinant, since it raises the question of why norms are formed at all, from the point of view of the group. Steinor (1954), in the investigation described above, found greater conformity to perceived norms when greater pressure to conform was experienced. Festinger and Thibaut (1951) found greater convergence in experimental groups when greater pressure towards uniformity was introduced in the instructions. Gerard (1953) obtained the same result, his pressure to uniformity being created by the expectation of a subsequent discussion of the question with some politicians.

The relation of an individual's judgment to those of other group members is a determinant of his change of judgment. Festinger and his colleagues (1952) and several other investigators have found that deviates change more than members whose judgments are near the mode for the group. Goldberg (1954) showed that conforming took place regularly to the extent of about 30% of the degree of deviation, in groups of two to four members judging the I.Q. of Negroes from photographs. Thus conforming is proportional to initial deviation. The numbers of people disagreeing with the deviate also determines the amount of influence: Asch (1952) discovered that two and three opponents in his above-threshold perceptual situation increased the amount of conforming, but that larger majorities did not enhance the effect. The presence of another deviate reduced the effect.

The extent to which the group is a reference group is an important determinant of norm-formation. Kelley (1952) has distinguished between two senses in which the term 'reference group' is used. In the first place, a reference group is a group to which a person wishes to conform and which may be able to exert certain sanctions. Secondly, a reference group may be one used as a standard for the purposes of self-perception, as described previously (p. 104 f.). It is the first sense with which we are concerned here. It is useful to extend the term 'reference group' to groups of which a person is not a member, but to which he refers his opinions: when this occurs it is clearly an instance of 'private' behaviour. The classical study of reference groups is Newcomb's Bennington College investigation (1943). He found that those who were keen on being accepted in the college community also conformed to the norm of political radicalism, whereas those more concerned with life at home tended to deviate. Festinger, Schachter and Back (1950) discovered more deviants among those whose important group memberships were centred elsewhere than on the housing estate under investigation. Similarly, Kelley and Volkhart (1952) found a negative correlation between valuation of membership and attitude change in response to counter-propaganda, among troops of boy scouts.

Previous learning also influences individual conforming behaviour. Sherif (1935a) found that previous autokinetic judgments made alone reduced the effects of social influence. Kelman (1950) and Mausner (1954) showed that telling subjects during previous trials in the autokinetic situation that they were 'right' or 'wrong' reduced and increased respectively the amount of social influence. The effects of personality differences have been discussed above.

(b) *The Rejection of Deviates*

An issue which must be discussed, in view of its importance for the explanation of norm-formation, is the rejection of deviates. During the discussion of leadership the question of how far leaders had to conform to the norms was postponed. This is the reverse side of the present problem. Several field studies have found correlations between popularity and conformity—e.g. Newcomb (1943) in Bennington College, and Kelley and Volkhart (1952) in scout troops. The result has been established in a laboratory experiment in which paid accomplices acted the part of deviates (Schachter 1951). There is also an interesting study by McCandless (1942), in which it was found that the correlation between popularity and rated dominance decreased in a democratically led group and increased in a control group. There are several studies of friendship which show that people choose friends who choose the same values (e.g. Precker 1952). These findings go a long way towards establishing the generalisation that deviates are rejected while conformers become popular. One possible limitation on this has been suggested by Hughes (1946), who noticed that high-status members do not have to conform so closely as the barely accepted newcomers. Evidence is needed to resolve this paradox. Another interesting point is how far a leader can change the norms, an activity which seems to be involved to some extent in the notion of leadership. Merei (1949) found that leaders among groups of children were not able to change established norms amongst weaker children, and Sherif (1935a) discovered that a leader would cease to be a leader if he tried to change the norm. Nevertheless, there must be some conditions under which a leader can influence norms, and it would be interesting to know what they are.

(c) *The Explanation of Norm-formation*

A considerable amount of knowledge has been accumulated about the empirical conditions of norm-formation, and this has been reviewed above. A theory of norm-formation should account for the basic phenomenon itself, and in addition for all the particular determinants. Three theories will be discussed, one due to Festinger, one due to the author and one to French. There are many other theories, but they fail to meet the basic criteria for a scientific explanation, so that there is no need to examine empirical evidence in order to test them (Argyle 1953c).

Festinger's theory (1954) is too long to be given here in full, but some of the main postulates will be given.

Hypothesis I: There exists, in the human organism, a drive to evaluate his opinions and his abilities.

Hypothesis II: To the extent that objective, non-social means are not available, people evaluate their opinions and abilities by comparisons respectively with the opinions and abilities of others.

Hypothesis III: The tendency to compare oneself with some other specific person decreases as the difference between his opinion or ability and one's own increases.

Derivation B: The availability of comparison with others whose (from I, II, III) opinions or abilities are somewhat different from one's own will produce tendencies to change one's evaluation of the opinion or ability in question.

Derivation C: A person will be less attracted to situations where others (from I, IIIB) are very divergent from him than to situations where others are close to him for both abilities and opinions.

Derivation D: The existence of a discrepancy in a group with respect (from I, II, III) to opinions or abilities will lead to action on the part of members of that group to reduce the discrepancy.

Derivation D_1: When a discrepancy exists with respect to opinions or abilities there will be tendencies to change one's own position so as to move closer to others in the group.

Derivation D_2: When a discrepancy exists with respect to opinions or abilities there will be tendencies to change others in the group to bring them closer to oneself.

Hypothesis VI: The cessation of comparison with others is accompanied by hostility or derogation to the extent that continued comparison with those persons implies unpleasant consequences.

Corollary V_A: Cessation of comparison with others will be accompanied by hostility or derogation in the case of opinions. In the case of abilities this will not generally be true.

Hypothesis VIII: If persons who are very divergent from one's own opinion or ability are perceived as different from oneself on *attributes consistent with the divergence*, the tendency to narrow the range of comparability becomes stronger.

This theory comprises a considerable range of data, altogether thirteen empirical generalisations, including several successful predictions from the theory. There is no space here to detail all these results. In other respects however the theory is rather unsatisfactory.

(*a*) Not all the hypotheses are at a lower level of analysis from the deductions made from them. The hypotheses are of a complex nature, some of them simply being generalisations about groups (e.g. VI, VII, and VIII).

(*b*) There is no economy of derivation. A theory should explain many diverse results by means of a few simple principles. Here nine hypotheses are required to produce thirteen generalisations.

(*c*) The combination of principles concerning opinions and abilities in the same theory is not illuminating. The sections dealing with the evaluation of abilities are concerned solely with experiments on the level of aspiration, and it is necessary to bring in two postulates (IV and V) to account for the differences between opinions and abilities.

The author's theory of norm-formation (Argyle 1953*c*) is less elaborate, being primarily devised as an exercise in theory-construction.

Hypothesis I: Group members satisfy individual needs by attaining the group goal.

Hypothesis II: Attainment of the group goal will not occur unless the members co-operate; in some cases this will entail acting similarly.

Derivation A: The majority will dislike the deviating minority, since their deviation threatens to frustrate the needs of the majority (I, II).

Derivation B: Norms will be formed more readily in co-operative groups (I, II), and

Derivation C: on issues relevant to the group purposes (I, II), and

Derivation D: in groups and on issues where parallel as opposed to complementary action is demanded (I, II).

Hypothesis III: There is a need, in the human organism, for acceptance by groups.

Derivation E: People learn to conform in order not to be rejected (A, III).

Derivation F: Members are more likely to conform if they have a strong need for acceptance in a group (III, E).

Derivation G: Social influence will be less for private than for public behaviour, i.e. where there is no fear of rejection (III, E).

The central part of this theory is Derivation A. The empirical evidence for this has been examined above. This statement cannot stand as an hypothesis in a reductive theory since it is at the group level, so Hypotheses I and II are postulated very tentatively to explain it. Hypothesis III receives independent confirmation from the studies of job satisfaction quoted at the beginning of the chapter. Derivations C, E, and F had already been established. Derivations B and G were new predictions and have subsequently been confirmed. Derivation D is new and follows logically from the earlier propositions, but it is difficult to see how it could be tested empirically. The theory also points to a new direction of research on delinquency: if delinquents are regarded as persistent deviates in society, this may be because they choose deviant reference groups (such as gangs), or because they have no need for acceptance (psychopaths?), because they have had inadequate experience of group life and have not learnt the effects of deviance, or because they are imperceptive and cannot tell when they are being rejected. Such types would of course call for radically different methods of treatment.

A third theory, which explains some of the data, is due to J. R. P. French (1954). It is postulated that if A likes B, then B can influence A. Two established results follow immediately from this: norm-formation is greater in cohesive groups, and popular people tend to be leaders. Of greater interest however is the fact that the 'influence structure' can be taken to be the sociometric structure with the directions of arrows reversed: the extent of changes of behaviour for each member of a group can be predicted if this structure and the initial behaviour of each member are known.

Other Changes with Time

An important way in which groups change over time is in the direction of greater stability; a pattern of interaction is developed which is fairly stable over time. Hunt and Solomon (1942), for example, found that sociometric choices fluctuated quite a lot during the first four weeks of a camp, but remained fairly constant after that. Klein (1952) observed three groups of six over ten meetings of an hour; she found that the members came to agree with one another over the relative status of each member in the group.

Evidence was brought forward earlier to show that frequent interaction leads to increased liking, and that when a group is newly formed the members will come to like each other. However, as Loomis and Beegle (1950) showed, sociometric choice is progressively based more on personal compatibility and less on sheer spatial proximity with the passage of time. A further interesting aspect of group development is that sociometric choice becomes differentiated for different activities: Lippitt (1948) found that the correlation between scores for work and play diminished from ·70 to ·55 during the first three weeks of a discussion group.

Bales and his co-workers at Harvard have produced several interesting findings about the phases through which a discussion group moves. Heinecke and Bales (1953) observed ten groups over four sessions each, and found that emotional behaviour not directed towards the task became more common in successive meetings, and that showing of agreement decreased. Riecken and Homans (1954, p. 823) interpret this as indicating that a more permissive atmosphere develops in which explicit agreement is unnecessary. An alternative explanation might be that these laboratory groups got bored with the task in later meetings.

Bales and Strodtbeck (1951) studied the changes of group behaviour within single meetings of twenty-two discussion groups. They found that 'orientation' behaviour was most frequent at the beginning, 'evaluative' behaviour in the middle, and 'control' behaviour and agreements at the end. This confirms the idea that discussion groups collect information, evaluate solutions, and then decide upon one.

The most important way in which groups change, of course, is through the activity of a leader. This will be dealt with in the following chapter.

CHAPTER VI

HUMAN RELATIONS IN INDUSTRY AND OTHER SOCIAL ORGANISATIONS

THIS CHAPTER IS concerned with behaviour in industrial, military, and similar social organisations. The important aspects of behaviour here for practical purposes are such things as efficiency, absenteeism, and the rest: the first section discusses the measurement of these, at the same time breaking down the notion of 'morale' into simpler elements. The remainder of the chapter is concerned with the causal influence of those factors specific to organisations and not present in small groups—the formal organisation with its hierarchy of positions, its selection and training methods, and its incentive system, as well as the influence of leaders at various levels on those under their charge.

There are many kinds of social organisation,[1] but most of the research aimed at establishing scientific generalisations has been carried out in industry, the Services, and other administrative hierarchies. Anthropologists have studied the complex organisation of primitive societies, especially their family structure, but they have been primarily interested in describing the organisation of particular tribes rather than in arriving at generalisations (cf. Radcliffe-Brown 1950). Again, sociologists have examined the class systems of modern communities, but they too have worked largely at a descriptive level (cf. Pfautz 1953). In addition to field investigations of industrial, military, and administrative organisations, a number of laboratory experiments on structured groups will also be reported.

The field of research covered by this chapter lies between Industrial Psychology on the one hand, and Industrial Relations and Economics on the other. In other words, it is not concerned with individual skill, selection, or training—the traditional subject-matter of Industrial Psychology—save in so far as these show up in the purely social activities of supervisors and managers. Nor is there any discussion of economic factors such as the degree of capitalisation or the state of employment, and very little is said

[1] The terms 'social organisation' and 'social structure' will be used synonymously.

about industrial relations matters such as the joint consultation arrangements and the organisation of the unions.

Human Relations in Industry is not yet established and accepted as a *scientific* discipline. The non-scientific work is probably better known than the investigations discussed in this chapter. In Great Britain, one of the most prominent research teams is that of the Tavistock Institute of Human Relations, much of whose work is of the clinical and interpretative type criticised earlier (p. 19 f.). In America, the Harvard School of Business Administration is equally well known, but continues to publish case-studies, from which, as has been argued previously (p. 40 ff.), it is impossible to draw any valid conclusions, although they may yield valuable suggestions. Many workers in the field of Public Administration adopt a similar procedure. For some reason the more scientific studies are relatively little known, and it is hoped that this collection of valid investigations in the field of administration will be convincing to those sceptical of the use of scientific methods in this area.

The problem of the generality of results is important here, because different functional relationships may be found in different organisations. For example, the correlation between job satisfaction and output has been found to be sometimes positive, sometimes negative, while in some studies there was no relation at all. Clearly, further variables must be studied, and the effects of these will not be discovered until comparative studies are done in several organisations whose precise differences are known. Meanwhile the results accumulate, so that increasingly intelligent guesses can be made. This variation between organisations also upsets the measuring instruments: basic correlations—for example, between the answers to the same two questions—vary widely in different investigations. Finally, the unsettled state of the empirical results makes them difficult to explain, therefore it may be felt that theorising should be delayed until completely general laws have been found. On the other hand, not all the results vary between organisations, and a theory is likely to be concerned with the variable results as well, and may be able to predict what the further unknown variables are likely to be.

THE DEPENDENT VARIABLES

The aspects of behaviour in social organisations to which practical considerations have directed attention are output, absenteeism, labour turnover, job satisfaction, informal organisation, and style of leadership. While the methods of measurement described previously still apply, it is necessary to discuss the particular problems that arise specifically in connection with these variables. This will also serve as an introduction to some of the problems of social organisations.

Output

Human Relations in Industry, like other branches of Industrial Psychology, has received support partly since it has been able to discover ways of increasing output, which has traditionally been the major dependent variable. The measurement is straightforward when all the workers to be compared are producing a number of equivalent units, using the same equipment and making no mistakes: output is then simply the number of units produced per man, or per department, in a given time. In practice, however, allowance must be made for mistakes and a correction made for the quality of what is produced. This can be done by taking into account the time required to correct the mistakes, or the wastage of material or diminished value of the product.

It is often desirable to compare the output of individuals, departments, or firms which are not producing the same product or are using different capital equipment. Economists are able to calculate differences of net output in terms of cost, though this depends on the state of the market where different products are concerned: in any case, how hard the men are working is only one factor in the costs. In factories using the piece-work method of payment, each job has a 'standard' time assessed by the time-study department. It is thus possible to compare the rate of work at different jobs either by finding how much work is turned out in relation to the standard times, or by obtaining direct ratings by time-study men of the speed of work.[1] The first method, if piece-work tickets are studied, would make allowance for wastage, while the second would not. The objection to the use of time-study methods is the low reliability of the standards established in this way. Rodgers and Hammersley (1954), in an investigation of thirty-one trained practitioners, found that only two-thirds of them gave times within 21% of the mean. Although five-sixths of this variance was due to the use of different systems of allowances and so forth, only two-thirds of the observers trained in the same way differed from the mean by less than 9%. On the other hand, in a recent unpublished investigation it has been

---

[1] This is done in terms of the '60–80 scale': 60 is the effort-rating given to a man walking at 3 m.p.h.

claimed that two-thirds of a large sample of time-study engineers differed from the mean by less than 1%. Heron (1952) found a correlation of ·92 between individual rate of output of a standard product, and individual earnings based on time-study values for a variety of products, showing that the time-study values were accurate in this case. The low reliability of orthodox time-study may be avoided by means of one of the standardised sets of times for different movements which have been established. This cuts out doing any actual timing—the time can be looked up once the movements are known. It is too early as yet to say how reliable such methods are, or whether they are satisfactory for comparing different work processes.

Not everybody in the organisations that have been studied has been engaged on 'production jobs'—that is to say, actually turning out material units of production. The efficiency of those who are supervising others can be measured in terms of the output, job satisfaction, etc., of those under them. For workers not on production jobs, merit ratings can be used. The important aspects of the performance must first be decided, so that rating scales can be devised for their measurement. Reliability checks and multiple measurements are more important here than for more objective measurements, such as of absenteeism. Sometimes the efficiency of whole departments is assessed in this way: for example Katz and others (1951), in their study of the supervision of railway gangs, obtained ratings of the relative output of pairs of gangs equated for the conditions of work. The ratings were shown to be of high reliability between different judges.

Of course the efficiency, or value to the organisation, of a man or of a department is not only a question of output. Rates of absence, for example, would also have to be taken into account. In a later section there will be a discussion of attempts to obtain general measures of 'satisfactoriness'.

Absenteeism

The absence rate of an individual or department is the percentage of days lost in relation to the total assigned to be worked. This is fairly straightforward, and may normally be extracted from existing records. The total absence rate can be divided up into excused and voluntary absenteeism, and it has been shown that these are quite differently caused. Two methods have been used for distinguishing voluntary absenteeism from the rest. The usual method is simply to make use of records showing the reasons given for absence, when such records exist or can be instituted. Using this method, Kerr and his collaborators (1951) found that high voluntary absenteeism was associated with low job satisfaction, whereas excused absenteeism was unrelated to either of these but was greater under incentive motivation. The weakness of this method of measuring voluntary absence is that it depends on verbal reports and may be quite invalid: apparent variations in voluntary absence may in reality be variations in honesty.

The second method of assessing voluntary absenteeism is that suggested by Behrend (1951). She made use of the fact that over a wide range of British industry absenteeism falls steadily throughout the week, so that it is highest on Monday and lowest on Friday for a five-day week. Behrend's 'Blue Monday Index' is the difference between Friday's and Monday's attendances per hundred workers. She demonstrated that the Blue Monday Index depends on the type of work, and varies between departments, whereas total absence rates depend on age and are largely due to sickness. Again, the two indices did not correlate with one another. Research by the Acton Society in the coal industry (Acton Society Trust 1953) has shown that there are local variations in the pattern of weekly absenteeism and that the trend found by Behrend in the Midlands does not hold in Scotland and Wales. A more general way of measuring voluntary absenteeism is to use the difference between the two days of the week which consistently have the largest and smallest attendance. With such modification, Behrend's Index is a very useful and objective measure of voluntary absenteeism.

A further refinement which can be applied to measures of absenteeism as well as to other measurements has been used by Handyside (1953c). Variations from week to week for a given department may be greater than variation between different departments. Consequently, if departments are to be compared, an analysis of variance should be carried out to discover the relative importance of these two different sources of variation, otherwise weekly differences may be counted as inter-departmental ones. In any case, the larger the *unit* and the longer the period studied, the more reliable will be the figures obtained.

Labour Turnover

The total labour turnover of a department or firm is the number of workers leaving during a year expressed as a percentage of the average number employed. People may leave an organisation for four main reasons. They may be *dismissed* because they are (1) unsatisfactory or (2) redundant, and they may *resign* for (3) avoidable and (4) unavoidable reasons. Ministry of Labour figures of labour turnover are totals due to all four causes, but other figures may refer only to (1) and (3), the avoidable kinds of labour turnover, which account for about 75% of turnover in this country (Raphael et al. 1938; Social Survey 1952). The Ministry of Labour however do not count many of the people who stay less than a month. It has often been found that the most recently employed workers are more liable to leave a firm than are those who have built up a period of service with it. J-shaped curves are obtained if the length of service of leavers is plotted against their numbers (Rice et al. 1950). Those staying less than a month comprise as much as 14% of the leavers (Long 1951), and it is often desirable to include them in turnover figures. In the years 1945–9 the average total labour turnover figure for Great Britain was 12% for men and 13% for women (Social Survey 1952).

Another index sometimes used instead of labour turnover is *labour stability*. This is simply the percentage of workers with a firm at one date who are still there a year later. The advantage of this index is that it indicates the number of permanent workers, whereas labour turnover may be inflated if there are a lot of short-term leavers.

Like absenteeism, labour turnover is an important index of the efficiency of firms and departments: whereas absenteeism means wasted time, turnover entails extra training. Both have been found to be sensitive to social factors in the organisation.

Job Satisfaction

The three measures so far considered have depended on records of overt behaviour. Job satisfaction, however, is a 'state of mind' and can be measured only by verbal methods, i.e. by interview or questionnaire. All kinds of attitude scales have been used for this purpose. The principal ones are as follows:

(*a*) Hoppock (1935) devised one of the earliest scales, and this has been more widely used than any other. His method of scale-construction is rather similar to that of Likert, in that multiple-choice questions are selected by item-analysis. Different forms of the scale have between four and ten questions, and the total score is calculated by adding up scores on separate questions, the multiple choices being numbered 1–5 or 1–7. The addition of ranked scores was shown to be justified in view of the fact that scores thus obtained had a correlation of ·997 with the sums of standard scores.[1]

[1] Standard scores are scores expressed as differences from the mean and divided by the standard deviation.

(b) In recent years job satisfaction scales have been drawn up by factor analysis. A number of questions are administered to the population under survey and a general factor extracted. The questions contributing most to this factor are then used as a job satisfaction scale, the total scores being obtained by addition as before. As Heron (1954a) has pointed out, the correlation between any given pair of questions may vary between different investigations: a variation from ·18 to ·71 in the correlation between the same two questions used by himself and Carlsson (1951) being quoted. This indicates that it may not always be satisfactory to use the same job satisfaction scale in different investigations without a pilot enquiry, and the results of different researches will not be strictly comparable. Some investigators have extracted group factors. Morse (1953), for example, distinguished Intrinsic job satisfaction, Financial and Job Status satisfaction, and Involvement with the company. However, examination of the correlation patterns reveals that the average intercorrelations *within* each area of satisfaction are scarcely any higher than the correlations *between* the three group factors (p. 19), so that there is really very little support for such a tripartite division. The same objection does not apply however to Heron's factors (op. cit.), and furthermore he discovered that while scores on one of his group factors correlated with labour turnover, scores on the other factors did not.[1]

(c) On the other hand, if it is desired to raise job satisfaction by the removal of specific grievances, a check-list of objects for complaint can be circulated. Handyside (1953a) has suggested that priorities for action can be derived from the replies to such a list by multiplying frequencies of mention of different topics by the average scale-value of intensity of feeling.

(d) A new scale for measuring job satisfaction has recently been constructed at Oxford (Argyle and Gardner, unpublished Report to the Department of Scientific and Industrial Research). The items correlating most highly with general and group factors in previous scales were listed and placed in groups of verbal equivalents. By the selection of one question from each group a list of fifteen items was obtained. These items are administered by questionnaire and factor-analysed.

These scales have face validity from the nature of the questions asked, for example "How do you like working here?", and they have

---

[1] Personal communication.

internal validity from the nature of the methods of scale-construction used. Is it also possible to establish their validity against some external criterion? There is a certain amount of evidence that job satisfaction as measured in this way correlates with low labour turnover (Kerr 1952, and Heron quoted above), and with low voluntary absenteeism (Kerr 1952). These correlations can be regarded as providing either external or experimental validation of job-satisfaction scales, depending on whether absenteeism and turnover are regarded as defining criteria, or as predicted concomitants.

Informal Organisation

The notion of informal organisation has been used to include a variety of aspects of social interaction in organisations. The measurement of three different aspects of it will be considered here: communication channels, patterns of friendship, and status.

(1) *Communication Channels*

Several techniques have been used to find out the actual, as opposed to the formal, channels of communication. The questionnaire method has been used by Jacobsen and Seashore (1951), who asked with whom executives spent most of their time, and what they discussed. This is certainly the easiest way of obtaining a picture of communication channels, and Stogdill and Elton (Stogdill et al. 1953c) found that the estimated distribution of time of Naval officers correlated with logged time from ·41 to ·86 for different men. Carlson (1951) used a self-recording method whereby executives filled in a standard form every time they telephoned, wrote a letter, interviewed anyone, etc. On this form was recorded the place of work, the person contacted, the mode of communication, the kind of question discussed, and the action taken. A number of categories was provided for the last three items, of which the executive ticked one. These records can be analysed in several ways—to show the major channels, the short-cuts and blockages, the people who discuss certain issues, and how they do it. Though laborious, this method is more valid than the simple questionnaire technique. As a matter of fact both Carlson (op. cit.) and Burns (1954) found that many executives did not mind filling in forms, and quite missed them when the investigation was over. A third way of analysing communication channels has been suggested by Davis (1953). Called by him 'Ecco Analysis', it consists in tracing back communications to their sources: each communicator fills in a form, specifying the nature of the message, its source, and the time and medium of communication. The particular interest of this method is that it is able to reveal delays and distortions of information, whereas the previous methods only show which channels are used.

(2) *Patterns of Friendship*

The sociometric method was discussed in Chapter II (p. 21). Certain elaborations on the method have been devised for the study of social organisations. Wechsler and his collaborators (1952), for example, used an extended sociometric method which distinguishes between various activities for which a partner is being chosen, and between the modes of: prescribed, thought to be prescribed, actual, desired, and rejected relationships. Of these, the first taken is from organisation charts, the third is a communication-channel question, and the last two are orthodox sociometric questions. From the answers to these questions various indices are calculated, e.g. satisfaction with social relationships, and accuracy of perception of the organisation. This seems to be a promising approach, but little use has been made of it as yet.

(3) *Status*

In social organisations, status is primarily determined by a person's position or rank. There are also however differences of status between people of the same rank, while *categories* of people may have a status bearing no relation to their pay or authority—as in the case of office and manual workers.

Methods of measuring status in various contexts have been discussed elsewhere (Argyle 1953b), so only a brief account will be given here. There are three general ways of measuring status in a social group. (a) One may observe the subject's social interactions with others, noting in particular the deferential, non-reciprocal, order-giving aspects of behaviour. While feasible with small groups in the laboratory, this method is of very limited application in the field, though Warner and Lunt (1941) succeeded in stratifying the upper classes of 'Yankee City' on the basis of direct observation. It might be possible to analyse communications recorded by the Carlson technique to show status differences, but Burns (1954) has shown that what may seem to be an 'instruction' to the giver, is often regarded as 'advice' or 'information' by the recipient. (b) A person's status can be taken as the judgment of others about his status. This is the most widely used method, and was applied in industry by Jacobsen and Seashore (1951). The principal limitation of the method is that it is possible only in social groups small enough for the members to know one another. This is sometimes the case inside social organisations, but is possible in the class system of society at large only for small communities like those studied by Warner. On a larger scale it is possible to survey people's estimation about the status, not of individuals, but of categories of individuals, such as their occupations. This has been done by Hall and Jones (1950), and the idea is explored further in another place (Argyle loc. cit.). (c) A person's status can be taken as his own opinion of his status. It has been shown that people have exaggerated ideas of their own status (compared with measurements of the other kinds) (Green 1948), and that these perceptions are open to distortion by motivational factors (Hyman 1942). It must be concluded that while self-perceptions of status have some interest in themselves, they are not the primary concern of the student of informal organisation.

In the above discussion, status was never defined. As with other empirical concepts the definition lies in the method of measurement, so that it has three different definitions. There is evidence that the first two methods yield substantially the same results, while the third one measures something different.

The Style of Leadership of Supervisors and Executives

Great interest has been taken in the behaviour of executives both as a causal and a dependent variable. Its measurement therefore becomes a matter of importance. There are two principal methods—interview or questionnaire, given to the person himself or to other people in the organisation.

Various scales have been devised[1] for administration to executives themselves. Katz and his colleagues (1951) made use of ratings based on an open-ended interview. Such scales require validation, for they may not reflect supervisory behaviour accurately. As with job satisfaction scales, there is face and internal validity, but no external validation has been carried out. It is important in this instance to establish the validity of these measures either against direct observations of behaviour, or by finding their relationship with the

[1] cf. File and Remmers (1945); Castle (1953); Shartle and Stogdill (1953).

efficiency, job satisfaction, etc., of the people for whom the executive is responsible. Confidence in the scales is increased when it can be shown that they agree with the ratings of superiors (File and Remmers 1946), but these cannot be regarded as a very satisfactory criterion, as will be explained below. Another criterion which may be used consists of questions asked of those supervised. For example, Morse (1953, p. 133) checked ratings of closeness of supervision based on interviews of foremen against answers to the question "Do you make decisions on the job you are doing?", administered to those supervised. D. T. Campbell (1953) did a similar check, but found a conflict between the different measurements (pp. 164–5).

Rating scales have been drawn up for completion by the men working under a supervisor or executive. Some of these have been compiled by attitude-scaling methods. Hemphill (1950*b*), for example, drew up a Likert-type scale by factor analysis, measuring two dimensions of supervisory behaviour. Jackson (1953) devised a set of Guttman scales for assessing nine areas of behaviour and found that supervisors received the same scores from different groups of workers when they were changed round. This method is methodologically superior to the technique of interviewing supervisors themselves, since it is a matter of rating on the basis of observation as opposed to introspection. It is not so satisfactory as using an independent observer, since the people concerned are caught up in the social organisation themselves, and their ratings will reflect other factors besides the behaviour of the person rated. Furthermore, when other variables, such as job satisfaction, are being recorded by interviewing the same people who carry out the rating, it means that the two measurements are not made independently. It is dangerous to assert a causal relationship between two variables if they were not recorded independently. Apart from such considerations this method is probably the best means of assessing supervisory behaviour, in the absence of any external validation for the first method.

A third method often used is that of ratings by superiors. These ratings are usually of 'efficiency', rather than of any particular style of behaviour, and hence different ideas as to what is desirable reduce the meaningfulness of such measures. Ratings by seniors on particular traits however would be a useful supplement to ratings by juniors, since they are concerned with rather different aspects of the behaviour of the person being studied.

RELATIONS BETWEEN THE DEPENDENT VARIABLES

The variables discussed in the last section do not vary independently of one another. On the other hand, functional relationships between them cannot be interpreted causally in view of the fact that none of them can be manipulated independently of the others: they are effects, not causes.[1] Correlations appear between them because they are affected by some of the same determinants: it is a case of A varying with B because both are influenced by C. In general then it would be supposed that explanation of the relations between the dependent variables should be in terms of the independent determinants of each dependent variable. In some cases, however, there is an obvious psychological connection between two measures, as with job satisfaction and labour turnover, so that the two can be regarded as a unified response affected by similar causes.

A further use which can be made of these relationships is to calculate indices based on the combination of a number of correlated measures to give measurements of satisfactoriness.

Job Satisfaction and Output

Great interest has been shown in this relationship, partly because of the theory that one way to increase output is to make the workers happy, partly because it indicates to some extent how far the aims of management and men are compatible. More will be said on both these topics below.

The nature of the relation between job satisfaction and output is by no means clear. Bernberg (1952), with workers in an aircraft factory, and Kristy (1952) with post office workers, found no relationship between the job satisfaction and efficiency of individuals. Heron (1954a) found a positive correlation of ·31 between job satisfaction and a general index of satisfactoriness (see below) for 144 bus conductors. Katz et al. (1951) found a negative relation between job satisfaction and ratings of output for *work-teams* on the railway; Katz et al. (1950) found no relation for *groups* of clerical workers, and Giese and Ruter (1949) found a positive correlation of ·19 for *departments* in a retail firm. These last results are for groups and would have to be compared with the others cautiously, since personality factors would be largely eliminated. The evidence is at least enough to refute the widely held belief that happy workers and high output necessarily go together. Probably the extent and direction of the

[1] This does not apply to the style of leadership of supervisors.

correlation depend on further factors in the organisation, as yet unknown. Morse (1953, p. 127) suggests that more positive correlations will occur with more skilled tasks, but the studies quoted above do not clearly display this tendency.[1]

Does this mean that the aims of management and men are independent, and sometimes incompatible? The important point is that management is in a position to manipulate a number of variables: as will be shown later some of these will increase both output *and* job satisfaction, others increase one but not the other. The relation depends on the relative values of these variables.

What of the idea that increased job satisfaction leads to greater output? As argued above, this could not be regarded as a causal relationship. Furthermore, there is little evidence for there being any general relation between these two. It is however worth noting that if there were a significant relationship, it would be possible to explain this psychologically, that is to say by means of a same-level explanation. Something like this may have been in the minds of exponents of the original proposition. Such a theory might go: "The less satisfied workers are frustrated (by definition): they will therefore become aggressive (frustration-aggression hypothesis): the company may be chosen as an object for aggression because the source of frustration tends to be the object of aggression: aggression may take the form of reducing output." Such a theory could be verified by seeing if low-output workers had more hostile attitudes towards the company than high-output workers.

A second explanation of the relation between job satisfaction and output has been put forward by Morse (1953). It is suggested that job satisfaction depends on the strength of needs and the amount of environmental gratification; "the greater the amount the individual gets, the greater his satisfaction and, at the same time, the more the individual still desires, the less his satisfaction" (p. 28). Output, she suggests, depends on seven factors, of which one is need-strength. Hence individuals with strong needs will produce more (the other six factors being equal), and will also be more satisfied if *the amount of environmental gratification is high*. If it is low there will be a negative relation between satisfaction and output. (pp. 125-7).

This is the best kind of explanation for the relation between two dependent variables: same-level, or deductive, theories are put for-

---

[1] Further studies relating job satisfaction and output are reported in the review by Brayfield and Crockett, *Psychological Bulletin*, 1955, pp. 396-424.

ward to account for the relation of each dependent variable to its determinants. The relation between two such variables then follows.

Job Satisfaction, Labour Turnover and Absenteeism

Three investigations by Kerr (1947, 1952) all show a correlation between labour turnover and low job satisfaction, for departments. Argyris (1954) was able to predict individual leavers from ratings of the extent to which workers' needs were satisfied in the organisation. As a matter of fact, this relation is so understandable that labour turnover has been regarded as a criterion for validating measures of job satisfaction.

The same thing applies to voluntary absenteeism. Kerr and associates (1952) found that in departments with high job satisfaction, voluntary absenteeism was low, but absence due to illness was high. If this interesting result is confirmed, the theoretical problem will be raised of why satisfied workers should be sick.

General Measures of Individual Efficiency

Output is not the only criterion of an individual worker's efficiency, and for those not engaged on direct production jobs, output figures are not available. Other criteria may be, for example: absenteeism, lateness, amount of overtime worked, merit ratings by supervisors, complaints received from the public, errors and accidents, etc. Various ways of combining such measurements are discussed by Ghiselli and Brown (1948, pp. 84–7). The two most important methods are: (*a*) Value judgments of experts and (*b*) factor analysis. In method (*a*), managers, or others, rate the criteria in order of importance. The first difficulty with this is that the experts fail to agree and the inter-expert reliability may be around ·2 or ·4 (Ghiselli and Brown, loc. cit.). In the second place, the experts, even if they agree, may not be right. Fiske (1951) suggests a systematic attempt to relate the criteria to the goals of the organisation; this would however entail both empirical research and agreement on these goals. In (*b*) the centroid method can be used to extract a general factor, and the criteria may be weighted according to their correlation with it, as in the measurement of morale. Heron (1954*a*) obtained a single measure for the 'satisfactoriness' of bus conductors by this method, though he did not weight the separate criteria.

Such indices based on a combination of criteria are more valuable than either single merit ratings or measures of output alone.

The 'Morale' of Groups

We are not concerned here with individuals, although 'morale' has often been used to refer to the state of motivation, well-being, or satisfaction of individuals.

Morale has also been used in various ways to characterise groups. To begin with, it has been used by various writers as a synonym for variables to which we have given other names—such as job satisfaction, or output. More often, however, it has been used to refer to some combination of variables characterising departments. When people talk of a 'good group' or a 'happy ship', they are referring to a combination of efficiency and job satisfaction. It has however been shown above that these two variables have little or no relation to each other, so that it may be claimed that morale in this sense does not exist, i.e. it is not a dimension along which groups may usefully be classified. Morale has been used, again, for a combination of co-operativeness, or cohesion, and other variables such as output or job satisfaction. Apart from the redundancy of terminology here, the actual relations between these variables are complex, as was shown at the beginning of Chapter V.

The senses of morale listed above are of no classificatory value, but there are two others more worthy of consideration. The first is the attitude of the workers in a department towards the organisation as a whole. The Bank Wiring Observation Room is a familiar instance of a keen group whose goals differed from those of the management (Roethlisberger and Dickson 1939). Uhrbock (1934) developed a Thurstone-type scale with items such as "A man can get ahead in this company if he tries", to measure morale in this sense. This is the same as the 'Company Involvement' part of the Michigan job satisfaction scales. The second sense of morale worth pursuing is the development of general measures of efficiency for departments or firms, analogous to those discussed above for individuals. This has been done by Giese and Ruter (1949) and Burns (1951), who factor-analysed a large number of measures of efficiency, including job satisfaction. Such a general factor would, of course, be of less interest when some of the measures correlate negatively or not at all. As with job satisfaction scales, the correlations between the items vary in different organisations, though the same remedy could be applied.

THE ORGANISATIONAL STRUCTURE

Any social organisation contains a number of *positions* or *offices* which endure while particular occupants come and go. The existence of such positions may be regarded as the basic characteristic of a social organisation, as opposed to informal groups, crowds, and other collections of people. The unique feature of social organisations for social psychologists is that behaviour seems to be determined more by the social structure than by individual personality. As a simple example of this, Whyte's study of Chicago restaurants (1948) may be instanced. He found a widespread tendency for waitresses to cry, that is to say they cried more frequently than either the customers or the cooks. This is quite general—the occupants of similar positions behave similarly, and in a different way from those in different positions. Furthermore, the interactions between members of an organisation are largely governed by the positions of those concerned.

The shared behaviour for occupants of a position is sometimes called the *role* for that position, especially when this behaviour is distinct from the behaviour in adjacent positions (Argyle 1953b). This is very similar to the notion of a group norm, and is in fact the same thing if group-membership is classed as a position. This should be distinguished from *role-playing*, which refers to the deliberate acting out of a role and is an attribute of individual behaviour, whereas *role* is an organisational concept. The exact differences in behaviour for different positions depend on the type of organisation. In the case of industry, the *rank* of a person is an important aspect of his position: those of higher rank have greater job satisfaction (Harrell 1949, Chapter XII), lower absenteeism (Behrend 1951), greater intelligence (Whitfield and Himmelweit 1944), and greater emotional stability (Guilford 1952). Stogdill and his co-workers (1953a) have carried out an extensive survey of differences in the way Naval officers of different ranks and branches spend their time: there is a characteristic profile of time-distribution for each position.

The factors making for similarities of behaviour within similar positions may be considered under three headings—selection, training, and structure. Only certain kinds of person are admitted to each position, either as a result of deliberate selection machinery or through self-selection processes. This defines the range of individual differences for each position in an organisation. Secondly, most organisations have special training schemes for their members, which have the effect of moulding people in the required way and of making them more like one another. In addition to formal training, the guidance, training, and social pressures experienced on the job have a similar and probably even greater effect. Thirdly, everyone responds to the demands of his position, which may be regarded as a complex pattern of stimuli. The relevant aspects of a position here are such things as: the nature of the incentive system, the channels of authority and communication, and the requirements of the job.

Each of these three factors of selection, training, and structure will be considered in the sections that follow. The behaviour characteristic of a position may be a result of any or all of them. Whyte thought that his waitresses cried because of their position in the structure—they came under the conflicting authorities of the cooks and the customers. It might conceivably, however, have been a product of training or selection, and detailed research would be needed to establish the true cause.

Before going on to examine these three processes, it is as well to consider the residual individual differences between occupants of similar positions. While the range of such differences is small compared with that in the general population, individual differences may still be considerable. Three types of distribution may be found in social organisations. Where there are strong institutional pressures towards a certain form of behaviour a J-shaped curve is usually found—most people conform and successively fewer deviate more extremely. This kind of pattern has been found in the case of such things as lateness (F. H. Allport 1934), absenteeism (Walker 1947), and accidents (Greenwood and Woods 1919). Abilities, and any other aspects of personality which may be involved in selection, will show a distribution with a cut-off point which is more or less sharp depending on the efficiency of selection (cf. Whitfield and Himmelweit 1944). For higher posts the cut-off will be at the lower end of the distribution, but for lower posts an upper cut-off is sometimes used in selection, to avoid intelligent people becoming disgruntled with repetitive work. Attitudes, and other aspects of behaviour which are the object neither of institutional pressures nor of selection processes, will be distributed much as they are in the general population—often in a normal, or near-normal manner (cf. Viteles 1954, Part 4).

Such variability in behaviour is related to age, sex, and those personality traits which can be measured by psychological tests. For example, job satisfaction increases with age (save for 17–25, when it decreases), is greater among women, and is less for neurotics (cf. Harrell 1949, Chapter XII). Stogdill (1953*b*) has studied the problem of which aspects of organisational behaviour are determined primarily by position and which by personality (i.e. by the residual individual differences). His method was ingenious: the behaviour of newly-promoted Naval officers was compared with (*a*) the previous behaviour of these men in their old positions, and (*b*) the previous behaviour of the old occupants of the positions. It was thought that if the new behaviour was most like (*a*) it must be determined by personality, while if more similar to (*b*) it must be due to the position. The results showed that personality determined leadership score, and time spent supervising, reading, and attending conferences. Position determined popularity, and time spent in personal contacts and research. While these results are highly specific to the organisation in question, the technique is useful and the findings suggestive.

Selection for Leadership

Although selection operates at all levels in the hierarchy, the discussion in this section will be restricted to the selection of leaders, i.e. foremen, managers, officers, and so forth. The task of leaders is largely a social one, and as such is more relevant to the topic of this book than is the work of other members of social organisations. As stated above, part of the explanation of why members of positions have the kind of abilities, personality, attitudes, and background that they have depends on the manner in which people enter and are promoted within the concern. This is partly because only certain sorts of people apply (self-selection), partly because of the selection system in force. Even when there is no formal procedure, or where nepotism predominates, it is still the case that a certain type of person is being selected. The overall effects of selection and self-selection can be examined simply by a comparison of the occupants of different positions. For instance, Whitfield and Himmelweit (1944) compared the intelligence-test scores of Army recruits from different occupations: teachers scored 40, shop assistants 23, miners 15, etc. This method is, of course, only possible for relatively stable personality characteristics, or for background factors such as father's profession. Nor does it isolate the influence of selection as opposed to self-selection. Both of these difficulties can be overcome by studying people before selection (to cut out the effect of experience), and comparing them with those not selected. Stouffer and his colleagues (1949, p. 258 f.) found that in the U.S. Army the men promoted were those with initially favourable attitudes towards authority.

It is not intended to review here the results of selection in particular organisations, since there are as yet no general findings about the types of person selected in different kinds of organisation. Instead, it is proposed to describe the methods of selection for supervision and management that are used, and summarise the empirical findings concerning the success of these methods.

(1) *Traditional Methods*

In industry the great majority of firms use unsystematic procedures of *ad hoc* nomination, on the basis of existing knowledge of the available people in the firm (N.I.I.P. 1951, pp. 39–40). The results of these procedures as shown in our study were that 16% of supervisors selected in this way were rated as 'first class' by managers and psychologists, and 44% as 'good', the remainder being judged 'satisfactory' or 'weak' (op. cit., p. 41). Handyside and Duncan (1954) found correlations of ·23 and ·18 against a composite criterion based on promotions and managerial ratings, two and four years after selection was carried out in this way, in one firm.

In the British Army, officer selection was traditionally conducted by a board interview by senior officers. Out of 491 officers selected in this way, 22% were later found to be above average, 41·3% average, and 36·6% below average, corresponding to a correlation of about ·2 (Vernon and Parry 1949, p. 124).

It may be concluded that traditional methods of selection for supervisory positions in social organisations are extremely unsatisfactory, and are little better than choosing at random from the available candidates. Modern systematic methods of selection have used intelligence and other tests, group discussion, and interviews. The value of these will be considered in turn. There is no space here to discuss these methods in full: an attempt will simply be made to assess the principal findings.

(2) *Tests*

As shown in Table I, various kinds of verbal tests make a considerable contribution to selection schemes. The low figure of ·22 found by Vernon for the Civil Service Selection Board is highly significant statistically: like all the correlations in this follow-up study it is low, because the candidates were very highly selected and thus the range of the qualities measured was small. A number of investigators have found correlations between File's test for supervisors, and intelligence, but these were not very adequate studies as Heron points out (1954*b*), apart from the dubious validity of File's test. There is also evidence that higher ranks of social organisations have higher I.Q.s than the lower ranks, so that intelligence tests would be expected to be useful here.

TABLE I
Validation Studies of Systematic Selection Methods

Authors	Personnel Selected	N	Verbal Tests	Group Situations	Interview	Whole
Vernon and Parry (1949)	British Army officers	500	—	—	—	·35
Morris (1949)		—	·35	—	—	·58
Reeve (1949)		—	—	—	—	·58
O.S.S. (1948)	American Army officers	511	—	—	—	·08 to ·53*
Vernon (1950)	Civil servants	633	·22	·44	·47 (using previous data)	·58
Arbous and Maree (1951)	Administrative trainees	219	—	·60	—	·60
Handyside and Duncan (1954)	Industrial supervisors	44	·59	·57	·17 to ·66† for different interviewers	·72 (after four years)

* Depending on which criterion was used.
† Depending on the interviewer.

In the selection methods which were the object of the follow-up studies summarised in Table I, intelligence tests were used. It is found that for any given selection purpose, some tests are more useful than others. Further, as Castle and Garforth point out (1951), scores on most tests decline with age, so that it is advisable to test all personnel on entering the organisation. Alternatively a correction could be applied or vocabulary tests used (scores on which are unaffected by age).

Other tests, such as Strong's Vocational Interest Blank, have been used in selection, though not usually with as much success as intelligence tests. Progress may be expected with tests for supervision, like File's and Castle's, when they have been validated, and with dimensions of personality such as Eysenck's 'neuroticism', which has been used successfully in student selection (Himmelweit and Summerfield 1951).

(3) *Group Situations*

The War Office Selection Boards started the use of groups for selection in this country. Both leaderless groups and groups with candidates appointed as leaders were used. The groups had to solve problems such as getting over a barbed-wire fence without touching it, and with the help of a few logs. Group discussions were also used, and in all sessions trained observers made systematic notes upon the behaviour of the candidates, these later being converted into single ratings. The Civil Service Selection Boards arranged committee situations resembling the work of civil servants, and management-selection schemes have discussion of industrial problems. One difficulty with this method is that individuals behave differently in different groups. This could be solved by the observation of people in two or three different groups, or by the use of a group that is standard, apart from the single individual being tested. This latter method was adopted by part of the American Army (Office of Strategic Services 1948): candidates were placed in a group of three, where the two other members were permanent staff who always played the standard and irritating parts of 'Zippy' and 'Buster', and did their best to be unhelpful in dealing with the group task.

Whereas intelligence tests have a high reliability, the same is not true of the judgment of observers of group situations. Inter-observer reliabilities of ·6 to ·7 have been reported in the literature (Arbous and Maree 1951). This is lower than the reliability of interaction recording, and it may therefore be suggested that higher reliabilities might be obtained by the use of such methods.

As can be seen from Table I, the validity of group discussions is between ·4 and ·6, so that this can be regarded as a useful selection method.

(4) *The Interview*

The validity figures obtained for the interview are included in Table I, but discussion of this question may be found in Chapter IV, where the accuracy of social perception is considered (p. 95 ff.).

(5) *Some Comments on the Interpretation of these Validities*

It is not possible to accept any of the validity coefficients quoted at their face value. In the first place, the criteria used are extremely unsatisfactory (Arbous 1953, Chapter I). This difficulty was most acutely realised by the O.S.S. Staff in their selection of officers for the American Army (1948). They made use of four sets of ratings, at different points and by different people in the officers' later careers: these criteria correlated with one another only to the extent of ·46 to ·59. The test-retest reliability of ratings of civil servants was ·6 over two years (Vernon 1950)—scarcely distinguishable from the predictive success of the C.S.S.B. (·58). While objective methods appear to be superior to traditional ones, the criterion used to establish this fact is itself very similar to the traditional selection methods. The criteria suffer from the same two defects as the old-fashioned selection—low reliability and low validity.

If the criterion is itself of low validity, obviously the true value of a selection method will not be revealed. It would be most desirable to make use of criteria more objective than ratings: possible objective criteria are discussed below. The low reliability of the criterion also reduces the size of the correlation between test and criterion. A correction for 'attenuation' can be made when the reliability of the criterion is known.[1]

The second main problem about the interpretation of the follow-up validities of selection schemes arises from the contraction of the sample after selection. It would, of course, be ideal to allow all candidates to proceed to a point at which they could be assessed on the job, but this is generally impractical. If there was a curvilinear relation between success and test scores, those failed on the tests might have done better than those just passing. This would be un-

[1] cf. Guilford, op. cit., p. 528 f.

usual, and it is assumed that the correlation obtaining for those who pass would continue for those who fail. If this were so, and if follow-up data were available for the failures, the value of this correlation would be larger, owing to the greater range of variation studied. A correction for such selectivity can be applied, and as far as is known the figures given above have all been corrected in this way. Similarly, when the applicants already come from a very highly selected, and therefore homogeneous, population, the correlation is likely to be reduced. This probably applies to the Civil Service candidates.

Although the situation with respect to the follow-up studies is far from satisfactory, there can be no question of the superiority of the new methods. Typical findings are that the old-fashioned techniques have a predictive success of about ·2, while that of the new methods is more like ·6, this being an underestimate in view of the unreliability of the criterion.

The Training of Leaders

In the last section the influence of selection methods in determining the type of person to be found in an organisation was discussed. A second part of the explanation of the behaviour of members of an organisation lies in their experiences after selection—the influence of further learning. This may be considered in two parts—formal training schemes, and the result of experience and social pressures encountered on the job.

Training schemes for managers and supervisors are widely used in England and America (Anglo-American Council on Productivity 1951; British Institute of Management 1954). These courses vary in length from six-year undergraduate and post-graduate courses in America to courses of a week or fortnight. A variety of methods is used, the principal ones being: (*a*) Formal lectures and instruction in economics, psychology, 'human relations', work-study, etc. (*b*) Role-playing. Here students take parts in realistic situations, for example in that of a supervisor reprimanding a worker for being late (Maier 1952). (*c*) Case-studies. A class of students is presented with some administrative problem and has to make suggestions as to what went wrong and how it could be put right (Andrews 1953). (*d*) Syndicate discussions. Students learn from each other by discussing various problems, sometimes writing a 'brief' or joint essay, embodying their conclusions. At higher levels of industry the tendency has been to concentrate on the last two methods, making minimal use of the teaching staff. Role-playing is largely confined to America at present. Another tendency at all levels has been to concentrate on influencing the behaviour of students, as opposed to their mere knowledge, and to emphasise 'human relations'.

It is a very curious fact that while so much formal training is going on, few follow-up studies have been made either to compare the advantages of different methods, or to see if they are of any use at all. There is little doubt that these courses are enjoyed by those who attend them, and that the firms who send representatives always appear to be satisfied. This does not provide scientific evidence however about the influence of the courses. Most follow-up studies carried out so far have used scores on tests for supervision as the criterion. Since these tests have not yet been properly validated, the investigations are inadequate, though Karn's finding (1949) that scores on File's test were increased by a psychology course but not by a course in English gives some experimental validity to both the test and the course. Castle (1953) found significant improvements on his attitude scale for some courses, but not for others.

There are only three follow-up studies published so far in which objective criteria of supervisory performance have been used. Hariton (1951) measured attitudes of the men towards their foremen in four divisions of an electric power transmission system employing forty-one foremen in all. The foremen in two divisions were trained and there was a tendency for the men in these divisions to become more satisfied with them, though this was not significant. In fact, one division became less satisfied than before, and Hariton obtained some evidence that this difference between the two trained batches was due to the amount of support given to the new methods of supervision by higher management. Fleishman (1953a) found rather similar results in a study of 122 foremen at International Harvester. Foreman behaviour was measured by a questionnaire to the men consisting of a modification of Hemphill's questions, and measuring the two factored dimensions 'Consideration' and 'Initiating Structure'. Similar measurements were made of the second-line leaders by means of questions to the foremen. Fleishman found that while the training course seemed to make very little difference to foremen behaviour, foremen appeared to be influenced by the way in which they were treated by their own superiors.

Finally, Handyside (1954), working at the N.I.I.P., carried out a follow-up study of forty supervisors in relation to output, job satisfaction, labour turnover, absenteeism, and lateness in the departments under their charge. Productivity rose about 8% for the sections controlled by the trained supervisors, and not for the others; labour turnover fell temporarily, while absenteeism, lateness, and job satisfaction were not affected. There was little change of attitude on the part of the trained supervisors, as measured on Castle's scale. However, Handyside suggests that the change may have been due to increased co-operation between the supervisors and the production-planning department.

The difficulties of comparing output in different departments are, of course, removed when the same departments are studied at different points in time. Handyside's investigation, with its measurement of all the major objective indices, is the ideal way of finding the effects of training on foremen. The method could also be used for more senior leaders who are in charge of definite sections, but not for 'Staff' or 'Functional' leaders who are not. In the case of the latter it might still be possible to assess the aspects of efficiency for which the leader is responsible, and to measure these.

The results of Fleishman's and Hariton's studies suggest that influence by senior leaders may be of greater importance than training courses. Certainly experience of the job, together with the various social pressures brought to bear on the occupant, would be expected to be powerful factors in moulding his behaviour. The deliberate planning of promotion sequences is a recognised technique of 'management development'. However, there is no scientific material on this subject, apart from what is reported elsewhere about the influence of second-line on first-line leaders.

If there were any substantial results on the conditions for such social learning, they could probably be accounted for by means of extension of the laws of learning found to hold in experimental psychology.

The Influence of the Formal Structure

(1) *Incentive Systems*

All activity satisfies some need, with the possible exception of some kinds of frustration behaviour (Maier 1949), and the 'displacement activity' observed in animals by the ethologists (Tinbergen 1951). However, this chapter is not concerned with those types of behaviour. The motivational situation with which we are faced is very simple: a person is in a state of need; the environment is then so structured that for the person to gratify this need he must first go through certain preliminary activities. The gratification offered is called the 'incentive', and the preliminary activity is the 'work' he is being persuaded to perform. In this section the influence of incentives on performance in formal organisations will be considered.

A word may be said first about human motivation. The behaviour of insects, birds, and other lower animals depends largely upon instinct. They have innate needs for food, sex, etc., together with an innate neural organisation which produces fairly standard patterns of response to stimuli when the same state of motivation exists (Tinbergen, op. cit.). Humans have few instincts (apart from breathing and aspects of sexual behaviour): their biological needs are innate but the means of satisfying them are learnt, largely from the culture pattern. Peoples of different cultures eat different things and in different ways.

Human beings have other needs in addition to innately biological ones—needs for money, status, power, etc. The *existence* and *strength* of such needs vary between different societies and between different people in the same society. For example, the Kwakiutl of British Columbia have an exaggerated need for status (Benedict 1935), whereas the Arapesh have none at all (Mead 1935). As with biological needs, the *means of satisfying* these needs also varies: the behaviour which bestows status amongst the Kwakiutl—viz. destroying one's canoes and 'money'—would not do so in this country, and vice versa. It is thought on the basis of experiments with animals that these 'social' needs are acquired through their association with biological needs—e.g. having money brings about biological satisfactions and eventually becomes desired as an end in itself. However, this is far from proved, and furthermore there is no accepted means of measuring social needs. Hence the situation is that while industrial research on incentives can provide valuable evidence about social needs, it is not possible to draw on any body of established knowledge about human motivation to explain these results.

There have been two kinds of research on incentives in social organisations—the introspective and the objective. In the introspective method, people are asked what they feel is most important to them about their job. The National Industrial Conference Board (1947) carried out a survey in which employees were asked to mark the five most important out of a list of seventy-one 'morale factors'. General Motors advertised a competition in which prizes were offered for a letter on "My job and why I like it": content analyses were carried out on the 174,064 replies (Evans and Laseau 1950). This method is open to all the objections raised against the introspective method in previous chapters: the main point here is that people may not be consciously aware of their needs. If different surveys are compared, strikingly contradictory results are found. While 'wages' headed the list in both the surveys mentioned above, they have come eighth and even lower in other surveys. There is substantial scientific evidence to support the first finding, but many industrial sociologists have been misled by the other results and have underestimated the importance of wages as compared with human factors. The variability of introspective surveys is no doubt due to variations in local conditions of pay, security, etc.

The objective studies of incentives are the kinds of investigation which are discussed in the rest of this chapter. It is proposed to review now the evidence for the efficacy of wage incentives, fear of unemployment, and 'internal incentives'.

(a) *Wages*. There are different incentives to do different things: whereas *time pay* can be regarded as an incentive to stay with the firm, *payment by results* is strictly an incentive to work harder. There can also be incentives for other specific purposes, such as the bonus given in the mines to those who work a full week—this is an incentive for full attendance.

Seventy-three per cent. of manual workers in Great Britain are given straight time pay, together with all supervisory staff and members of other organisations, like the Army. It would not be expected that increased time pay would increase output, and there is no evidence that it does. There is evidence however that labour turnover is reduced by increased time pay: Scott and Clothier (1941, p. 452) give figures for labour turnover at a Ford factory showing that after an increase of wages, labour turnover dropped from 370% to 16%; no control figures are presented, unfortunately. There is some evidence that job satisfaction is increased with greater time pay. Hoppock (1935) and others (Harrell 1949, Chapter XII) have shown that job satisfaction increases as pay, social status, and level of skill increase: the separate influence of the three factors is not shown by these studies, however. A survey by Centers and Cantril (1946) showed that while over half of the people in a representative sample in the U.S.A. were dissatisfied with their incomes, the higher a person's income the more likely he was to be satisfied with it, and that he wanted a smaller proportionate increase.

There are all kinds of payments by results—piece-work, merit rating, bonuses, targets, and profit sharing. Many workers are on a combination of payment by time and by results. There are several pieces of evidence to the effect that wage incentives lead to increased output, lower labour costs, and higher pay. A Government survey in America, published in *Modern Industry* (1946), showed that 514 wage-incentive schemes produced an average increase of output of 39%, a decrease in labour costs of 11·6%, and a wage increase of 17·7%. Other surveys show the same (Viteles 1954, pp. 25–9; Lynton 1949, p. 93), but lack control groups and so, strictly speaking, fail to allow for other changes, such as new working methods or personnel practices. However, the extent and immediacy of the changes reported make it likely that the wage incentive was largely responsible.

There is one experiment on this question. Wyatt (1934) studied a group of ten girls engaged in weighing and wrapping chocolates. During nine weeks worked on time pay, output levelled off at 12% higher than at the beginning. Introduction of a bonus produced a 46% increase, and the introduction of a flat piece-rate fifteen weeks later led to a further increase of 30%. This is an unsatisfactory experiment for the same reasons as the Hawthorne experiment—too few groups, artificial conditions, and many uncontrolled factors. It may be noted that reversion to the bonus system produced a further increase of about 12%—a fact which is also reminiscent of the Relay Assembly Test Room.

It is not seriously doubted that men work harder under wage incentives, though more detailed evidence about the effect on total costs would be valuable. There is little doubt that wages are increased, but trade unions have often been opposed to wage incentives for various reasons. Many workers, of course, cannot be paid in this way—maintenance men, office workers, and foremen, for instance; there are increased administrative problems, and the calculation of wages becomes very complex.[1]

It would be of great interest to have some information about the effects of different kinds of wage-incentive system. It has been found, for instance, that group piece-work is more effective for smaller groups (Marriott 1949), and in the same investigation there was some indication that output is even higher under individual piece-work. Again, it would be valuable to know the effects of such methods as merit rating, not only on output, but on relations with supervisors.

The explanation of the effects of incentives has been considered previously. The reason why large groups work less hard under group piece-work must be that it is more difficult to increase one's own pay, either by individual effort or by exhortation of others.

[1] Thus costs may actually be increased under piece-work.

(b) *Fear of Unemployment.* This incentive can be studied by comparing behaviour under different economic conditions. In bad times the danger of unemployment is increased. There is no clear evidence that output is increased under these conditions, and Lynton has shown (1949, Chapter IV) that there are serious indirect effects which tend to reduce output—increased restriction of output, resistance to change, together with distraction and worry. The fear and memory of unemployment are probably major factors behind non-co-operative behaviour on the part of workers.

Absenteeism (Behrend 1951) and labour turnover (Long 1951) are certainly greater under full employment. Discipline is said to be worse, but is in fact very little worse (Lynton, op. cit., p. 68). Job satisfaction is greater when the fear of unemployment is absent (cf. Viteles 1954, p. 307). The principal cause of fear of unemployment is, of course, economic conditions, but it is possible to minimise it by guaranteeing employment for long periods and having no lay-offs.

(c) *'Internal' Incentives.* In addition to the orthodox incentives, knowledge of results and the setting of standards may also act to increase output. Knowledge of results is used during training in order to speed learning by drawing attention to mistakes. The incentive use of knowledge of results is quite a different matter, since the knowledge given is simply a total score and does not enable any correction of methods to take place. The only rigorous demonstrations of this are in laboratory studies of fatigue. Mackworth (1950), for instance, found that subjects reading dials and listening to signals over a period of two hours missed more stimuli when no knowledge of results was given. Bingham (cf. Viteles 1954, pp. 144–5) observed that large savings occurred in a power station in which gauges had been installed to show how efficiently the boilers were working, but there were other changes as well. Bingham reports that rivalry between the shifts took place, and the men tried to improve upon their own records. The explanation of the effects of knowledge of results as an incentive must be to classify it either as competition or as attempts to reach one's own level of aspiration.

Mace (1935) showed that setting standards or targets in addition to knowledge of results could act as an incentive. He compared the speeds of performance of subjects working at various laboratory tasks under a number of different sets of instructions. He found that setting a definite objective to be reached produced better results than simply telling the subjects to do their best or improve on their own past performance. He showed that such standards can be manipulated and may affect any aspect of performance—speed, accuracy, variability, etc. An earlier experiment by Crawley (1926) showed that knowledge of results as well as a target increased output at a weight-lifting task by 13%. It would be interesting to have confirmation of these results in connection with the setting of targets for individuals or groups in industry.

(d) *Social Incentives.* Some recent writers on industrial psychology have suggested that economic needs are of only secondary importance, on the strength of introspective surveys, though, as has been shown above, these results cannot be accepted at their face value. The incentives which are thought to be more important are the so-called social incentives. Four kinds of social incentive may be distinguished — promotion, welfare arrangements, treatment by leaders, and organisation of working groups. The question of "incentives for what?" must be raised again at this point. It is established that each of these four variables is related to job satisfaction as well as to absenteeism and labour turnover. Administrators and managers have believed in the past that increased job satisfaction would result in higher output. While this belief may have had beneficial results on job satisfaction, it is doubtful whether the expected increases of output ever occurred. Earlier in this chapter it was shown that there is no evidence for any universal positive relationship between job satisfaction and output, while on general grounds there is no reason why, for example, improved welfare should make people work harder. The hope of promotion would have this effect (though being promoted probably would not), but it is doubtful if this acts as an incentive for the lower levels of organisations as much as it does at higher ones. Ambition is to some extent a middle-class trait (Davis and Gardner 1941). The effect of different aspects of group organisation on output and job satisfaction is discussed in Chapter V (p. 1181 ff.): while all the dimensions considered influence job satisfaction, output is affected only under certain specific conditions. The influence of leadership is dealt with later in this chapter, where an attempt is made to define those characteristics of leadership which result in greater output or satisfaction.

(2) *The Formal Structure of Communication and Authority*

A great deal has been written about the formal structure of industry, based on the experience of managers (e.g. Dale 1952), but this cannot count as scientific knowledge. Our problem is how certain variable dimensions of the formal structure influence output, job satisfaction, and the rest. The many possible dimensions of organisations which might be considered will be grouped as follows: length of communication channels, size of the organisation and of its sub-units, conflicts of authority, and delegation of authority.

(a) *Length of Communication Channels.* A formal structure may vary in the number of steps of communication between positions through which messages have to pass. Bavelas (1951) has suggested the quantitative concept of 'dispersion', which is calculated by the addition of all the communication steps between each position and every other position. The effect of different degrees of dispersion on laboratory groups was illustrated by a series of ingenious experiments. Groups of five people had to solve problems for which information distributed amongst them was needed. Groups in different experimental conditions were allowed to use different channels of communication. Leavitt (1951) compared, for example, groups of five communicating (*a*) in a closed circle, so that each person could communicate with his neighbours, (*b*) in a wheel pattern, so that a central person communicated with the four others, and (*c*) in a Y pattern. He found that the wheel pattern solved the problems most quickly, required fewer messages, and made the smallest number of errors. The wheel pattern, of course, had the smallest 'dispersion', i.e. the shortest lines of communication. On the other hand, subjects apart from the person in the central position of the wheel pattern, who was the most satisfied of all, enjoyed the circle pattern more. Thus job satisfaction in this experiment appeared to be related to the 'centrality' of position—the length of communication lines to other positions. All these results were confirmed in an experiment by Smith (cf. Bavelas 1951), comparing the circle pattern with a straight-line pattern. Heise and Miller (1951) investigated the effect of introducing noise in communication channels of three-men groups. The groups with two-way communication between all members were more efficient than all other patterns: increasing the amount of noise emphasised the differences in efficiency between the different patterns. Mohanna, working at Oxford, has investigated the effect of the popularity of the person at the central position in the wheel pattern. He found that the wheel pattern is more efficient than the circle when the central person is popular, but less efficient when he is unpopular.

In the context of real social organisations, bad relations in the line of command will result in poor communication. Gardner (1944) has described the way in which members of social organisations are nervously looking upwards while their superiors assess them, and how bad news is held up or distorted in order to keep the good opinion of those higher up. It would be expected that where the social distances between levels in the hierarchy are small, communication would be improved. In a laboratory experiment on groups with status divisions, Kelley (1951) found low-status members more ready to communicate upwards about irrelevant matters, and unwilling to criticise high-status members. Burns (1954), in an industrial study using Carlson's technique, found that when a senior executive thought he had given instructions or a decision to a junior, the latter often regarded this as advice or information.

(b) *The Size of the Organisation and of its Sub-units.* Economists do not agree about the relative efficiency of firms of different sizes. Sargant Florence (1953, p. 68) showed that there is a tendency for larger firms to be more efficient, and he puts this down to greater mechanisation. On the other hand, Dennison (1947) maintains that there is an upper limit to the advantages of size and that the increased difficulties of management make for inefficiency.

Work by the Acton Society (1953) has shown that absenteeism is greater in larger concerns: this is true of coal-mines, factories, and retail stores. The accident rate is also greater in large mines, though it is less if there are several independent seams being worked; accidents at the coal face do not increase as the underground community increases above five hundred. Job satisfaction has also been shown to be greater in small firms and in small towns (Harrell 1949, Chapter XII). These results seem to indicate social effects related to size of the working community. There is some evidence that steps can be taken to increase the cohesiveness of large organisations. Trist and Bamforth (1951) suggest, on the basis of interviews with informants rather than on any quantitative analysis, that the reason for low output under the Longwall method of coal-mining is lack of social cohesion between three interdependent shifts which never meet. Paterson and Willett (1951) carried out an experiment to increase cohesiveness in mines. They organised group activities and propaganda against excessive individualisation; a system was then introduced of painting pit-props yellow to signify "I'm leaving this safe for my neighbours". The accident rate fell in the experimental sections and not in others, though there is a possibility that the yellow paint helped in lining up the supports.

A final problem which may be included in this section is that of the optimum size of the span of control. The span of control of a position is the number of people directly responsible to the occupant. Many experienced administrators have recommended that the span of control should be limited to five or six, and to even fewer at higher levels (cf. Florence 1953, pp. 149–51). A more typical figure in industry to-day is about eight to nine. Research by the Acton Society (1953) in British coal-mines showed that output increased as the ratio of men to supervisors diminished down to fifteen. It is not clear how far these results are a function of the size of the group and how far they depend on the span of control. This problem does not present itself at senior levels, but there is no objective evidence here.

(c) *Conflicts of Authority*. It is widely held by writers on organisation that one person should not be under two authorities, since these are liable to give conflicting instructions. While it would be thought that careful limitation of spheres of authority would solve the problem, this may not prove satisfactory, as Westerlund's experiment (1952), reported below, indicates. Whyte (1948) thought that the explanation of why the waitresses in Chicago restaurants cried was that they were under the dual and conflicting authority of customer and cook. Similarly Homans (1951) explains the practice of mother-in-law avoidance often found in primitive society as being a means of avoiding conflict between mother and husband—both of whom have power over the wife. Each of these instances however is capable of other explanations, and the generalisation in question has yet to be demonstrated.

In large organisations it is common to have both 'line' and 'staff' executives, the former being in the direct line of command, the latter being specialists in a largely advisory capacity. This may be a source of conflicting authority for lower-level leaders. Westerlund (1952) carried out an experiment on the effects of changing over to a single 'line' supervisor from a multitude of 'staff' supervisors for groups of telephone operators. He found increased output for some of the experimental sections, together with generally improved relations within the working groups.

(d) *Delegation of Authority*. The most direct evidence on the effect of greater delegation of authority is provided by the studies of second-line leaders reported later. It was shown that both output and job satisfaction are increased in the sections controlled by leaders who delegated authority. Further evidence on this point comes from surveys conducted by Sears, Roebuck, and Company, from which the conclusion is apparently that job satisfaction is greater in companies where authority is delegated (Worthy 1950). Unfortunately, insufficient details are provided for this conclusion to be evaluated. Lastly, there is the heroic experiment by Morse, Reimer, and Tannenbaum (1951), who altered the amount of delegation of authority in different directions in two firms. The degree of delegation was measured by responses to a questionnaire enquiry 'To what extent do your supervisors decide ———?', and 'To what extent do your peers decide ———?', for various issues. Delegation was changed by means of training and instruction. The outcome of the investigation was another 'Hawthorne effect', in that the efficiency of both organisations was increased; however, job satisfaction was increased only in the organisation where delegation was increased.

Evidence is given later to show that job satisfaction, and in some cases output, are increased by first-line leaders who allow their men to participate in decisions. With the setting up of formal machinery such as works councils and joint consultative committees, the opportunities for worker participation have been increased. There is as yet no follow-up data by means of which to assess the success of these measures. A survey by the N.I.I.P. (1952) of joint consultation in Great Britain showed that a wide range of topics was discussed in most firms, and replies to a questionnaire to the firms indicated considerable "effectiveness" of the discussion. It was also found that different joint consultative structures had different degrees of efficiency. In firms of more than a thousand, a simple works council was not so satisfactory as either a hierarchy of committees or a works council supplemented by separate committees for each department. Large firms with one works council received nothing but complaints, and there were no helpful suggestions concerning the detailed work of each department.

The findings on the influence of the social structure are not established in sufficient generality or detail to warrant great efforts to explain them. It is however worth indicating the type of explanation that would be possible. Supposing that it were established that conflicts of authority led to high labour turnover and low job satisfaction in the position concerned, this is quite easily explained by extension of the generalisations about conflict situation developed by experimental psychologists (cf. Underwood 1949, Chapter XVIII). The general principle is to consider the implications for social interaction of a given structure, and then to explain this by means of other psychological findings.

SUPERVISION AND MANAGEMENT

The Influence of the First-line Leader

Some of the most careful research in the field of human relations has been concerned with the influence of the first-line leader. In most of this work the style of leadership has been the principal variable. The effects of training have been discussed separately, and the relation of test scores to leadership effectiveness has been described in the section on selection of leaders.

(1) *Studies of Children and Students*

Nearly all of the *experiments* on leadership have made use of children or students as subjects: investigations of military, industrial, and community leadership have used the statistical field-study approach. The classic study is, of course, Lewin, Lippitt, and White's experiment (Lippitt 1940) of autocratic, democratic, and laissez-faire leadership. In the two phases of the experiment, six matched groups of five boys experienced the different styles of leadership in different orders. This experiment broke much new ground—in the use of standardised leader roles, the application of interaction recording to small-group behaviour, and in the arrangement of a realistic experimental situation. The main defect of the experiment lies in the insufficient number of groups studied. It is not surprising to find that while autocratic leadership led to aggressive behaviour in the first two groups which were set up, it did not do so in the four groups used in the second phase of the experiment. With so few groups, significant results cannot be obtained, but the differences found were as follows: autocratic leadership resulted in greater dependence on the leader, lower cohesiveness and scapegoating of individuals, irritability and discontent, and more work being done—though only when the leader was watching. These results have been obtained in repetitions of the experiment by other investigators of children's groups.

Further studies have confirmed that American children prefer 'democratic', 'non-directive', or 'group-centred' teaching, but obtained conflicting results on the academic success of pupils taught by these methods. Similarly, there is conflicting evidence as to whether lectures or class discussions result in better examination results (Roseborough 1953, p. 278), though the evidence indicates that the discussion method results in improved social adjustment (M. J. Asch 1951, Thompson 1944). Experiments by Preston and Heintz (1949) and Bovard (1951a) showed that non-directive leadership produced more friendly groups, and facilitated norm-formation. As was reported earlier (p. 127 f.), cohesive groups form group standards more readily, so this may be the basic mechanism.

A number of experiments have been carried out on children and college students concerning the relative effectiveness of different verbal incentives. Hurlock (1924) found that praise and reproof at first had equally beneficial effects on repeated intelligence-test scores of children, but that after the second time praise was by far the better incentive. Similarly, in several experiments summarised by Moore (1939, p. 302), public praise produced improved work in 87·5% of the students studies and private reprimand in 66·3%, while public reprimand and all kinds of ridicule and sarcasm produced worse results.

(2) Industrial Studies

The most important investigations here are those recently carried out by the Survey Research Center of the University of Michigan, into work-teams in the Chesapeake and Ohio Railway (Katz et al. 1951), the Prudential Insurance Company (Katz et al. 1950; Morse 1953), and the Caterpillar Tractor Company (Katz and Kahn 1951). There are related studies by Pelz (1949, 1951) and Fleishman (1953a). In the three principal field studies, a number of matched work-teams were compared for output, job satisfaction, and foreman behaviour. For example, in the railway investigation, forty matched pairs were chosen out of 180 sections of track, so that the conditions of work were as far as possible identical for each pair. In each study the foremen were interviewed and the men given a questionnaire on job satisfaction and the behaviour of their foremen. Output of the teams was measured by ratings in the railway study and by time-study units in the other two researches. These three investigations are models of research technique in respect of the careful equating of groups and the numbers involved, and of the care taken to obtain meaningful measurements of foreman behaviour and job satisfaction. In the light of recent developments the measurement of job satisfaction could now be improved by means of factor analysis, while the whole question of measuring foreman behaviour needs further investigation. Some of the results of these researches are that output is greater when the foreman spends his time on leadership activities, and is 'employee-centred' as opposed to 'production-centred'. Job satisfaction is greater when the foreman takes the role of leader and gives 'general' as opposed to 'close' supervision.

Another series of investigations into the effect of different kinds of leadership in industrial productivity was carried out at the University of Southern California by Comrey and Pfiffner. They studied successively a number of state forests, the offices of a state department, the repair shop of a Naval air station, and the Lockheed Aircraft Corporation. Many of the results did not turn out to be statistically significant, but Comrey, Pfiffner, and High (1954) have presented a summary of the consistently significant results in the several studies. The measurement of output was only by ratings in the earlier studies, and these had a rather low reliability (unlike those in Katz's railway research), and the questions given to the men were not about the same dimensions of foremanship as those given to the foremen, so that no check is provided. The final conclusion of this programme is that higher output results from foremen who say that they have adequate authority, and who claim to like their men and who exert general supervision. These foremen are reported by their men to be more competent at their job and to be more employee-oriented.[1]

In a survey of eight thousand workers in a public utility, Pelz (1949) found that job satisfaction was increased when supervisors took a personal interest, recognised good work, and encouraged employee participation in decisions. Fleishman (1953b) found a correlation between grievance rates and supervisors who scored low on the dimension of 'consideration' (employee-centred) and high on 'initiating structure' (exerting pressure for production).

Absenteeism also is affected by supervision, as was suggested by Fox and Scott's earlier study (1943). Behrend (1951) found that voluntary absence, though not sickness absence, varied between departments equated for type of work and composition of the labour force. Katz and Kahn (1952) showed that workers with high absence rates were less likely to say "I feel free to discuss important things about my job with my supervisor", and Wickert (1951) found that more labour turnover occurred amongst people who felt that they did not have sufficient scope for making decisions.

The statistical field studies reported here provide strong evidence of a relation between style of supervision and output, job satisfaction, and absenteeism. Due to the nature of such studies however

[1] The actual traits here were: Communication downwards, job helpfulness, lack of arbitrariness, public relations, and sympathy.

they cannot decide the direction of causation—i.e. it is just as possible that foremen become more employee-centred when their men work hard as that the reverse process occurs. The best way of discovering the direction of causation is to do an experiment. The experiments on the influence of leadership on groups of children and students show that causation here may be from leader to group rather than vice versa; there is also one experiment in an industrial setting. Feldman (1937) arranged for twenty-two foremen to be changed round so that the foremen of high-output sections went to low-output ones. It was found that the rank order of output of the foremen's sections remained the same, i.e. output depended on the foremen, not on the men. The order of output differences involved was from 6% to 18%. Furthermore, Jackson (1953) found that foremen supervised in the same way when in charge of different groups, showing that style of supervision is not a dependent variable.

(3) *Military Studies*

There are four investigations of the commanders of aircrews in the American Air Force. The Ohio researches into the American Navy were concerned with higher levels of leadership and will be discussed later. Adams (1954) found that the commanders of aircrews which were rated as more efficient scored low on the F-scale (for authoritarianism), except at the extreme equalitarian end of that scale. Berkowitz (1953) showed that efficient aircrews were commanded by officers scoring high on a factor called "Maintenance of crew co-ordination and team-work". Halpin (1954) discovered that crews rated as efficient had leaders scoring low on the factor named "consideration" (employee-centred) and high on "initiating structure" (pressure for output). Satisfaction of crews depended on these two factors in the reversed senses.[1] Finally, Roff (1950) found that pilots rated highly by their colleagues scored high on measures of sincerity, impartiality, and strictness of ground discipline.

(4) *The Use of Group Decision by Leaders*

Studies on group decision have been collected together in this section, although they are drawn from different contexts. The first experiments on group decision were concerned with changing the behaviour of group members. A leader trained in the art would conduct a discussion in such a way that the group decided

---

[1] This provides another instance of a negative relation between efficiency and satisfaction.

'spontaneously' to make the change desired by the leader. The originator of this technique was Lewin (1943b), who was in charge of research during the war aimed at discovering how to change the food habits of American housewives. Three similar experiments, each using about six groups of from fifteen to fifty housewives, compared the effectiveness of individual instruction, lectures and group decisions, in making the women use more milk, different kinds of meat, etc. The group decision proved to be by far the most effective method of changing food habits (at least up to four weeks later), even though the women were strangers to each other. As Lewin himself recognised, these experiments were unsatisfactory since only the group-decision subjects were told that there would be a check-up on their change of habits.

Some industrial group-decision experiments were conducted in the Harwood Manufacturing Company by Bavelas and by Coch and French. In Bavelas's experiment (cf. French 1950) twenty-four experimental groups of from four to twelve workers participated in decisions about levels of output and set new production goals. During four months, output went up 18%, while that of equated control groups was unchanged. However, as Viteles observes (1954, pp. 167–8), the experimental groups were provided with knowledge of results, which is also likely to affect output. Coch and French (1948) applied the group-decision technique to the problem of changing jobs—which usually led to lowered output and to labour turnover. Two experimental groups of workers participated in discussions and decisions concerning the details of the change; they increased output by 14% and none left. Out of the control group, 17% left and output fell 17%. However, there were too few groups in this experiment, and it seems that better training was received by the experimental groups (Viteles, op. cit., p. 169).

In a recent experiment, Levine and Butler (1952) equated the experimental conditions better than had been done in the other industrial studies, but used only three experimental groups. The experiment compared the effects of lectures and group decisions in training supervisors to rate their men without halo effect. How the accuracy of these ratings was measured is by no means clear, and only one of the two experimental groups showed any change after its decision: the other experimental group and the lecture group showed no change.

Maier has tried to show that a practised leader is more able to bring about the required change. In one experiment (1950) he found that groups under trained leaders could solve problems better. However, the trained leaders knew the correct answers, so the experiment does not show that training in the social technique was the causal factor. In a second experiment (1953), foremen trained in the group-decision method of leadership were divided into groups of four and given a role-playing test in which one had to persuade the others to accept a change of work-methods. The change was accepted more often than among groups of untrained foremen, but it must be noted that the group as well as the leader received instruction in this experiment. Other evidence, perhaps for the importance of the technique of the leader, is provided by French (1950), who was unable to achieve results as successful as those of Bavelas until he had had a year's practice.

A number of experiments has been carried out to isolate exactly what it is about group decisions which produces the changed behaviour. McKeachie (1954) found that discussion and decision both weakened forces towards agreement, as shown by a greater difference between attitudes and perceived norms, but also increased the accuracy of perception of what the norm was. This experiment was concerned with the norm-formation aspects of group decision, not with the change of group behaviour. Bennett (1952) experimented with methods of persuading people to come as subjects for an experiment. Discussion and commitment made no difference, but making a group decision and perceiving unanimity in the group were related to increased attendance as subjects. This result may however be interpreted as showing that more favourable groups will be more likely to attend. Hare (1953) found that scout-leaders who permitted more participation had a greater influence over the opinions of their groups. This result provides a neat demonstration of the paradox of group decisions—the more the group is allowed to do as it likes, the more likely it is to follow the leader.

(5) *The Explanation of these Results*

The results on first-line leadership are very similar in each of the fields distinguished. The leader who allows the group members to participate in decisions and who takes a personal interest in the members produces greater satisfaction among them. It is not difficult to see why satisfaction should be increased, though knowledge of the specific needs satisfied would make this explanation more valuable. Clearly there is a widespread need to have a say in what happens—and this is likely to lead to the satisfaction of other needs.

Furthermore, the leader who takes a personal interest is obviously likely to satisfy the needs of the members. This is supported by Pelz's finding (1951) that only powerful leaders can increase job satisfaction by behaving democratically. It should also be noted that cohesiveness is increased by this kind of leadership, and this may be one reason why satisfaction is greater.

Democratic or non-directive leadership is reported to increase industrial output and military efficiency (though not to facilitate *learning* among children and students). This could be explained via job satisfaction—leaders who see to the satisfactions of their men are liked, and by French's theory (p. 158) more able to exert influence. This would be confirmed if the same leaders produced both efficiency and job satisfaction, which often does not prove to be the case. Halpin (1954), for example, found that employee-centred aircrew commanders had contented but inefficient crews. Explanations using cohesiveness as an intermediate variable[1] can only be part of the story, for the same reason.

This problem may be taken in conjunction with group decision: why is group decision a good way of coercing groups and why does participation lead to greater efficiency? Lewin's theory (1947) is that group decisions are able to change the whole field of forces maintaining a social norm in existence; the forces are unfrozen, shifted, and frozen at a different point. In other words, the forces towards conformity will demand conformity towards a different norm. This goes far to explain why it is easier to change groups than individual members of them—the group controls stronger forces than the leader possesses and can exert strong pressures to make individuals conform. McKeachie's results (1954) indicate that discussions may do the 'unfreezing' part, and Bennett's (1952) give some evidence that decision may do the 'freezing'. However, it is still necessary to suppose that the leader must exert some subtle positive influence in the intervening period.

From the published results it looks as if the form of leadership which is most effective varies with the criterion and also with the precise conditions—for example, pressure for output is probably useful when there is no wage incentive and harmful when there is. Authoritarian leadership is probably more acceptable in larger groups (Hemphill 1950*a*) and with authoritarian group members

[1] This is used in the economists' sense of a variable which is *causally* intermediate—unlike an intervening variable which can only be said to be *logically* intervening (cf. p. 63 ff.).

(Sanford 1950). Theorising will be easier when these relationships are known in greater detail.

The Influence of the Second-line Leader

(1) *The Influence of Second-line on First-line Leaders*

In some of the Michigan researches, no relationship was found between foreman behaviour and job satisfaction. However, Pelz (1951), in a study of a power station, divided foremen into those who had high and low influence in the organisation—on the basis of answers to questions about contact with superiors and sharing in higher decisions. He found a significant correlation between employee-centred supervision and job satisfaction of the men in the case of the powerful foremen, but not for the others. This is a very interesting finding from the point of view of the explanation of the influence of the first-line leader. Similarly, Stogdill and Scott (Stogdill et al. 1953c, Chapter VIII) found that when second-line leaders in the Navy described themselves as high in 'authority',[1] first-line leaders (junior officers) regarded themselves as low or uncertain in 'responsibility'. Similarly, when seniors delegated a lot of authority downwards, their juniors were high in responsibility and authority, and also delegated authority themselves.

The transmission downwards of the practice of delegation, as found by Stogdill, is an example of what is probably a general tendency: junior leaders tend to lead in a similar way to their immediate seniors. In the Michigan studies of the railway and office-work-teams, it was found that foremen exerted pressure when pressure was exerted on them. Another demonstration of this tendency is provided by Fleishman's follow-up study of a foreman training course (1953a) described above, in which it was found that the major determinant of foreman behaviour was not the training course but the leadership style of the foreman's supervisor. When the latter was incompatible with the principles taught on the course, the course was ineffective.

(2) *The Influence of the Second-line Leader on his Section*

A number of studies of the influence of the second-line leader on the effectiveness of his section have been carried out by Stogdill and his associates at Ohio, using ships in the U.S. Navy as units. Stogdill

---

[1] 'Authority', 'Responsibility', and 'Delegation' were measured by Thurstone-type scales administered to the leaders themselves. See Shartle and Stogdill (1953), Chapter X.

and his colleagues (1953c, Chapter IX), in a study of eleven ships, found that Operational Readiness scores of the ships correlated with the Responsibility, Authority, and Delegation scores of the Commanding Officer and the Executive Officer, and that such correlations were highest for the C.O., next highest for the Executive Officer, and lower for other officers. However, the fact that such relationships are highest for the senior person concerned does not mean to say that junior executives do not have an important influence over their own sub-sections. On the other hand, Campbell (1953) found that Responsibility, Authority, and Delegation scores of the sixty-eight officers on ten submarines did not correlate significantly with the official ratings of the officers, but did relate to nominations for leadership by subordinates. The way officers spend their time also proved to be important: those spending more time in personal contacts, consulting assistants, reading, and answering mail were universally judged to be better leaders. The reverse was the case for those spending more time in technical operations and at meetings off the ship. Finally, Miller (Stogdill et al. 1953c, Chapter IV) studied the principals of two hundred and five high schools. Those who were rated by their teachers as being more democratic, and by their superintendents as being more adequate, spent more time on "supervision to see that the work gets done" and less on "pupil control". (The principals estimated their own distribution of time.) On the other hand, principals spending more time on research were rated as more democratic by their teachers but less adequate by the superintendents.

This concludes all that will be reported of the Ohio research under Stogdill, and a few general comments will be made. (*a*) In most of the investigations too few ships were included: it is most unsatisfactory to work out elaborate statistical analyses on ten ships or ten C.O.s. (*b*) No decision has yet been reached on an overall measure of ship effectiveness, though D. T. Campbell (1953) used sixteen different criteria: it is difficult to draw any general conclusions from the results as they stand. Similarly, while many different measures of officer behaviour are used, no conclusions are reached about the most useful ones. (*c*) No reliabilities, e.g. for Operational Readiness ratings, are found. (*d*) There are a large number of scattered results, but no attempt is made to explore their interrelations. Individual results are explained by means of vague and *ad hoc* psychological theorising.

Despite these remarks, however, the Ohio studies must be recognised as the most important work to date on leadership at senior levels.

(3) *The Explanation of these Results*

Once more little can be produced to explain the results. Pelz's findings were discussed at the end of the account of first-line supervision. The conditioning of first- by second-line leaders can readily be understood in terms of the findings on social influence presented earlier (p. 108 f.), where it was shown that people will imitate those of greater prestige in the group—rank being a major source of prestige. The finding by Stogdill and Scott (Stogdill et al. 1953c), if it be accepted, that there is a negative correlation for both Responsibility and Delegation scores between senior and junior officers on *small* ships, provides an interesting complication to this view. The authors account for the negative correlation for Responsibility by saying: "It seems understandable that juniors might feel a reduction of their own responsibility if their C.O. and X.O. assume a high degree of responsibility.... In a primary group ... the behaviour of one member is likely to have an immediate and direct effect upon the behaviour of other members of the group. In a stratified organisation interactions are likely to be more highly formalised" (loc. cit., p. 65). A mechanism is postulated which counteracts the social-influence process: when a person takes on more responsibility those in contact with him must take on less. No explanation is offered for the delegation findings.

REFERENCES

A

Acton Society Trust, 1953, *Size and Morale*.
ADAMS, S., 1954, "Social Climate and Productivity in Small Military Groups", *Amer. Sociol. Rev.*, **19**, 421–5.
ADORNO, T. W., et. al., 1950, *The Authoritarian Personality*. New York: Harper.
AIDMAN, T., 1951, "An Objective Study of the Changing Relationship between the Present Self and the Ideal Self Pictures as Expressed by the Client in Non-directive Therapy". Ph.D. thesis, U. of Chicago (quoted by Seeman & Raskin (1953), p. 212).
ALLPORT, F. H., 1920, "The Influence of the Group upon Association and Thought", *J. Exp. Psychol.*, **3**, 159–82.
— 1924, *Social Psychology*. Boston: Houghton Mifflin.
— 1934, "The J-curve Hypothesis of Conforming Behaviour", *J. Soc. Psychol.*, **5**, 141–83.
ALLPORT, G. W., 1937, *Personality: A Psychological Interpretation*. London: Constable.
ALLPORT, G. W., & KRAMER, B. M., 1946, "Some Roots of Prejudice", *J. Psychol.*, **22**, 9–39.
ALLPORT, G. W., & VERNON, P. E., 1931, "A Test for Personal Values", *J. Abnorm. Soc. Psychol.*, **26**, 231–48.
ANDREWS, K. R. (ed.), 1953, *Case Study Method of Teaching Human Relations and Administration*. Harvard U.P.
ANGELL, R. C., & FREEDMAN, R., 1953, "The Use of Documents, Records, Census Materials and Indices". Chap. VII in Festinger & Katz (1953).
Anglo-American Council on Productivity, 1951, *Education for Management*.
ARBOUS, A. G., 1953, *Selection for Industrial Leadership*. London: O.U.P.
ARBOUS, A. G., & MAREE, J., 1951, "Contribution of Two Group Discussion Techniques to a Validated Test Battery", *Occ. Psychol.*, **25**, 73–89.
ARGYLE, M., 1952, "Methods of Studying Small Social Groups", *Brit. J. Psychol.*, **43**, 269–79.
— 1953a, "The Relay Assembly Test Room in Retrospect", *Occ. Psychol.*, **27**, 98–103.
— 1953b, "The Concepts of Role and Status", *Sociol. Rev.*, **44**, No. 3.
— 1953c, "The Explanation of Norm-formation in Small Groups". Abstract of paper to *B.P.S. Quart. Bull.*, No. 20, p. 8. Roneoed.
— 1955, "Deductive Theories in Sociology", *Sociol. Rev.*, **3**, 219–34.
— 1957, "Social Pressure in Public and Private Situations", *J. Abnorm. Soc. Psychol.*, **54**, 172–175.
ARGYRIS, C., 1952, *An Introduction to Field Theory and Interaction Theory*. Yale: Labor and Management Center.

1954, "The Fusion of an Individual with the Organisation", *Amer. Sociol. Rev.*, **19**, 267–72.
ASCH, M. J., 1951, "Nondirective Teaching in Psychology: an Experimental Study", *Psychol. Monogr.*, **65**, No. 4.
ASCH, S. E., 1946, "Forming Impressions of Personality", *J. Abnorm. Soc. Psychol.*, **41**, 258–90.
1952, *Social Psychology.* New York: Prentice-Hall.
ASCH, S. E., BLOCK, H., & HERTZMAN, M., 1940, "Studies in the Principles of Judgements and Attitudes. II—Determinants of Judgements by Group and by Ego Standards", *J. Soc. Psychol.*, **12**, 433–65.
AVELING, F., & HARGREAVES, H., 1921, "Suggestibility With and Without Prestige in Children", *Brit. J. Psychol.*, **18**, 362–88.

B

BACK, K. W., 1951, "Influence through Social Communication", *J. Abnorm.-Soc. Psychol.*, **46**, 9–23.
BALDWIN, A. L., 1946, "The study of Individual Personality by means of Intra-individual Correlation", *J. Pers.*, **14**, 151–68.
BALES, R. F., 1950, *Interaction Process Analysis. A Method for the Study of Small Groups.* Cambridge, Mass.: Addison-Wesley.
1951, "A Set of Hypothetical Interaction Matrices for Group Sizes 2 to 10". Roneoed.
1953, "The Equilibrium Problem in Small Groups", pp. 111–61 in *Working Papers in the Theory of Action*, by Parsons, T., Bales, R. F., & Shils, E. A. Glencoe, Ill.: The Free Press.
BALES, R. F., & GERBRANDS, H., 1948, "The 'Interaction Recorder' ", an Apparatus and Check List for Sequential Content Analysis of Social Interaction", *Hum. Relat.*, **1**, 456–63.
BALES, R. F., & STRODTBECK, F. L., 1951, "Phases in Group Problem-solving", *J. Abnorm. Soc. Psychol.*, **46**, 485–95.
BALES, R. F., et al., 1951, "Channels of Communication in Small Groups", *Amer. Sociol. Rev.*, **16**, 461–8.
BARKER, R., DEMBO, T., & LEWIN, K., 1941, "Frustration and Regression. An Experiment with Young Children", *U. Ia. Stud. Child Welf.*, **18**, No. 1.
BARRON, F., 1952, "Some Personality Correlates of Independence of Judgment", *J. Pers.*, **21**, 287–97.
BASS, B. M., 1950, "The Leaderless Group Discussion Technique", *Personnel Psychol.*, **3**, 17–32.
BASS, B. M., & WURSTER, C. R., 1953, "Effects of the Nature of the Problem on LDG performance", *J. App. Psychol.*, **37**, 96–9.
BATESON, G., 1944, "Cultural Determinants of Personality". Chap. XXIII in Hunt (1944).
BAVELAS, A., 1948, "A Mathematical Model for Group Structures", *App. Anth.*, **7**, No. 3, 16–30.
1951, "Communication Patterns in Task-oriented Groups". Chap. X in Lerner & Lasswell (1951).

REFERENCES

BEHREND, H., 1951, *Absence under Full Employment*. U. of Birmingham Mimeographed.
BELL, G. B., & FRENCH, R. L., 1950, "Consistency of Individual Leadership Position in Groups of Varying Memberships", *J. Abnorm. Soc. Psychol.*, 45, 764–7.
BELL, G. B., & HALL, H. E., 1954, "The Relationship between Leadership and Empathy", *J. Abnorm. Soc. Psychol.*, 49, 156–7.
BENEDICT, R., 1935, *Patterns of Culture*. London: Routledge.
BENNE, K. D., & SHEATS, P., 1948, "The Dynamics of the Discussion Group", *J. Soc. Issues*, 4 (2), 41–9.
BENNETT, E. B., 1952, "Group Discussion, Decision, Public Commitment, and Perceived Unanimity as Factors in the Effectiveness of 'Group Decision' ", *Amer. Psychol.*, 7, 315.
BERENDA, R. W., 1950, *The Influence of the Group on the Judgments of Children. An Experimental Investigation*. New York: King's Crown Press.
BERGMANN, G., 1953, "Theoretical Psychology", *Ann. Rev. Psychol.*, 1953.
BERGMANN, G., & SPENCE, K. W., 1941, "Operationism and Theory in Psychology", *Psychol. Rev.*, 48, 1–14.
1944, "The Logic of Psychophysical Measurement", *Psychol. Rev.*, 51, 1–24.
BERKOWITZ, L., 1953, "An Exploratory Study of the Roles of Aircraft Commanders". *Human Resources Research Center Bull.*, 53–65.
BERNBERG, R. E., 1952, "Socio-psychological Factors in Industrial Morale. I—The Prediction of Specific Indicators", *J. Soc. Psychol.*, 36, 73–82.
BIERI, J., 1953, "Changes in Interpersonal Perceptions following Social Interaction", *J. Abnorm. Soc. Psychol.*, 48, 61–6.
BLOCK, J., 1953, "The Assessment of Communication: Role Variation as a Function of Interactional Content", *J. Pers.*, 21, 272–86.
BLOCK, J., & BLOCK, J., 1952, "An Interpersonal Experiment on Reactions to Authority", *Hum. Relat.*, 5, 91–8.
BOS, M. C., 1937, "Experimental Study of Productive Collaboration", *Acta Psychologica*, 3, 315–426.
BOVARD, E. W., 1951a, "Group Structure and Perception", *J. Abnorm. Soc. Psychol.*, 46, 398–405.
1951b, "The Experimental Production of Interpersonal Affect", *J. Abnorm. Soc. Psychol.*, 46, 521–8.
BOVARD, E. W., & GUETZKOW, H., 1950, "A Validity Study of Rating Scales as a Device to Distinguish Participants in Stable and Temporary Groups". U. of Michigan. Mimeographed.
BRAITHWAITE, R. B., 1953, *Scientific Explanation*. C.U.P.
British Institute of Management, 1954, *Education and Training in the Field of Management*.
BROWN, I. S., 1950, "Training University Students in Group Development and Experiment". Ph.D. thesis, U. of California at Los Angeles (quoted by Swanson (1951)).
BROWN, J. F., 1936, *Psychology and the Social Order*. New York: McGraw-Hill.

REFERENCES

BRUNER, J. S., & GOODMAN, C. C., 1947, "Values and Need as Organising Factors in Perception", *J. Abnorm. Soc. Psychol.*, **42**, 33–44.
BRUNER, J. S., & TAGIURI, R., 1954, "The Perception of People". Chap. 17 in Lindzey (1954).
BRUNSWIK, E., 1945, "Social Perception of Traits from Photographs", *Psych. Bull.*, **42**, 535–6.
BURNS, R., 1951, "Employee Morale—its Meaning and Measurement". *Proc. 4th Ann. Meeting Ind. Relations Res. Ass.* 52–68.
BURNS, T., 1954, "The Directions of Activity and Communication in a Departmental Executive Group: a Quantitative Study in a British Engineering Factory with a Self-recording Technique", *Hum. Relat.*, **7**, 73–97.
BURTT, H. E., 1938, *The Psychology of Advertising*. Boston: Houghton Mifflin.
BUTLER, J. M., 1952, "The Interaction of Client and Therapist", *J. Abnorm. Soc. Psychol.*, **47**, 366–78.

C

CALDWELL, O. W., & WELLMAN, B. L., 1926, "Characteristics of School Leaders", *J. Ed. Res.*, **14**, 1–13.
CAMERON, N. A., 1947, *The Psychology of Behavior Disorders*. Boston: Houghton Mifflin.
CAMPBELL, D. T., 1953, *A Study of Leadership among Submarine Officers*. Personnel Res. Bd., Ohio State University.
CAMPBELL, H., 1952, "Group Incentive Schemes: the Effects of Lack of Understanding and of Group Size", *Occ. Psychol.*, **26**, 15–21.
CANNELL, C. F., & KAHN, R. L., 1953, "The Collection of Data by Interviewing". Chap. VIII in Festinger & Katz (1953).
CANTRIL, H. A. (ed.), 1944, *Gauging Public Opinion*. Princeton U.P.
CARLSON, S., 1951, *Executive Behaviour*. Stockholm: Strömbergs.
CARLSSON, G., 1951, "An Analysis of Morale Dimensions. Preliminary Report". U. of Michigan. Roneoed.
CARTER, L., et al., 1951a, "A Note on a New Technique of Interaction Recording", *J. Abnorm. Soc. Psychol.*, **46**, 258–60.
1951b, "The Relation of Categorisations and Ratings in the Observation of Group Behavior". *Hum. Relat.*, **4**, 239–54.
CARTER, L., & NIXON, M., 1949, "An Investigation of the Relation between Four Criteria of Leadership Ability for Three Different Tasks", *J. Psychol.*, **27**, 245–61.
CARTWRIGHT, D., & ZANDER, A. (eds.), 1953, *Group Dynamics. Research and Theory*. New York: Row, Petersen.
CASTLE, P. F. C., 1953, "The Evaluation of Human Relations Training for Supervisors", *Occ. Psychol.*, **27**, 191–205.
CASTLE, P. F. C., & GARFORTH, F. I. DE LA P., 1951, "Selection, Status and Training of Supervisors", *Occ. Psychol.*, **25**, 109–23.
CATTELL, R. B., 1948, "Concepts and Methods in the Measurement of Group Syntality", *Psychol. Rev.*, **55**, 48–63.
CATTELL, R. B., SAUNDERS, D. R., & STICE, G. F., 1953, "The Dimensions of Syntality in Small Groups", *Hum. Relat.*, **6**, 331–56.

CENTERS, P., & CANTRIL, H., 1946, "Income Satisfaction and Income Aspiration", *J. Abnorm. Soc. Psychol.*, **41**, 64–9.

CHAPIN, F. S., 1940, "An Experiment on the Social Effects of Good Housing", *Amer. Sociol. Rev.*, **5**, 868–79.

1947, *Experimental Designs in Sociological Research.* New York: Harper.

CHAPIN, F. S., et al., 1954, "Group Structure and Function as Related to the Personality Characteristics and Interests of Group Members". *O.N.R. Report.*

CHAPMAN, D. W., & VOLKMANN, J., 1939, "A Social Determinant of the Level of Aspiration." *J. Abnorm. Soc. Psychol.*, **34**, 225–38.

CHAPPLE, E. D., & ARENSBERG, C. M., 1940, "Measuring Human Relations. An Introduction to the Study of the Interaction of Individuals", *Genet. Psychol. Monogr.*, **22**, 3–147.

CHILD, I. L., 1954, "Socialization". Chap. XVIII in Lindzey (1954).

CHOWDHRY, K., & NEWCOMB, T. M., 1952, "The Relative Ability of Leaders and Non-leaders to Estimate Opinions of their own Groups", *J. Abnorm. Soc. Psychol.*, **47**, 51–7.

COCH, L., & FRENCH, J. R. P., 1948, "Overcoming Resistance to Change", *Hum. Relat.*, **1**, 512–32.

COFFEY, H., et al. (eds.), 1950, "Community Service and Social Research: Group Psychotherapy in a Church Programme", *J. Soc. Issues*, **6**, No. 1.

COFFIN, T. E., 1941, "Some Conditions of Suggestion and Suggestibility", *Psychol. Monogr.*, **53**, No. 4.

COHEN, M. R., & NAGEL, E., 1939, *An Introduction to Logic and Scientific Method.* London: Routledge. Abridged edition.

COMBS, A. W., & TAYLOR, C., 1952, "The Effect of the Perception of Mild Degrees of Threat on Performance", *J. Abnorm. Soc. Psychol.*, **47**, 420–4.

COMREY, A. L., PFIFFNER, J. M., & HIGH, W. S., 1954, *Factors Influencing Organisational Effectiveness. A Final Report.* U. of Southern California.

COOK, P. H., 1951, "Methods of Field Research", *Aust. J. Psychol.*, **3**, 84–98.

COWEN, E. L., 1952, "The Influence of Varying Degrees of Psychological Stress on Problem-solving Rigidity", *J. Abnorm. Soc. Psychol.*, **47**, 512–19.

CRAWLEY, S. L., 1926, "An Experimental Investigation of Recovery from Work", *Arch. Psychol.*, No. 85.

CRUTCHFIELD, R. S., & GORDEN, D. A., 1947, "Variations in Respondents' Interpretations of an Opinion Poll Question", *Int. J. Opin. and Att. Res.*, **1**, No. 3, 1–12.

D

DALE, E., 1952, *Planning and Developing the Company Organisation Structure.* American Management Association.

DARLEY, J. G., GROSS, N., & MARTIN, W. E., 1951, "Studies of Group Behavior: Stability, Change and Interrelations of Psychometric and Sociometric Variables", *J. Abnorm. Soc. Psychol.*, **46**, 565–76.

REFERENCES

DASHIELL, J. F., 1930, "An Experimental Analysis of Some Group Effects", *J. Abnorm. Soc. Psychol.*, **25**, 190–9.
1935, "Experimental studies of the Influence of Social Situations on the Behavior of Individual Human Adults", pp. 1097–1158 in *Handbook of Social Psychology*, ed. C. Murchison. Worcester: Clark U.P.
DAVIS, A., GARDNER, B. B. & M. R., 1941, *Deep South; a Social Anthropological Study of Caste and Class*. U. of Chicago Press.
DAVIS, K., 1953, "A Method of Studying Communication Patterns in Organisations", *Personnel Psychol.*, **6**, 301–12.
DENNISON, S. R., 1947, "The Problem of Bigness", *Cambridge Journal*, **1**, 109–25.
DEUTSCH, J. A., 1953, "A New Type of Behaviour Theory", *Brit. J. Psychol.*, **44**, 304–17.
1954, "A Machine with Insight", *Quart. J. Exp. Psychol.*, **6**, 6–11.
DEUTSCH, M., 1949a, "A Theory of Cooperation and Competition", *Hum. Relat.*, **2**, 129–52.
1949b, "An Experimental Study of Cooperation and Competition", *Hum. Relat.*, **2**, 199–231.
DOLLARD, J., et al., 1939, *Frustration and Aggression*. Yale U.P.
DOLLARD, J., & MILLER, N. E., 1950, *Personality and Psychotherapy*. New York: McGraw-Hill.
DOOB, L. W., 1937, "Poor Whites: a Frustrated Class", pp. 445–84 in *Caste and Class in a Southern Town*, by Dollard, J. Yale U.P.
DREYER, A. S., 1954, "Aspiration Behavior as Influenced by Expectation and Group Comparison", *Hum. Relat.*, **7**, 175–90.
DURKHEIM, E., 1895, *The Rules of Sociological Method*. Trans Solovay, S. A., & Mueller, J. H. Glencoe, Ill.: The Free Press (1938).
1897, *Suicide*. Trans Spaulding, J. A., & Simpson, G. Glencoe, Ill.: The Free Press.

E

EDWARDS, A. L., 1950, *Experimental Designs in Psychological Research*. New York: Rinehart.
EKDAHL, A. G., 1929, "Effects of Attitude on Free Word Association-time", *Genet. Psychol. Monogr.*, **5**, 253–338.
ELLIS, A., 1946, "The Validity of Personality Questionnaires", *Psychol. Bull.*, **43**, 385–440.
ESCALONA, S. K., 1945, "Feeding Disturbances in Very Young Children", *Amer. J. Orthopsychiat.*, **15**, 76–80.
ESTES, S. G., 1937, *The Judgment of Personality on the Basis of Brief Records of Behavior*. Cambridge, Mass.: Harvard Coll. Library.
EVANS, C. E., & LASSAU, LA V. N., 1950, "My Job Contest", *Personnel Psychol. Monogr.*, No. 1.
EYSENCK, H. J., 1947, *The Dimensions of Personality*. London: Kegan Paul.
1952, *The Scientific Study of Personality*. London: Routledge & Kegan Paul.
1954, *The Psychology of Politics*. London: Routledge & Kegan Paul.

EZRIEL, H., 1951, "The Scientific Testing of Psycho-analytic Findings and Theory", *Brit. J. Med. Psychol.*, **24**, 30–4.

F

FELDMAN, H., 1937, *Problems in Labor Relations*. New York: MacMillan.

FESTINGER, L., 1954, "A Theory of Social Comparison Processes", *Hum. Relat.*, **7**, 117–40.

FESTINGER, L., & KATZ, D., 1953, *Research Methods in the Behavioral Sciences*. New York: Dryden.

FESTINGER, L., & KELLEY, H. H., 1951, "Changing Attitudes through Social Contact". U. of Michigan. Mimeographed.

FESTINGER, L., PEPITONE, A., & NEWCOMB, T., 1952, "Some Consequences of De-individuation in a Group", *J. Abnorm. Soc. Psychol.*, **47**, 382–9.

FESTINGER, L., SCHACHTER, S., & BACK, K., 1950, *Social Pressures in Informal Groups*. New York: Harper.

FESTINGER, L., & THIBAUT, J., 1951, "Interpersonal Communication in Small Groups", *J. Abnorm. Soc. Psychol.*, **46**, 92–9.

FESTINGER, L., TORREY, J., & WILLERMAN, B., 1954, "Self-evaluation as a Function of Attraction to the Group", *Hum. Relat.*, **7**, 161–73.

FESTINGER, L., et al., 1952, *Theory and Experiment in Social Communication*. U. of Michigan.

FIEDLER, F. E., 1949, "A Comparative Investigation of Early Therapeutic Relationships Created by Experts and Non-experts of the Psychoanalytic, Non-directive, and Adlerian schools". Ph.D. thesis, U. of Chicago (quoted by Mowrer (1953), pp. 216–17).

FIEDLER, F. E., WARRINGTON, W. G., & BLAISDELL, F. J., 1952, "Unconscious Attitudes as Correlates of Sociometric Choice in a Social Group", *J. Abnorm. Soc. Psychol.*, **47**, 790–6.

FILE, Q. W., & REMMERS, H. H., 1945, *How Supervise? Forms A and B*. New York: Psychological Corporation.

1946, "Studies in Supervisory Evaluation", *J. App. Psychol.*, **30**, 421–5.

FISHER, R. A., 1949, *The Design of Experiments*. Edinburgh: Oliver & Boyd.

FISKE, D. W., 1951, "Values, Theory, and the Criterion Problem", *Personnel Psychol.*, **4**, 93–8.

FLEISHMAN, E. A., 1953a, "Leadership Climate, Human Relations Training and Supervisory Behavior", *Personnel Psychol.*, **6**, 205–22.

1953b, "The Description of Supervisory Behaviour", *J. App. Psychol.*, **37**, 1–6.

FLORENCE, P. S., 1953, *The Logic of British and American Industry*. London: Routledge & Kegan Paul.

FOURIEZOS, N. T., HUTT, M. L., & GUETZKOW, H., 1950, "Measurement of Self-oriented Needs in Discussion Groups", *J. Abnorm. Soc. Psychol.*, **45**, 682–90.

FOX, J. B., & SCOTT, J. F., 1943, "Absenteeism: Management's Problem", *Harvard Bus. Res. Stud.*, No. 29. Harvard U.P.

FRENCH, J. R. P., 1944, "Organised and Unorganised Groups under Fear and Frustration", *U. Ia. Stud. Child Welf.*, **20**, 229–308.

REFERENCES

1950, "Experiments on Changing Group Productivity", in *Experiments in Social Process*, ed. Miller, J. G. New York: McGraw-Hill.
1953, "Experiments in Field Settings". Chap. III of Festinger and Katz (1953).
1954, "A Small Theory of Leadership". Pages to A.P.A. Mimeographed.
FRENCH, T. M., 1944, "Clinical Approach to the Dynamics of Behavior". Chap. 7 in Hunt (1944).
FRENKEL-BRUNSWIK, E., 1951, "Personality Theory and Perception". Chap. XIII in *Perception: An Approach to Personality*, ed. Blake, R. R., & Ramsey, G. V. New York: Ronald.

G

GAGE, N. L., & SUCI, G., 1951, "Social Perception and Teacher-pupil Relationships", *J. Exp. Psychol.*, 42, 144–52.
GARDNER, B. B., 1944, *Human Relations in Industry*. Chicago: Irwin.
GARDNER, B. B., & WHYTE, W. F., 1946, "Methods for the Study of Human Relations in Industry", *Amer. Sociol. Rev.*, 11, 506–12.
GERARD, H. B., 1953, "The Effect of Different Dimensions of Disagreement on the Communication Process in Small Groups", *Hum. Relat.*, 6, 249–71.
1954, "The Anchorage of Opinions in Face-to-face Groups", *Hum. Relat.*, 7, 313–25.
GHISELLI, E. E., & BROWN, C. W., 1948, *Personnel and Industrial Psychology*. New York: McGraw-Hill.
GIBB, C. A., 1949, "The Emergence of Leadership in Small Temporary Groups of Men". Ph.D. thesis. U. of Illinois, quoted in Gibb (1954), p. 902.
1950, "The Research Background of an Interactional Theory of Leadership", *Aust. J. Psychol.*, 2, 19–42.
1954, "Leadership", Chap. XXIV in Lindzey (1954).
GIBB, J. R., 1951, "The Effects of Group Size and of Threat Reduction upon Creativity in a Problem-solving Situation", *Amer. Psychol.*, 6, 324.
GIESE, W. J., & RUTER, H. W., 1949, "An Objective Analysis of Morale", *J. App. Psychol.*, 33, 421–7.
GILLESPIE, J. F., 1953, in *Group Report of a Programme of Research in Psychotherapy*, pp. 105–19, ed. Snyder, W. U. Pennsylvania State College.
GOLDBERG, G. C., 1954, "Three Situational Determinants of Conformity to Social Norms", *J. Abnorm. Soc. Psychol.*, 49, 325–9.
GOLDMAN-EISLER, F., 1951, "The Measurement of Time-sequences in Conversational Behaviour", *Brit. J. Psychol.*, 42, 355–62.
GOODACRE, D. M., 1951, "The Use of a Sociometric Test as a Predictor of Combat Unit Effectiveness", *Sociometry*, 14, 148–52.
GORDEN, K. H., 1924, "Group Judgments in the Field of Lifted Weights", *J. Exp. Psychol.*, 3, 398–400.
GORDEN, R. L., 1952, "Interaction between Attitude and the Definition of the Situation in the Expression of Opinions", *Amer. Sociol. Rev.*, 17, 50–8.

GOUGH, H. G., 1948, "Associated Theory of Psychotherapy", *Amer. Sociol. Rev.*, **53**, 359–66.

GOULD, R., 1939, "An Experimental Analysis of 'Level of Aspiration' ", *J. Psychol.*, **6**, 265–79.

GREEN, G. H., 1948, "Insight and Group Adjustment", *J. Abnorm. Soc. Psychol.*, **43**, 49–61.

GREENWOOD, E., 1945, *Experimental Sociology. A Study in Method*. New York: King's Crown Press.

GREENWOOD, M., & WOODS, H. M., 1919, "The Incidence of Industrial Accidents upon Individuals, with Specific Reference to Multiple Accidents". *I.F.R.B.*, No. 4.

GREER, F. L., 1954, "Interpersonal Knowledge and Individual and Group Effectiveness", *J. Abnorm. Soc. Psychol.*, **49**, 411–14.

GROSSACK, M. M., 1954, "Some Effects of Cooperation and Competition upon Small Group Behavior", *J. Abnorm. Soc. Psychol.*, **49**, 341–8.

GROSSER, D., POLANSKY, N. A., & LIPPITT, R., 1951, "A Laboratory Study of Behavioral Contagion", *Hum. Relat.*, **4**, 115–42.

GUETZKOW, H., 1950, "Unitising and Categorising Problems in Coding Qualitative Data", *J. Clin. Psychol.*, **6**, 47, 58.

GUETZKOW, H., & GYR, J., 1954, "An Analysis of Conflict in Decision-making Groups", *Hum. Relat.*, **7**, 367–82.

GUILFORD, J. P., 1950, *Fundamental Statistics in Psychology and Education*. New York: McGraw-Hill.

1952, "Temperament Traits of Executives and Supervisors Measured by the Guilford Personality Inventories", *J. App. Psychol.*, **36**, 228–33.

GUMP, P. V., 1944, "A Statistical Investigation of One Psychoanalytic Approach and a Comparison of it with Non-directive Therapy". Ph.D. thesis, Ohio State University (quoted by Seeman & Raskin (1953), p. 208).

GUNTER, R., 1951, "Binocular Fusion of Colours", *Brit. J. Psychol.*, **42**, 363–72.

GYR, J., 1951, "Analysis of Committee Member Behavior in Four Cultures", *Hum. Relat.*, **4**, 193–202.

H

HALL, J., & JONES, D. C., 1950, "Social Grading of Occupations", *Brit. J. Sociol.*, **1**, 31–55.

HALMOS, P., 1952, *Solitude and Privacy*. London: Routledge & Kegan Paul.

HALPIN, A. W., 1954, "The Leadership Behavior and Combat Performance of Airplane Commanders", *J. Abnorm. Soc. Psychol.*, **49**, 19–22.

HANDYSIDE, J. D., 1953a, "Raising Job Satisfaction: a Utilitarian Approach", *Occ. Psychol.*, **27**, 89–97.

1953b, "An Estimate of the Size of Primary Working Groups in British Industry", *Occ. Psychol.*, **27**, 107–8.

1953c, "Two Studies in Supervision: Supervision in a Cotton-spinning Mill". N.I.I.P. Report, No. 10.

1954, "The Effectiveness of Supervisory Training: a Survey of Recent Experimental Studies". Paper to British Psychological Society.

REFERENCES

HANDYSIDE, J. D., & DUNCAN, D. C., 1954, "Four Years Later: a Follow-up on an Experiment in Selecting Supervisors", *Occ. Psychol.*, **28**, 9–23.

HARE, A. P., 1952, "A Study of Interaction and Consensus in Different Sized Groups", *Amer. Sociol. Rev.*, **17**, 261–7.

1953, "Small Group Discussions with Participatory and Supervisory Leadership", *J. Abnorm. Soc. Psychol.*, **48**, 273–5.

HARITON, T., 1951, "Conditions Affecting the Effects of Training Foremen in Human Relations". Ph.D. thesis, U. of Michigan (quoted by Viteles (1954), p. 446).

HARRELL, T. W., 1949, *Industrial Psychology*. New York: Rinehart.

HAYTHORN, W., 1953, "The Influence of Individual Members on the Characteristics of Small Groups", *J. Abnorm. Soc. Psychol.*, **48**, 276–84.

HEBB, D. O., 1949, *The Organisation of Behavior*. London: Chapman & Hall.

HEINECKE, C., & BALES, R. F., 1953, "Developmental Trends in the Structure of Small Groups", *Sociometry*, **16**, 7–39.

HEISE, G. A., & MILLER, G. A., 1951, "Problem Solving by Small Groups Using Various Communication Nets", *J. Abnorm. Soc. Psychol.*, **46**, 327–35.

HEMPHILL, J. K., 1950a, "Relations between the Size of the Group and the Behaviour of 'Superior' Leaders", *J. Soc. Psychol.*, **32**, 11–22.

1950b, *Leader Behavior Description*. Ohio State University. Personnel Res. Bd.

HEMPHILL, J. K., & WESTIE, C. M., 1950, "The Measurement of Group Dimensions", *J. Psychol.*, **29**, 325–42.

HERON, A., 1952, "The Establishment for Research Purposes of Two Criteria of Occupational Adjustment", *Occ. Psychol.*, **26**, 78–85.

1954a, "Satisfaction and Satisfactoriness", *Occ. Psychol.*, 140–53.

1954b, "Industrial Psychology", *Ann. Rev. Psychol.*, **5**, 203–28.

1956, "Rigorous Methods in Clinical Studies of Individual Change." Paper to British Psychological Society. *Abstract Quart. Bull.*, *B.P.S.* No. 29, p. 8.

HEWITT, D., & PARFITT, J., 1953, "A Note of Working Morale and Size of Group", *Occ. Psychol.*, **27**, 38–42.

HEYNS, R. W., & ZANDER, A. F., 1953, "Observation of Group Behavior". Chap. IX in Festinger & Katz (1953).

HILGARD, E. R., & MARQUIS, D. G., 1940, *Conditioning and Learning*. New York: Appleton-Century-Crofts.

HIMMELWEIT, H. T., 1947, "A Comparative Study of the Level of Aspiration of Normal and Neurotic Persons", *Brit. J. Psychol.*, **37**, 41–59.

1950, "Frustration and Aggression. A Review of Recent Experimental Work". Chap. VIII in *Psychological Factors of Peace and War*, ed. Pear, T. H. London: Hutchinson.

HIMMELWEIT, H. T., & SUMMERFIELD, A., 1951, "Student Selection—an Experimental Investigation. II", *Brit. J. Sociol.*, **2**, 59–75.

HITES, R. W., & CAMPBELL, D. T., 1950, "A Test of the Ability of Fraternity Leaders to Estimate Group Opinion", *J. Soc. Psychol.*, **32**, 95–100.

HOBHOUSE, L. T., GINSBERG, M., & WHEELER, G. C., 1915, *The Material Culture and Social Institutions of the Simpler Peoples*. London Monographs on Sociology, No. 3.

HOFFMAN, M. L., 1953, "Some Psychodynamic Factors in Compulsive Conformity", *J. Abnorm. Soc. Psychol.*, **48**, 383–93.

HOFFMAN, P. J., FESTINGER, L., & LAWRENCE, D. H., 1954, "Tendencies toward Group Comparability in Competitive Bargaining". *Hum. Relat.*, **7**, 141–59.

HOLLANDER, E. P., 1954, "Authoritarianism and Leadership Choice in a Military Setting", *J. Abnorm. Soc. Psychol.*, **49**, 365–70.

HOLT, R. R., 1945, "Effects of Ego-involvement upon Levels of Aspiration", *Psychiatry*, **8**, 299–317.

HOMANS, G. C., 1951, *The Human Group*. London: Routledge and Kegan Paul.

HOPPOCK, R., 1935, *Job Satisfaction*. New York and London: Harper.

HORNEY, K., 1945, *Our Inner Conflicts*. New York: Norton.

HOROWITZ, M. W., LYONS, J., & PERLMUTTER, H. V., 1951, "Induction of Forces in Discussion Groups", *Hum. Relat.*, **4**, 57–76.

HORTON, D., 1943, "The Functions of Alcohol in Primitive Societies", *Quart. J. Stud. Alcohol.*, **4**, 292–303.

HORWITZ, M., 1954, "The Recall of Interrupted Group Tasks: an Experimental Study of Individual Motivation in Relation to Group Goals", *Hum. Relat.*, **7**, 3–38.

HOVLAND, C. I., 1954, "Effects of the Mass Media of Communication". Chap. XXVIII in Lindzey (1954).

HOVLAND, C. I., LUMSDAINE, A. A., & SHEFFIELD, F. D., 1949, *Experiments on Mass Communication*. Princeton U.P.

HUGHES, E. C., 1946, "The Knitting of Racial Groups in Industry", *Amer. Sociol. Rev.*, **11**, 512–19.

HULL, C. L., 1951, *Essentials of Behavior*. Yale U.P.
1953, *A Behavior System*. Yale U.P.

HUNT, J. MCV., 1944, *Personality and the Behavior Disorders*. New York: Ronald.

HUNT, J. MCV., & SOLOMON, R. L., 1942, "The Stability and Some Correlates of Group Status in a Summer Camp of Young Boys", *Amer. J. Psychol.*, **55**, 33–45.

HURLOCK, E. B., 1924, "The Use of Praise and Reproof as Incentives for Children", *Arch. Psychol.*, No. 71.

HURWITZ, J. I., ZANDER, A. F., & HYMOVITCH, B., 1953, "Some Effects of Power on the Relations among Group Members". Chap. XXXII of Cartwright & Zander (1953).

HUTTE, H. A., 1953, *De Invloed van Moeilijk te Verdragen situaties op groepsverhoudingen*. Leiden: Stenfert Kroese.

HYMAN, H. H., 1942, "The Psychology of Status", *Arch. Psychol.*, **38**, No. 269.
1951, "Interviewing as a Scientific Procedure". Chap. XI in Lerner & Lasswell (1951).

I

ICHHEISER, G., 1930, "Ueber die Veränderung der Leistungsbereitschaft durch das Bewusstsein einer Zuschauer zu haben". *Psychotech. Zsch.*, **5**, 52–3.

Information and Education Division, 1945, "Opinions about Negro Infantry Platoons in White Companies of Seven Divisions", pp. 502–6 in *Readings in Social Psychology*, ed. Swanson, G. E., et al. New York: Holt.

J

JACKSON, J. M., 1953, "The Effect of Changing the Leadership of Small Work Groups", *Hum. Relat.*, **6**, 25–44.
JACOBSEN, E., & SEASHORE, S. E., 1951, "Communication Practices in Large Organisations", *J. Soc. Issues*, **7**, No. 3, 28–40.
JAHODA, G., 1953, "Social Class Attitudes and Levels of Occupational Aspiration in Secondary Modern School Leavers", *Brit. J. Psychol.*, **44**, 95–107.
JAHODA, M., DEUTSCH, M., & COOK, S. W., 1951, *Research Methods in Social Relations*. New York: Dryden.
JANIS, I. L., & FESHBACH, S., 1953, "Effects of Fear-arousing Communications", *J. Abnorm. Soc. Psychol.*, **48**, 78–92.
JAQUES, E., 1948, "Interpretative Group Discussion as a Method of Facilitating Social Change", *Hum. Relat.*, **1**, 533–49.
JENNINGS, H. H., 1950, *Leadership and Isolation*. New York: Longmans.

K

KARN, H. W., 1949, "Performance on the File-Remmers Test *How Supervise?* before and after a Course in Psychology", *J. App. Psychol.*, **33**, 534–9.
KATZ, D., & BRALY, K. W., 1935, "Racial Prejudice and Racial Stereotypes", *J. Abnorm. Soc. Psychol.*, **28**, 280–90.
KATZ, D., & KAHN, R. L., 1951, *The Caterpillar Tractor Co. Study*. 6 vols. U. of Michigan. Mimeographed.
1952, "Some Recent Findings in Human Relations Research". U. of Michigan. Mimeographed.
KATZ, D., MacCOBY, N., & MORSE, N. C., 1950, *Productivity, Supervision and Morale in an Office Situation*. U. of Michigan.
KATZ, D., et al., 1951, *Productivity, Supervision and Morale among Railroad Workers*. U. of Michigan.
KELLEY, H. H., 1950, "The Warm-cold Variable in First Impressions of Persons", *J. Pers.*, **18**, 431–9.
1951, "Communication in Experimentally Created Hierarchies".
1952, "Two Functions of Reference Groups", pp. 410–14 in *Readings in Social Psychology*, ed. Swanson, G. E., et al. New York: Holt.
KELLEY, H. H., & THIBAUT, J. W., 1954, "Experimental Studies of Group Problem-solving and Process". Chap. XXI in Lindzey (1954).
KELLEY, H. H., & VOLKHART, E. H., 1952, "The Resistance to Change of Group-anchored Attitudes", *Amer. Sociol. Rev.*, **17**, 453–65.
KELLY, E. L., & FISKE, D. W., 1951, *The Prediction of Performance in Clinical Psychology*. U. of Michigan Press.

KELMAN, H. C., 1950, "Effects of Success and Failure on 'Suggestibility' in the Autokinetic Situation", *J. Abnorm. Soc. Psychol.*, **45**, 267–85.
KERR, W. A., 1947, "Labour Turnover and its Correlates", *J. App. Psychol.*, **31**, 366–71.
1948, "On the Validity and Reliability of the Job Satisfaction Tear Ballot", *J. App. Psychol.*, **32**, 275–81.
1952, "Summary of Validity Studies of the Tear Ballot", *Personnel Psychol.*, **5**, 105–13.
KERR, W. A., KOPPELMEIER, G. J., & SULLIVAN, J. J., 1951, "Absenteeism, Turnover and Morale in a Metals Fabrication Factory", *Occ. Psychol.*, **25**, 50–5.
KEYS, A., et al., 1945, *Experimental Starvation in Man*. U. of Minnesota.
KINSEY, A. C., POMEROY, W. P., & MARTIN, C. E., 1948, *Sexual Behavior in the Human Male*. Philadelphia: Saunders.
KLEIN, J. F. H., 1952, "The Development of Relationships in Small Groups". Ph.D. thesis, U. of Birmingham (quoted by Riecken & Homans (1954), p. 820).
KLUCKHOHN, C., 1954, "Culture and Behavior". Chap. XXV of Lindzey (1954).
KLUCKHOHN, F. R. C., 1940, "The Participant-observer Technique in Small Communities", *Amer. J. Sociol.*, **46**, 331–43.
KLUGMAN, S. F., 1944, "Cooperative versus Individual Efficiency in Problem-solving", *J. Ed. Psychol.*, **35**, 91–100.
KOCH, S., 1941, "The Logical Character of the Motivation Concept", *Psychol. Rev.*, **48**, 15–38, 127–54.
1951, "Theoretical Psychology. 1950: an Overview", *Psychol. Rev.*, **58**, 295–305.
1952, review of Parsons & Shils (1951).
KÖHLER, O., 1927, "Ueber den Gruppenwirkungsgrad der menschlichen Kürperarbeit und die Bedingung optimaler Kollectivkraftreaktion", *Indust. Psychotech.*, **16**, 406–14 (quoted by Dashiell (1935), pp. 1113–15).
KRECH, D., & CRUTCHFIELD, R. S., 1948, *Theory and Problems of Social Psychology*. New York: McGraw-Hill.
KRISTY, N. F., 1952, "Criteria of Occupational Success among Post Office Counter Clerks". Ph.D. thesis, U. of London (quoted by Heron (1954a)).
KUPER, L., 1953, *Living in Towns*. London: Cresset.

L

LANZETTA, J. T., et al., 1954, "Some Effects of Situational Threat on Group Behavior", *J. Abnorm. Soc., Psychol.*, **49**, 445–53.
LAZARUS, R. S., & McCLEARY, R. A., 1951, "Autonomic Discrimination without Awareness: a Study of Subception", *Psychol. Rev.*, **58**, 113–22.
LEAVITT, H. J., 1951, "Some Effects of Certain Communication Patterns on Group Performance", *J. Abnorm. Soc. Psychol.*, **46**, 38–50.
LEEPER, R. W., 1948, "A Motivational Theory of Emotion to Replace 'Emotion as Disorganised Response' ", *Psychol. Rev.*, **55**, 5–21.

REFERENCES

LEEPER., R. W., 1951, "Cognitive Processes". Chap. XIX in *Handbook of Experimental Psychology*, ed. Stevens, S. S. Harvard U.P.
LEIGHTON, D., & KLUCKHOHN, C., 1947, *Children of the People*. Harvard U.P.
LERNER, D., & LASSWELL, H. D., 1951, *The Policy Sciences*. Stanford U.P.
LEUBA, C., & LUCAS, C., 1945, "The Effects of Attitudes on Descriptions of Pictures", *J. Exp. Psychol.*, 35, 517–24.
LEVI, I. J., 1930, "Student Leadership in Elementary and Junior High School, and its Transfer into Senior High School", *J. Educ. Res.*, 22, 135–9.
LEVINE, J., & BUTLER, J., 1952, "Lecture vs. Group Decision in Changing Behaviour", *J. App. Psychol.*, 36, 29–33.
LEWIN, K., 1931, "The Conflict between Aristotelian and Galilean Modes of Thought in Contemporary Psychology", *J. General Psychol.*, 5, 141–77 (also pp. 1–42 of *Dynamic Theory of Personality*, 1935. New York: McGraw-Hill).
  1936, *Principles of Topological Psychology*. New York: McGraw-Hill.
  1938, *The Conceptual Representation and Measurement of Psychological Forces*. Contr. to Psychol. Theory, 1, No. 4, ed. Adams, D. K., & Lundholm, H. Duke U.P.
  1940, "Formalisation and Progress in Psychology", *U. Ia. Stud. Child Welf.*, 16, 7–42.
  1943a, "Defining the 'Field at a Given Time' ", *Psychol. Rev.*, 50, 292–310.
  1943b, "Forces behind Food Habits and Methods of Change", *Bull. Nat. Res. Co.*, 108, 35–65.
  1947, "Frontiers in Group Dynamics: Concept, Method and Reality in Social Science; Social Equilibria and Social Change", *Hum. Relat.*, 1, 5–41.
  1952, *Field Theory in Social Science*. London: Tavistock.
LEWIN, K., et al., 1944, "Level of Aspiration". Chap. X in Hunt (1944).
LEWIS, H. B., 1944, "An Experimental Study of the Role of the Ego in Work. I—The Role of the Ego in Cooperative Work", *J. Exp. Psychol.*, 34, 113–26.
LINDGREN, E. J., 1935, "Field Work in Social Psychology", *Brit. J. Psychol.*, 26, 174–82.
LINDZEY, G., 1954, *Handbook of Social Psychology*. Cambridge, Mass.: Addison-Wesley.
LIPPITT, R., 1940, "An Experimental Study of the Effects of Democratic and Autocratic Atmospheres", *U. Ia. Stud. Child Welf.*, 16, 45–195.
  1948, "A program of Experimentation on Group Functioning and Group Productivity", in *Current Trends on Social Psychology*, ed. Dennis, W. U. of Pittsburgh.
  1949, *Training in Community Relations*. New York: Harper.
LIPPITT, R., POLANSKY, N., & ROSEN, S., 1952, "The Dynamics of Power", *Hum. Relat.*, 5, 37–64.
LONG, J. R., 1951, *Labour Turnover under Full Employment*. U. of Birmingham. Roneoed.
LOOMIS, C. P., & BEEGLE, J. A., 1950, *Rural Social Systems*. New York: Prentice-Hall.

LORD, E., 1950, "Experimentally Induced Variations in Rorschach Performance", *Psychol. Monogr.*, **64**, No. 10.
LORENZ, K. Z., 1950, "The Comparative Method of Studying Innate Behaviour Patterns", pp. 221–68 in *Physiological Mechanisms in Animal Behaviour*, Symposia of the Society for Experimental Biology, No. 4. C.U.P.
LUCHINS, A. S., 1945, "Social Influence on Perception of Complex Drawings", *J. Soc. Psychol.*, **21**, 257–73.
LUNDBERG, G. A., & STEELE, M., 1938, "Social Attraction Patterns in a Village", *Sociometry*, **1**, 375–419.
LYNTON, R. P., 1949, *Incentives and Management in British Industry*. London: Routledge & Kegan Paul.

M

McCANDLESS, B. R., 1942, "Changing Relationships between Dominance and Social Acceptability during Democratisation", *Amer. J. Orthopsychiat.*, **12**, 529–35.
McCLELLAND, D. C., et al., 1953, *The Achievement Motive*. New York: Appleton-Century-Crofts.
MacCORQUODALE, J., & MEEHL, P. E., 1948, "On a Distinction between Hypothetical Constructs and Intervening Variables", *Psychol. Rev.*, **55**, 95–107.
McCURDY, H. G., & LAMBERT, W. E., 1952, "The Efficiency of Small Human Groups in the Solution of Problems requiring Genuine Cooperation", *J. Pers.*, **20**, 478–94.
McDOUGALL, W., 1908, *Introduction to Social Psychology*. London: Methuen.
McGEOCH, J. A., 1942, *The Psychology of Human Learning*. London: Longmans.
McINTYRE, C. J., 1952, "Acceptance by Others and its Relation to Acceptance of Self and Others", *J. Abnorm. Soc. Psychol.*, **47**, 624–5.
McKEACHIE, W. J., 1954, "Individual Conformity to Attitudes of Classroom Groups", *J. Abnorm. Soc. Psychol.*, **49**, 282–9.
McNEMAR, Q., 1946, "Opinion-attitude Methodology", *Psychol. Bull.*, **43**, 289–374.
MACE, C. A., 1935, "Incentives—Some Experimental Studies", I.H.R.B. Report, No. 72. H.M.S.O.
MACKWORTH, N. H., 1950, *Researches on the Measurement of Human Performance*. M.R.C. Report, No. 268. H.M.S.O.
MADGE, J., 1953, *The Tools of Social Science*. London: Longmans.
MAIER, N. R. F., 1931, "Reasoning in Humans. II—The Solution of a Problem and its Appearance in Consciousness", *J. Comp. Psychol.*, **12**, 181–94.
 1949, *Frustration. The Study of Behavior without a Goal*. New York: McGraw-Hill.
 1950, "The Quality of Group Decisions as Influenced by the Discussion Leader", *Hum. Relat.*, **3**, 155–74.
 1952, *Principles of Human Relations*. London: Chapman & Hall.
 1953, "An Experimental Test of the Effect of Training on Discussion Leadership", *Hum. Relat.*, **6**, 161–73.

REFERENCES

MALLER, J. B., 1929, *Cooperation and Competition. An Experimental Study in Motivation.* Teach. Coll. Contr. Educ.

MANN, F. C., 1951, "Human Relations Skills in Social Research", *Hum. Relat.*, **4**, 341–54.

MARQUIS, D. G., GUETZKOW, H., & HEYNS, R. W., 1950, "A Social Psychological Study of the Decision-making Conference", in *Groups. Leadership and Men*, ed. Guetzkow, H. Pittsburgh: Carnegie.

MARRIOTT, R., 1949, "Size of Working Group and Output", *Occ. Psychol.*, **23**, 47–57.

MASLING, J., GREER, F. L., & GILMORE, R. 1953, "Status, Authoritarianism and Sociometric Choice". O.N.R. Report.

MAUSNER, B., 1954, "The Effect of Prior Reinforcement on the Interaction of Observer Pairs", *J. Abnorm. Soc. Psychol.*, **49**, 65–8.

MAYO, E., & LOMBARD, G. F. F., 1944, "Teamwork and Labor Turnover in the Aircraft Industry of Southern California". Harvard Grad. Sch. Bus. Admin., *Bus. Res. Stud.*, No. 32.

MEAD, M., 1935, *Sex and Temperament in Three Primitive Societies.* New York: Morrow.

—— 1937, *Cooperation and Competition among Primitive Peoples.* New York: McGraw-Hill.

MEREI, F., 1949, "Leadership and Institutionalisation", *Hum. Relat.*, **2**, 23–39.

MERTON, R. K., 1949, *Social Theory and Social Structure.* Glencoe, Ill.: The Free Press.

MERTON, R. K., & KENDALL, P. L., 1946, "The Focussed Interview", *Amer. J. Sociol.*, **51**, 541–57.

MERTON, R. K., & KITT, A., 1950, "Contributions to the Theory of Reference Group Behavior", in *Continuities in Social Research*, ed. Merton, R. K., & Lazarsfeld, P. F. Glencoe, Ill.: The Free Press.

MILL, J. S., 1851, *A System of Logic.* London: Parker. 3rd edition.

MILLER, N. E., & DOLLARD, J., 1941, *Social Learning and Imitation.* London: Kegan Paul.

MILLS, T. M., 1953, "Power Relations in Three-person Groups", *Amer. Sociol. Rev.*, **18**, 351–7.

MINTZ, A., 1951, "Non-adaptive Group Behavior", *J. Abnorm. Soc. Psychol.*, **46**, 150–9.

Modern Industry, 1946, "Pay Plans for Higher Production" (quoted by Viteles (1954), p. 27).

MOEDE, W., 1920, *Experimentelle Massenpsychologie.* Leipzig: Hirzel (quoted by Dashiell, 1935, pp. 1106 f.).

MOORE, H., 1939, *Psychology for Business and Industry.* New York: McGraw-Hill.

MOORE, H. T., 1917, "Laboratory Tests of Anger, Fear and Sex Interests", *J. Psychol.*, **28**, 390–5.

MORENO, J. L., 1953, *Who Shall Survive?* New York: Beacon House.

MORRIS, B. S., 1949, "Officer Selection in the British Army, 1942–5", *Occ. Psychol.*, **23**, 219–34.

MORSE, N., 1953, *Satisfactions in the White-collar Job.* U. of Michigan.

MORSE, N. C., REIMER, E., & TANNENBAUM, A. S., 1951, "Regulation and Control in Hierarchical Organisations", *J. Soc. Issues*, **7**, No. 3, 41–5.

MOWRER, O. H., 1953, *Psychotherapy Theory and Research*. New York: Ronald.
MUKERJI, N. P., 1940, "An Investigation of Ability to Work in Groups and in Isolation", *Brit. J. Psychol.*, **30**, 352–6.
MUNSTERBERG, H., 1914, *Grundzüge der Psychotechnik*.
MURDOCH, G. P., 1949, *Social Structure*. New York: MacMillan.
MURPHY, L. B., 1937, *Social Behavior and Child Personality*. Columbia U.P.
MURRAY, E. J., 1954, "A Case Report in a Behavioral Analysis of Psychotherapy", *J. Abnorm. Soc. Psychol.*, **49**, 305–10.
MURRAY, H. A., 1933, "The Effect of Fear upon Estimates of the Maliciousness of Other Personalities", *J. Soc. Psychol.*, **4**, 310–29.
MUSCIO, B., 1916, "The Influence of the Form of a Question", *Brit. J. Psychol.*, **8**, 351–89.

N

National Industrial Conference Board, 1947, "Factors Affecting Employee Morale", *Studies in Personnel Policy*, No. 85.
N.I.I.P., 1951, *The Foreman*. London: Staples.
1952, *Joint Consultation in British Industry*. London: Staples.
NEWCOMB, T. M., 1943, *Personality and Social Change*. New York: Dryden.
1947, "Autistic Hostility and Social Reality", *Hum. Relat.*, **1**, 69–86.

O

Office of Strategic Services Staff, 1948, *Assessment of Men*. New York: Rinehart.
O'COMISKY, J. G., 1955, "Affective Reaction on Meeting People for the First Time". Paper to B.P.S.
OESER, O. A., 1939, "The Value of Teamwork and Functional Penetration as Methods in Social Investigation", pp. 402–17 in *The Study of Society*, ed. Bartlett, F. C., et al. London: Kegan Paul.
OLDFIELD, R. C., 1941, *The Psychology of the Interview*. London: Methuen.
ORLANSKY, H., 1949, "Infant Care and Personality", *Psychol. Bull.*, **46**, 1–48.

P

PAGE, D. P., 1935, "Measurement and Prediction of Leadership", *Amer. J. Sociol.*, **41**, 31–43.
PARSONS, T., & SHILS, E. A. eds., 1951, *Towards a General Theory of Action*. Harvard U.P.
PATERSON, T. T., & WILLETT, F. J., 1951, "An Anthropological Experiment in a British Colliery", *App. Anth.*, **10**, 19–25.
PEAK, H., 1953, "Problems of Objective Observation". Chap. VI of Festinger & Katz (1953).

PELZ, D. C., 1949, "The Effect of Supervisory Attitudes and Practices on Employee Satisfactions", *Amer. Psychol.*, **4**, 283–4.
1951, "Leadership within a Hierarchical Organisation", *J. Soc. Issues*, **7**, No. 3, 49–63.
1952, "Influence: a Key to Effective Leadership in the First-line Supervisor", *Personnel*, **3**, 209–17.
PEPITONE, A., 1950, "Motivational Effects in Social Perception," *Hum. Relat.*, **3**, 57–76.
PFAUTZ, H. W., 1953, "The Current Literature on Social Stratification: Critique and Bibliography", *Amer. J. Sociol.*, **58**, 391–418.
PHILLIPS, E. L., & AGNEW, J. W., 1953, "A Study of Rogers' 'Reflection' Hypothesis", *J. Clin. Psychol.*, **9**, 281–4.
PIAGET, J., 1926, *The Child's Conception of the World.* London: Kegan Paul.
POLANSKY, N. A., LIPPITT, R., & REDL, F., 1950, "An Investigation of Behavioral Contagion in Groups", *Hum. Relat.*, **3**, 319–48.
POTTER, S., 1952, *One-Upmanship.* London: Hart-Davis.
PRECKER, J. A., 1952, "Similarity of Values as a Factor in Selection of Peers and Near-authority Figures", *J. Abnorm. Soc. Psychol.*, **47**, 406–14.
PRESTON, M. G., & HEINTZ, R. K., 1949, "Effects of Participatory vs. Supervisory Leadership on Group Judgment", *J. Abnorm. Soc. Psychol.*, **44**, 345–55.
PROCTOR, C. H., & LOOMIS, C. P., 1951, "Analysis of Sociometric Data". Chap. XVII in Jahoda et al. (1951).

R

RADCLIFFE-BROWN, A. R., 1950, "Introduction", pp. 1–85 in *African Systems of Kinship and Marriage*, ed. Radcliffe-Brown, A. R., & Forde, D. London: O.U.P.
RAIMY, V. C., 1943, "The Self Concept as a Factor in Counselling and Personality Organisation", Ph.D. thesis, Ohio State University (quoted by Seeman & Raskin (1953), p. 209).
RAPHAEL, W., et al., 1938, "Report on an Enquiry into Labour Turnover in the London District", *Occ. Psychol.*, **12**, 196–214.
RASHEVSKY, N., 1947, *Mathematical Theory of Human Relations.* Bloomington, Ind.: Principia Press.
1951, *Mathematical Biology of Social Behavior.* U. of Chicago.
RASMUSSEN, G., & ZANDER, A., 1954, "Group Membership and Self-evaluation", *Hum. Relat.*, **7**, 239–51.
REEVE, G., 1949, "The Validation of Boards, Observers, and Selection Procedures". Chap. XX in *The Group Approach to Leadership Testing*, by Harris, H. London: Routledge & Kegan Paul.
RICE, A. K., HILL, J. M. M., & TRIST, E. L., 1950, "The Representation of Labour Turnover as a Social Process", *Hum. Relat.*, **3**, 349–71.
RIECKEN, H. W., & HOMANS, G. C., 1954, "Psychological Aspects of Social Structure". Chap. 22 in Lindzey (1954).
RIESMAN, D., & GLASER, N., 1948, "The Meaning of Opinion", *Pub. Op. Quart.*, **12**, 633–48.

RODGERS, W., & HAMMERSLEY, J. M., 1954, "The Consistency of Stopwatch Time-study Practitioners", *Occ. Psychol.*, **28**, 61–76.

ROETHLISBERGER, F. J., & DICKSON, W. J., 1939, *Management and the Worker*. Harvard U.P.

ROFF, M., 1950, "A Study of Combat Leadership in the Air Force by means of a Rating Scale: Group Differences", *J. Psychol.*, **30**, 229–39.

ROGERS, C. R., 1942, *Counselling and Psychotherapy*. Boston: Houghton Mifflin.

ROSEBOROUGH, M. E., 1953, "Experimental Studies of Small Groups", *Psychol. Bull.*, **50**, 275–303.

ROSENTHAL, D., & COFER, C. N., 1948, "The Effect on Group Performance of an Indifferent and Neglectful Attitude shown by One Member", *J. Exp. Psychol.*, **38**, 568–77.

RUESCH, J., 1949a, "Experiments in Psychotherapy. II—Individual Social Techniques", *J. Soc. Psychol.*, **29**, 3–28.

1949b, "Social Techniques, Social Status, and Social Change in Illness". Chap. X in *Personality*, ed. Kluckhohn, C., & Murray, H. A.

RUESCH, J., & PRESTWOOD, A. R., 1949, "Anxiety. Its Initiation, Communication and Interpersonal Management", *Arch. Neur. Psychiat.*, **62**, 527–50.

S

SACKS, E. L., 1952, "Intelligence Scores as a Function of Experimentally Established Social Relationships between Child and Examiner", *J. Abnorm. Soc. Psychol.*, **47**, 354–8.

SANFORD, F. H., 1950, *Authoritarianism and Leadership*. Philadelphia: Inst. for Res. in Human Relations.

SARBIN, T. R., 1954, "Role Theory". Chap. VI in Lindzey (1954).

SARBIN, T. R., & HARDYCK, C., 1953, "Contributions to Role-taking Theory: Role-perception on the Basis of Postural Cues". Quoted in Sarbin (1954), p. 230 f.

SARBIN, T. R., & WILLIAMS, J. D., 1953, "Contributions to Role-taking Teory V. Role-perception on the Basic of Limited Auditory Stimulhi". Quoted in Sarbin (1954) p. 230.

SCHACHTER, S., 1951, "Deviation, Rejection and Communication", *J. Abnorm. Soc. Psychol.*, **46**, 190–207.

1954, "Cross-cultural Experiments on Threat and Rejection". *Hum. Relat.*, **7**, 403–39.

SCHACHTER, S., ELLERTSON, N., & GREGORY, D., 1951, "An Experimental Study of Cohesiveness and Productivity", *Hum. Relat.*, **4**, 229–38.

SCHACHTER, S., & HALL, R., 1952, "Group-derived Restraints and Audience Persuasion", *Hum. Relat.*, **5**, 397–406.

SCHANCK, R. L., 1932, "A Study of a Community and its Groups and Institutions Conceived of as Behavior of Individuals", *Psychol. Monogr.*, **43**, No. 195.

SCHEIN, E. H., 1954, "The Effect of Reward on Adult Imitative Behavior", *J. Abnorm. Soc. Psychol.*, **49**, 389–95.

SCHONBAR, R. A., 1945, "The Interaction of Observer-pairs in Judging Visual Extent and Movement: the Formation of Social Norms in 'Structured' Situations", *Arch. Psychol.*, **41**, No. 299.

REFERENCES

SCHUTZ, W. C., 1953, "Construction of High Productivity Groups". Tufts College Dept. of Systems Analysis.
SCODEL, A., & MUSSEN, P., 1953, "Social Perceptions of Authoritarians and Non-authoritarians", *J. Abnorm. Soc. Psychol.*, **48**, 181–4.
SCOTT, W. D., CLOTHIER, R. C., MATHEWSON, S. B., & SPRIEGEL, W. R., 1941, *Personnel Management*. Chap. XIX. McGraw-Hill Book Co. Inc., New York.
SEARS, P. S., 1941, "Level of Aspiration in Relation to Some Variables of Personality: Clinical Studies", *J. Soc. Psychol.*, **14**, 311–36.
SEARS, R. R., 1936, "Experimental Studies of Projection: Attribution of Traits", *J. Soc. Psychol.*, **7**, 151–63.
1943, *Survey of Objective Studies of Psychoanalytic Concepts*. S.S.R.C. Bull. 51.
SEASHORE, S. E., 1954, "Group Cohesiveness as a Factor in Industrial Morale and Productivity". Paper to A.P.A. Minemographed.
SEEMAN, J., & RASKIN, N. J., 1953, "Research Perspectives in Client-centered Therapy". Chap. IX in Mowrer (1953).
SHARTLE, C. L., & STOGDILL, R. M., 1953, *Studies in Naval Leadership: Methods, Results and Applications*. Personnel Res. Bd., Ohio State University.
SHAW, M. E., 1932, "A Comparison of Individuals and Small Groups in the Rational Solution of Complex Problems", *Amer. J. Psychol.*, **44**, 491–504.
SHERIF, M., 1935a, "A Study of Some Social Factors in Perception", *Arch. Psychol.* No. 187.
1935b, "An Experimental Study of Stereotypes", *J. Abnorm. Soc. Psychol.*, **29**, 371–5.
1951, "A Preliminary Experimental Study of Inter-group Relations", pp. 382–424 in *Social Psychology at the Crossroads*, ed. Sherif, M., & Rohrer, J. H. New York: Harper.
SHERIF, M., & CANTRIL, H., 1947, *The Psychology of Ego-involvements*. London: Chapman & Hall.
SHILS, E. A., 1950, "Primary Groups in the American Army", in *Continuities in Social Research*, ed. Merton, R. K., & Lazarsfeld, P. F. Glencoe, Ill.: The Free Press.
SIMS, V. M., 1928, "The Relative Influence of Two Types of Motivation on Improvement", *J. Ed. Psychol.*, **19**, 480–4.
SKINNER, B. F., 1950, "Are Theories of Learning Necessary?", *Psychol. Rev.*, **57**, 193–216.
SMITH, F. V., 1951, *The Explanation of Human Behaviour*.
SMITH, K., 1953, "Distribution-free Statistical Methods and the Concept of Power Efficiency". Chap. XII in Festinger & Katz (1953).
SMITH, M. B., 1950, "The Phenomenological Approach in Personality Theory: some Critical Remarks", *J. Abnorm. Soc. Psychol.*, **45**, 516–22.
SNYDER, W. U., 1945, "An Investigation of the Nature of Non-directive Therapy", *J. General Psychol.*, **33**, 193–223.
SNYGG, D., & COMBS, A. W., 1949, *Individual Behavior*. New York: Harper.

SNYGG, D., & COOMBS, A. W., 1950, "The Phenomenological Approach and the Problem of 'Unconscious' Behavior: a Reply to Dr. Smith', *J. Abnorm. Soc. Psychol.*, **45**, 523–8.

Social Survey, 1952, "Labour Turnover in Great Britain, 1945–9". H.M.S.O.

SOLOMON, R. L., 1949, "An Extension of Control Group Design", *Psychol. Bull.*, **46**, 137–50.

SOROKIN, P., 1928, *Contemporary Sociological Theories*. New York: Harper.

SOUTH, E. B., 1927, "Some Psychological Aspects of Committee Work", *J. App. Psychol.*, **11**, 348–68, 437–64.

SPENCE, K. W., 1944, "The Nature of Theory Construction in Contemporary Psychology", *Psychol. Rev.*, **51**, 47–68.

STATON, T. F., 1948, "An Analysis of the Effect of Individuals on Seminar Discussion", *Amer. Psychol.*, **3**, 267.

STEINOR, D., 1954, "Primary Group Influences on Public Opinion", *Amer. Sociol. Rev.*, **19**, 260–7.

STEINZOR, B., 1949, "The Development and Evaluation of a Measure of Social Interaction", *Hum. Relat.*, **2**, 103–21, 319–47.

STERLING, T. D., & ROSENTHAL, B. G., 1950, "The Relation of Changing Leadership to the Changing Phases of Group Activity", *Amer. Psychol.*, **5**, 311.

STEVENS, S. S., 1939, "Psychology and the Science of Science", *Psychol. Bull.*, **36**, 221–63.

STEVENS, S. S., & DAVIS, H., 1937, *Hearing, its Psychology and Physiology*. New York: Wiley.

STOGDILL, R. M., 1948, "Personal Factors Associated with Leadership: a Survey of the Literature". *J. Psychol.*, **25**, 35–71.

STOGDILL, R. M., et al., 1953a, *Patterns of Leader Behavior: a Factorial Study of Naval Officer Performance*. Personnel Res. Bd., Ohio State University.

1953b, *The Prediction of Navy Officer Performance*. Personnel Res. Bd., Ohio State University.

1953c, *Aspects of Leadership and Organisation*. Personnel Res. Bd., Ohio State University.

STOUFFER, S., et al., 1949, *Studies in Social Psychology in World War II*, Vol. I. Princeton U.P.

1950, *Measurement and Prediction*. Princeton U.P.

STRODTBECK, F. L., 1951, "Husband-wife Interaction over Revealed Differences". *Amer. Sociol. Rev.*, **16**, 468–73.

1954, "The Family as a Three-person Group", *Amer. Sociol. Rev.*, **19**, 23–9.

STROOP, J. R., 1932, "Is the Judgment of the Group Better than that of the Average Member of the Group ", *J. Exp. Psychol.*, **15**, 550–62.

SWANSON, G. E., 1951, "Some Effects of Member Object-relationships on Small Groups", *Hum. Relat.*, 355–80.

T

TAFT, R., 1955, "The Ability to Judge People", *Psychol. Bull.*, **52**, 1–23.

REFERENCES

TAGIURI, R., BLAKE, R. R., & BRUNER, J. S., 1953, "Some Determinants of the Perception of Positive and Negative Feelings in Others", *J. Abnorm. Soc. Psychol.*, **48**, 585–92.

TALLAND, G. A., 1954, "The Assessment of Group Opinion by Leaders, and their Influence on its Function", *J. Abnorm. Soc. Psychol.*, **49**, 431–4.

TAYLOR, D. W., & FAUST, W. L., 1952, "Twenty Questions: Efficiency in Problem-solving as a Function of Group Size", *J. Exp. Psychol.*, **44**, 360–8.

THELEN, H. A., & WITHALL, J., 1949, "Three Frames of Reference: the Description of Climate", *Hum. Relat.*, **2**, 159–76.

THELEN, H. A., et al., 1954, *Methods for Studying Work and Emotionality in Group Operation*. U. of Chicago Human Dynamics Laboratory. Mimeographed.

THIBAUT, J., 1950, "An Experimental Study of the Cohesiveness of Underprivileged Groups", *Hum. Relat.*, **3**, 251–78.

THOMAS, D. S., et al., 1929, *Some New Techniques for Studying Social Behavior*. Teachers College, Columbia.

THOMPSON, G. G., 1944, "The Social and Emotional Development of Preschool Children under Two Types of Educational Program', *Psychol. Monogr.*, **56**, 258.

THORNDIKE, R. L., 1938, "The Effect of Discussion upon the Correctness of Group Decisions, when the Factor of Majority Influence is Allowed For", *Soc. Psychol.*, **9**, 343–62.

THORNTON, G. R., 1944, "The Effect of Wearing Glasses on Judgments of Personality Traits of People seen Briefly", *J. App. Psychol.*, **28**, 203–7.

THOULESS, R. H., 1951, *General and Social Psychology*. London: University Tutorial Press. 3rd edition.

THRASHER, F. M., 1927, *The Gang*. U. of Chicago Press.

THURSTONE, L. L., & CHAVE, E. J., 1929, *The Measurement of Attitudes*. U. of Chicago Press.

TIMMONS, W. M., 1942, "Can the Product Superiority of Discussion be Attributed to Averaging or Majority Influences?", *J. Soc. Psychol.*, **15**, 23–32.

TINBERGEN, N., 1951, *The Study of Instinct*. O.U.P.

TOLMAN, E. C., 1936, "Operational Behaviorism and Current Trends in Psychology", Proc. 25th Anniv. Celebr. Inaug. Grad. Stud. U. of S. Calif. Press (also Chap. V in *Psychological Theory*, ed. Marx, M.H.).

TOULMIN, S., 1953, *The Philosophy of Science*. London: Hutchinson.

TRAVIS, L. E., 1925, "The Effect of a Small Audience upon Eye-hand Co-ordination", *J. Abnorm. Soc. Psychol.*, **20**, 142–6.

TRIPLETT, N., 1898, "The Dynamogenic Factors in Pacemaking and Competition", *Amer. J. Psychol.*, **2**, 507–33.

TRIST, E. L., & BAMFORTH, K. W., 1951, "Some Social and Psychological Consequences of the Longwall Method of Coal-getting", *Hum. Relat.*, **4**, 3–38.

U

UHRBOCK, R. S., 1934, "Attitudes of 4,430 Employees", *J. Soc. Psychol.*, **5**, 365–77.
UNDERWOOD, B. J., 1949, *Experimental Psychology*. New York: Appleton-Century-Crofts.

V

VAN ZELST, R. H., 1952a, "Sociometrically Selected Work Teams Increase Production", *Personnel Psychol.*, **5**, 175–85.
1952b, "Validation of a Sociometric Regrouping Procedure", *J. Abnorm. Soc. Psychol.*, **47**, 299–301.
VERNON, M. D., 1952, *A Further Study of Visual Perception*. London: C.U.P.
VERNON, P. E., 1933, "Some Characteristics of the Good Judge of Personality", *J. Soc. Psychol.*, **4**, 42–58.
1950, "The Validation of Civil Service Selection Board Procedures", *Occ. Psychol.*, **24**, 75–95.
1953, *Personality Tests and Assessments*. London: Methuen.
VERNON, P. E., & PARRY, J. B., 1949, *Personnel Selection in the British Forces*. U. of London Press.
VITELES, M. S., 1954, *Motivation and Morale in Industry*. London: Staples.
VON NEUMANN, J., & MORGENSTERN, O., 1944, *Theory of Games and Economic Behavior*. Princeton U.P.

W

WALKER, K. F., 1947, "The Application of the J-curve Hypothesis of Conforming Behavior to Industrial Absenteeism", *J. Soc. Psychol.*, **25**, 207–16.
WAPNER, S., & ALPER, T. G., 1952, "The Effect of an Audience on Behavior in a Choice Situation", *J. Abnorm. Soc. Psychol.*, **47**, 222–9.
WARNER, W. L., & LUNT, P. S., 1941, *The Social Life of a Modern Community*. New Haven: Yale U.P.
WASHBURNE, J. N., 1935, "A Test of Social Adjustment", *J. App. Psychol.*, **19**, 125–44.
WATSON, G. B., 1928, "Do Groups Think More Efficiently than Individuals?", *J. Abnorm. Soc. Psychol.*, **23**, 328–36.
WECHSLER, I. R., TANNENBAUM, R., & TALBOT, E., 1952, "A New Management Tool: the Multi-relational Sociometric Survey", Inst. of Industrial Relations, U. of California, Los Angeles. Reprint No. 25.
WESTERLUND, G., 1952, *Group Leadership*. Stockholm: Nordisk Rotogravyr.
WHITE, R. W., 1944, "Interpretation of Imaginative Productions". Chap. VI of Hunt (1944).
WHITING, J. W. M., & CHILD, I. L., 1953, *Child Training and Personality*. Yale U.P.
WHITFIELD, J. W., & HIMMELWEIT, H. T., 1944, "Mean Intelligence Scores of a Random Sample of Occupations", *Brit. J. Indust. Med.*, **1**, 224–6.

REFERENCES

WHITTEMORE, I. C., 1924, 1925, "Influence of Competition on Performance: an Experimental Study", *J. Abnorm. Soc. Psychol.*, **19**, 236–53, **20**, 17–33.

WHYTE, W. F., 1943, *Street Corner Society. The Social Structure of an Italian Slum*. U. of Chicago Press.

—— 1948, *Human Relations in the Restaurant Industry*. New York: McGraw-Hill.

WICKERT, F. R., 1951, "Turnover, and Employees' Feelings of Ego-involvement in the Day-to-day Operation", *Personnel Psychol.*, **4**, 185–97.

WIENER, N., 1948, *Cybernetics*. New York: Wiley.

WILNER, D., & WALKLEY, R. P., 1952, "Residential Proximity and Intergroup Relations in Public Housing Projects", *J. Soc. Issues*, **8**, 45–69.

WILSON, A. T. M., 1947, "Some Implications of Medical Practice and Social Casework for Action Research", *J. Soc. Issues*, **3**, No. 2, 11–28.

WITTREICH, W. J., 1953, "A Preliminary Investigation of Certain Aspects of Perception Including the Honi Phenomenon", pp. 239–54 in *Human Behavior from the Transactional Point of View*, ed. Kilpatrick, F. P. Hanover Inst. for Associated Research.

WOLF, R. & MURRAY, H. A., 1937, "An Experiment in Judging Personalities", *J. Psychol.*, **3**, 345–65.

WOODWORTH, R. S., 1937, *Experimental Psychology*. New York: Holt.

WORTHY, J. C., 1950, "Factors Influencing Employee Morale", *Harv. Bus. Rev.*, **28**, 61–73.

WRIGHT, M. E., 1943, "The Influence of Frustration upon the Social Relations of Young Children", *Ch. Pers.*, **12**, 111–22.

WYATT, S., 1934, "Incentives in Repetitive Work", I.H.R.B. Report, No. 69.

Y

YOUNG, P. V., 1935, *Interviewing in Social Work*. New York & London: McGraw-Hill.

INDEX OF NAMES

Adams, S., 197
Adorno, T. W., 30, 101, 140
Agnew, J. W., 114
Aidman, T., 103
Allport, F. H., 107, 119, 176
Allport, G. W., 16, 41, 97, 102, 142
Alper, T. G., 106
Ames, A., 98
Andrews, K. R., 182
Angell, R. C., 26
Arbous, A. G., 179 ff.
Arensberg, C. M., 25
Argyle, M., 41, 47, 73 n., 114, 156 ff., 166, 168 f., 175
Argyris, C., 25, 173
Asch, M. J., 194
Asch, S. E., 88, 100, 109, 111 f., 140, 152, 154
Aveling, F., 110

Back, K., 124 f., 127, 149, 155
Baldwin, A. L., 41
Bales, R. F., 23 f., 29 f., 32, 113, 122, 136, 140 f., 144 f., 147, 159
Bamforth, K. W., 191
Barker, R., 24
Barron, F., 140
Bartlett, F. C., 100
Bass, B. M., 136, 141 ff.
Bateson, G., 146
Bavelas, A., 24, 190, 198
Beegle, J. A., 149, 159
Behrend, H., 164, 175, 188, 196
Bell, G. B., 138 f.
Bell, H. M., 102 f.
Benedict, R., 185
Benne, K. D., 35
Bennett, E. B., 199 f.
Berenda, R. W., 48

Bergmann, G., 27, 64, 65
Berkowitz, L., 197
Bernberg, R. E., 171
Bernreuter, R. G., 102 f.
Bieri, J., 98
Bingham, W. V., 188
Block, J., 113 f.
Bos, M. C., 123
Bouthilet, L., 88
Bovard, E. W., 150, 152, 194
Braithwaite, R. B., 69 ff.
Braly, K. W., 101
Brown, C. W., 173
Brown, I. S., 142
Brown, J. F., 91
Bruner, J. S., 15, 96, 99, 103
Brunswik, E., 96, 99 f.
Burns, R., 174
Burns, T., 168 f., 191
Burtt, H. E., 110
Butler, J. M., 117, 198

Caldwell, O. W., 137
Cameron, N. A., 114
Campbell, D. T., 139, 170, 202
Campbell, H., 121
Cannell, C. F., 17, 38
Cantril, H. A., 17, 37, 106, 146 f., 151, 186
Carlson, S., 25, 167 ff.
Carlsson, G., 166
Carter, L., 23 f., 29, 122, 136 ff.
Castle, P. F. C., 196 n., 180, 183 f.
Cattell, R. B., 30, 44, 134 f.
Centers, P., 186
Chapin, F. S., 44, 125
Chapman, D. W., 104
Chapple, E. D., 25, 113
Chave, E. J., 27

Child, I. L., 45
Chowdhry, K., 139
Clothier, R. C., 186
Coch, L., 198
Cofer, C. N., 142
Coffey, H., 142
Coffin, T. E., 110 f.
Cohen, M. R., 39, 69
Combs, A. W., 42, 85, 87, 106
Comrey, A. L., 196
Cook, P. H., 19 f.
Cowen, E. L., 106
Crawley, S. L., 189
Crutchfield, R. S., 17, 18, 20, 22, 62, 85, 87 f., 101 f.

Dale, E., 189
Darley, J. G., 125
Dashiell, J. F., 106, 107, 120
Davis, A., 189
Davis, H., 27
Davis, K., 168
Dembo, T., 24
Dennison, S. R., 191
Deutsch, J. A., 75, 77 f.
Deutsch, M., 9, 53, 128 ff.
Dickson, W. J., 14, 30, 36, 40, 47, 174
Dollard, J., 66 f., 109, 117
Doob, L. W., 37
Dreyer, A. S., 129
DuBois, C. A., 45
Duncan, D. C., 96, 178
Durkheim, E., 83 f.

Edwards, A. L., 51
Ekdahl, A. G., 106
Ellertson, N., 22, 126 f.
Ellis, A., 102 f.
Elton, C. F., 167
Escalona, S. K., 109
Estes, S. G., 96, 99
Evans, C. E., 185

Eysenck, H. J., 8, 19, 30, 41 f., 44, 50, 62, 110, 117, 134, 160, 180
Ezriel, H., 19

Faust, W. L., 121, 123
Feldman, H., 197
Feshbach, S., 111 f.
Festinger, L., 22, 31, 44, 106, 124, 127, 145, 149, 154, 155 ff.
Fiedler, F. E., 98
File, Q. W., 169 n., 170, 178, 180, 183
Fisher, R. A., 52
Fiske, D. W., 96, 173
Fleishman, E. A., 183 f., 195 f., 201
Florence, P. S., 191 f.
Fouriezos, N. T., 23, 29, 129
Fox, J. B., 124, 126, 196
Freedman, R., 26
French, J. R. P., 46, 50 f., 148, 156, 158 f., 198 ff.
French, R. L., 138
French, T. M., 42
Frenkel-Brunswik, E., 97, 100
Freud, S., 21, 61

Gage, N. L., 139
Gardner, B. B., 36, 189 ff.
Gardner, G., 166
Garforth, F. I. de la P., 180
Gerard, H. B., 154
Gerbrands, H., 24
Ghiselli, E. E., 173
Gibb, C. A., 135, 137 f.
Gibb, J. R., 121, 123
Giese, W. J., 171, 174
Gillespie, J. F., 115
Glaser, N., 37
Goldberg, G. C., 156
Goldman-Eisler, F., 113
Goodacre, D. M., 126
Goodman, C. C., 15
Gorden, D. A., 17
Gorden, K. H., 119
Gorden, R. L., 139, 153 f.

INDEX OF NAMES 231

Gough, H. G., 114
Gould, R., 103
Green, G. H., 169
Greenwood, E., 44
Greenwood, M., 176
Greer, F. L., 139
Gregory, D., 22, 126 f.
Gross, N., 125
Grossack, M. M., 130 f.
Grosser, D., 109
Guetzkow, H., 23, 24, 125, 129 ff., 152
Guilford, J. P., 27 n., 28 n., 51 n., 140, 175, 181 n.
Gump, P. V., 114
Gunter, R., 87
Guttman, L., 2, 8, 60 f., 170
Gyr, R., 130 f., 146

Hall, H. E., 139
Hall, J., 169
Hall, R., 153
Halmos, P., 142
Halpin, A. W., 197, 200
Hammersley, J. M., 162
Handyside, J. D., 96, 164, 166, 178, 183 f.
Hardyck, C., 99
Hare, A. P., 122, 199
Hargreaves, H., 110
Hariton, T., 183 f.
Harrell, T. W., 175 f., 186, 191
Haythorn, T. W., 125, 142
Hebb, D. O., 72
Heidbreder, E., 88
Heinecke, C., 145, 159
Heintz, R. K., 194
Heise, G. A., 148, 190
Hemphill, J. K., 40, 122, 126 f., 170, 183, 200
Heron, A., 41, 163, 166 f., 171, 173, 178
Hewitt, D., 121
Heyns, R. W., 22, 24, 33, 125, 130
High, W. S., 196

Hilgard, E. R., 71
Himmelweit, H. T., 67, 96, 103, 175 ff., 180
Hites, R. W., 139
Hobhouse, L. T., 44
Hoffman, M. L., 140
Hoffman, P. J., 145
Hollander, E. P., 137
Holloway, V. P., 131
Holt, R. R., 106
Homans, G. C., 25, 76, 124, 144, 159, 192
Hoppock, R., 165, 186
Horney, K., 21
Horowitz, M. W., 15, 33, 98
Horton, D., 73 f.
Horwitz, M., 128
Hovland, C. I., 111
Hughes, E. C., 155
Hull, C. L., 60, 63 ff., 78, 92
Hunt, J. McV., 159
Hurlock, E. B., 195
Hurwitz, J. I., 143
Hutte, H. A., 125, 129
Hyman, H. H., 16, 104, 169
Hymovitch, B., 143

Ichheiser, G., 106

Jackson, J. M., 170, 197
Jacobsen, E., 167, 169
Jahoda, G., 104
Jahoda, M., 38, 44
James, W., 88
Janis, I. L., 111 f.
Jaques, E., 19 f.
Jennings, H. H., 135
Jones, D. C., 169

Kahn, R. L., 17, 38, 195 f.
Kardiner, A., 45
Karn, H. W., 183
Katz, D., 44, 101, 136, 163, 169, 171, 195 f.

INDEX OF NAMES

Kelley, H. H., 98, 100 n., 104, 122, 143 f., 154 f., 191
Keelly, T. L., 166 n.
Kelly, E. L., 96
Kelman, H. C., 155
Kendalll,, P. L., 18
Kerr, W. A., 164, 167, 173
Keys, A., 16
Kinsey, A. C·, 14, 36 f.
Kitt, A. 105
Klein, J. F. H., 159
Kluckhohn, C., 6, 45
Kluckhohn, F. R. C., 35
Klugman, S. F., 120
Koch, S., 57, 64, 69, 79
Kohler, O., 119
Kohn, M., 78
Kramer, B. M., 102
Krech, D., 18, 20, 22, 62, 85, 87 f.. 101 f.
Kristy, N. F., 171
Kuper, L., 149

Lambert, W., 120, 123
Lauzetta, J. T., 148 f
Lassau, La V. N., 185
Lawrence, D. H., 145
Lazarus, R. S., 7
Leavitt, H. J., 190
Leeper, R. W., 88, 106
Lees, C., 73 n.
Leighton, D., 45
Leuba, C., 98
Levi, I. J., 138
Levine, J., 198
Lewin, K., 4, 24, 42, 61, 79 f., 84 f., 89 ff., 103, 194, 198, 200
Lewis, H. B., 129, 132
Likert, R., 20, 170
Lindgren, E. J., 35
Lindzey, G., 5
Lippitt, R., 4, 23, 46, 48 f., 109, 114, 125, 145, 148, 159, 194
Livingstone, F. R., 78
Lombard, G. F. F., 126

Long, J. R., 165, 188
Loomis, C. P., 21, 149, 159
Lord, E., 106
Lorenz, K. Z., 74 f., 78, 145
Lucas, C., 98
Luchins, A. S., 112
Lundberg, G. A., 144
Luria, A. R., 32
Lynton, R. P., 188

McCandless, B. R., 155
McCleary, R. A., 87
McClelland, D. C., 16, 97
MacCorquodale, J,. 63 ff., 71
McCurdy, H. G., 120, 123
McDougall, W., 108, 109
McGeoch, J. A., 62
McIntyre, C. J., 104
McKeachie, W. J., 153, 199 f.
McNemar, Q., 17
Mace, C. A., 188 f.
Mach, E., 59
Mackworth, N. H., 188
Madge, J., 13, 46
Maier, N. R. F., 87, 182, 184, 198 f.
Maller, J. B., 129 f.
Mann, F. C., 36
Maree, J., 179 f.
Marquis, D. G., 71, 125, 130
Marriott, R., 119, 187
Martin, W. E., 125
Masling, J., 137
Mausner, B., 155
Mayo, E., 126
Mead, M., 129, 185
Meehl, P. E., 63 ff., 71
Merei, F., 53, 155
Merton, R. K., 18, 57, 105
Mill, J. S., 39
Miller, G. A., 148, 190
Miller, N. E., 66 f., 108 f., 117
Mills, T. M., 145
Mintz, A., 108, 131, 133
Moede, W., 107, 129 f.
Mohanna, A. I., 190

INDEX OF NAMES

Moore, H., 195
Moore, H. T., 106
Moreno, J. L., 21, 124, 126
Morgenstern, O., 79 f.
Morris, B. S., 179
Morse, N., 166, 170, 172, 193, 195
Mukerji, N. P., 107
Munsterberg, H., 119
Murdoch, G. P., 42
Murphy, L. B., 108
Murray, E. J., 114 f.
Murray, H. A., 35, 98, 99
Muscio, B., 17
Mussen, P., 102

Nagel, E., 39, 69
Newcomb, T. M., 106, 139, 150, 154 f.
Nixon, M., 136 ff.

O'Comisky, J. G., 101
Oeser, O. A., 36
Oldfield, R. C., 115
Orlansky, H., 45

Page, D. P., 138
Pareto, V., 40
Parfitt, J., 121
Parry, J. B., 96, 178
Parsons, T., 62
Paterson, T. T., 191
Pavlov, I. P., 71
Peak, H., 20, 29
Pelz, D. C., 195 f., 200 f., 203
Pepitone, A., 15, 97, 105, 106
Pfautz, H. W., 160
Pfiffner, J. M., 196
Phillips, E. L., 114
Piaget, J., 60
Polansky, N. A., 109, 165
Potter, S., 115
Precker, J. A., 155
Preston, M. G., 194
Prestwood, A. R., 99, 108
Proctor, C. H., 21

Radcliffe-Brown, A. R., 160
Raimy, V. C., 103
Ramsey, F. P., 61
Raphael, W., 165
Rashevsky, N., 83
Raskin, N. J., 114
Rasmussen, G., 104
Redl, F., 145 n.
Reeve, G., 179
Reimer, E., 193
Remmers, H. H., 169 n., 170
Rice, A. K., 165, 176
Riecken, H. W., 144, 159
Riesman, D., 37
Rodgers, W., 162
Roethlisberger, F. J., 17 f., 30, 36, 40, 47, 174
Roff, M., 197
Rogers, C. R., 18
Rorschach, H., 106
Roseborough, M. E., 194
Rosen, S., 145 n.
Rosenthal, B. G., 138
Rosenthal, D., 142
Ruesch, J., 99, 108, 116
Ruter, H. W., 171, 174

Sacks, E. L., 106
Sanford, F. H., 138, 201
Sarbin, T. R., 99, 116
Saunders, D. R., 134
Schachter, S., 22, 65, 126 f., 149, 152, 153, 155 ff.
Schank, R. L., 153
Schein, E. H., 109
Schlick, F. A. M., 61
Schonbar, R. A., 152
Schutz, W. C., 115, 127
Scodel, A., 102
Scott, E. L., 201 f.
Scott, J. F., 124, 126, 196
Scott, W. D., 186
Seaman, J., 114
Sears, P. S., 103

INDEX OF NAMES

Sears, R. R., 97, 104
Seashore, S. E., 122, 126 f., 150, 167, 169
Shartle, C. L., 169 n.
Shaw, M. E., 120, 123
Sheats, P., 35
Sherif, M , 52, 53, 106, 111, 166 f., 150 ff, 155 f.
Shils, E. A., 62, 148
Sims, V. C., 129
Skinner, B. F., 59
Smith, F. V., 60, 79
Smith, K., 9, 28 n.
Smith, M. B., 87
Smith, S., 190
Snyder, W. U., 23, 113 f.
Snygg, D., 42, 84 f., 87, 89
Solomon, R. L., 50, 159
Sorokin, P., 42, 59
South, E. B., 121
Spence, K. W., 27, 64, 89 f.
Staton, T. F., 144
Steele, M., 144
Steinor, D., 127, 153 f.
Steinzor, B., 24
Sterling, T. D., 138
Stevens, S. S., 27, 55
Stice, G. F., 134
Stogdill, R. M., 135 ff., 143, 167, 169 n., 175 ff., 201 ff.
Stouffer, S., 8, 60 f., 177
Strodtbeck, F. L., 53, 145 f., 159
Strong, F. W., 180
Stroop, J. R., 119 f.
Suci, G., 139
Summerfield, A., 96, 180
Swanson, G. E., 16, 142, 144

Taft, R., 96
Tagiuri, R., 96, 99, 103, 105
Talland, G. A., 139
Tannenbaum, A. S., 193
Taylor, C., 106
Taylor, D. W., 123
Thelen, H. A., 24 f., 142

Thibaut, J., 122, 143, 148, 154
Thomas, D. S., 22 f.
Thompson, G. G., 194
Thorndike, R. L., 119
Thornton, G. R., 99
Thouless, R. H., 48
Thrasher, F. M., 147
Thurstone, L. L., 20, 26 ff., 103, 174
Timmons, W. M., 120
Tinbergen, N., 184 f.
Tolman, E. C., 63
Toulmin, S., 56 n., 61
Travis, L. E., 107
Triplett, N., 129 f., 133
Trist, E. L., 191

Uhrbock, R. S., 174
Underwood, B. J., 39, 52, 193

Van Zelst, R. H., 125 f.
Vernon, M. D., 97
Vernon, P. E., 16, 96, 99, 100 f., 103, 142, 178, 181
Viteles, M. S., 121, 187 f., 198
Volkhart, E. H., 155
Volkmann, J., 104
Von Neumann, J., 79 f.

Walker, K. F., 176
Walkley, R. P., 149
Wapner, S., 106
Warner, W. L., 168 f.
Washburne, J. N., 108
Watson, A., 84 n.
Watson, G. B., 120 f.
Weber, M., 40
Wechsler, I. R., 168
Wellman, B. L., 137
Westerlund, G., 192
Westie, C. M., 134
White, R. K., 194
White, R. W., 32
Whitfield, J. W., 175 ff.
Whiting, J. W. M., 45
Whittemore, I. C., 128 f., 131

Whyte, W. F., 36 f, 175, 192
Wickert, F. R., 196
Wiener, N., 61
Willett, F. J., 191
Williams, J. D., 99
Wilner, D., 149
Wilson, A. T. M., 20
Withall, J., 24 f.
Wittreich, W. J., 98
Wolf, R., 99
Woods, H. M., 176

Woodworth, R. S., 59, 88, 103
Worthy, J. C., 192
Wright, M. E., 148
Wurster, C. R., 143
Wyatt, S., 187

Young, P. V., 115

Zander, A. F., 22, 24, 33, 104, 143
Zeigarnik, B., 79, 90, 129, 132

SUBJECT INDEX

absenteeism, 163, 173, 176
accidents, 176
action research, 13 f.
Acton Society, 192
alcoholism, 73
ambiguity, 111
ambition, 189
America, 5, 145
analysis of variance, 50
Anglo-American Productivity reports, 182
anonymity, 22
anthropology, 6, 8, 21, 41 f., 160
anxiety, 149
Arapesch, 185
atomic hypothesis, 69
attitude, 15, 30, 176
audience, 33, 105 f.
authoritarian personality, 30, 122
authority, conflicts of, 192
  formal structure of, 189 ff.
axiomatic theories, 68 ff.

Bank Wiring Observation Room, 40, 174
batch, 40 n.
behaviour, 24
belief, 15
Blacky test, 142
Blue Monday Index, 164
British Institute of Management, 182

case studies, 40 ff., 182
categories, 61 f.
central tendency, 101
children, studies of, 194 f.

classification, 8
  of processes, 62
  of responses, 60 ff.
clinical explanation, 56
cohesiveness, *see* group
committee, 146
communication, barriers to, 150
  channels, 167 f., 190 f.
  formal structure of, 189 ff.
  in hierarchies, 143 f.
competition, *see* co-operation
concepts, 29 ff.
conditioning, 71
conforming, 140
conscious events, 85 f.
constant error, 101
control group, 49 f.
co-operation (and competition), 128 ff.
  and emotionality, 130
  and norm-formation, 131
  and output, 129 f.
  and satisfaction, 130 f.
correlational studies, 39 f., 44
co-workers, 107
cross-cultural differences, 53, 145 f.
crowds, 106 f., 131
cues, 99
culture, 145
  and personality, 45

delegation, 192 f.
delinquency, 147
Department of Scientific and Industrial Research, 166
design of investigations, 38 ff.
determinism, 55
deviate, 155 f.

SUBJECT INDEX

dimensional principle, 59 f.
dimensions, 61
discovery, 8

effort after meaning, 100
ego-involvement, 105 f.
emotional contagion, 108
equi-appearing intervals, 26 f.
equilibrium, 76
ethics, 34
ex post facto method, 44
experiment, 38 ff., 45 ff.
   after-only, 49 f.
   successive conditions, 48 f.
   natural, 44
experimental psychology, 5, 21
explanation, 58
   clinical, 56

factor analysis, 62, 134 f.
family, 146
foreman, 195 ff.
formal postulates, 77 ff.
formal structure, 184 ff.
friendship patterns, 168
frustration, 148 f.
functional explanation, 30
functional unity, 29

gang, 4
General Motors, 185
generalisation, 58 ff.
generality of results, 51
group, 82, 118
   cohesiveness, 123 ff.
      causes of, 124 f.
      and norm-formation, 127 f.
      and output, 126 f.
      and satisfaction, 125 f.
   decision, 197 ff.
   dimensions, 118 ff.
   discussion, 7 f., 23
   size, 118 ff.
      and interaction, 122

   and output, 118 f.
   and problem-solving, 120 f.
   and satisfaction, 121 f.
   spatial arrangement, 149 ff.
   task, 147 f.

halo effect, 100
Harvard School of Business Administration, 161
Hawthorne studies, 3, 17 f., 41, 47, 187, 193,
human instrument, 31 f.
hypothetical construct, 70 ff.
hypothetico-deductive method, 56 ff., 68 ff.

imitation, 108 f.
incentives, 108 f., 184 ff.
   internal, 188 f.
   social, 189
individual differences, 50 f., 135 ff.
industrial relations, 6
informal organisation, 167 ff.
information, 98 ff.
   theory, 61
insight, 103
instinctive behaviour, 74 f., 77 f.
intelligence, 176
   tests, 178 f.
interaction, 91
   continuous, 112 ff.
   recording, 22 f.
intervening variable, 63 ff., 92
interview, 14 ff., 115
   focused, 18
   non-directive, 17 f.
   reliability, 96
   validity, 96
interviewer roles, 36 ff.
introspection, 15
introversion, 140
intuitive methods, 1
investigations, design of, 38 ff.
investigator, disturbance by, 33 ff.

SUBJECT INDEX

J-curve, 176
job satisfaction, 165 ff., 171 ff.
  and absenteeism, 173
  and labour turnover, 173
  and output, 171 f.
judge, motivation of, 97 f.
  personality of, 96 f.
judgment, errors of, 100 f.
  of individuals and groups, 119 f.
jury, 120

Kwakiutl, 185

labour turnover, 164 f., 173, 176
  stability, 165
lateness, 176
leader, first-line, influence of, 194 ff.
  second-line, influence of, 201 ff.
  training of, 182 ff.
leadership, 135 ff.
  autocratic, 194
  democratic, 194 f.
  scales, 169 f.
    validity of, 169 f.
  style of, 169 f.
learning, 62 f., 155
levels of aspiration, 103 f.
  of explanation, 83
life-space, 61, 89 ff.

matching, 47
mathematics, 9, 65 f., 79 f.
measurement, 26 ff.
  instruments, 14 ff.
mechanisms, 74 ff.
merit rating, 163
military studies, 197
Mill's methods, 39 f.
miniature theories, 57
models, 69 f., 74 ff.
morale, 173
motivation, 16
  unconscious, 87

National Industrial Conference
  Board, 185
National Institute of Industrial
  Psychology, 183, 193
neuro-physiology, 72
neuroticism, 140
non-directive therapy, 114 f.
norm-formation, 122, 127 f., 130 f.,
  151 ff.

observation, 21 ff.
observer, entry of, 36
  roles, 34 ff.
operational definition, 27
operationism, 55
organisational structure, 174 ff.
output, 118 f., 129 f., 162 f., 171 ff.

participant observer, 35 f.
participation, 140 ff.
perception, 15, 35, 139
  of others, 95 ff.
  of self, 102 ff.
perceptual ambiguity, 111, 152
personality, 41 f., 145
  assessment, 95 f.
  psychology of, 5
  trait, 15, 41, 53
  and leadership, 136 ff.
phenomenal field, 42, 56, 84 ff.
philosophy, 54 f.
  of science, 55 f.
physics, 33, 55
Polynesia, 13
position, 142 f., 174 f.
prejudice, 149 f.
pressure to uniformity, 154
problem-solving, 120 f.
psychiatry, 8, 41
psychoanalysis, 18 ff., 42, 114 f.
psychoanalytic theory, 58 f.
psychotherapy, 117
public/private, 152 f.

SUBJECT INDEX

questionnaire, 14 ff., 102 ff.
  validity, 102 f.

ratings, 22 f.
records, 25 f.
reductive theories, 81 ff.
reference group, 103 f., 154 f.
Relay Assembly Test Room, 47
relevance, 152
reliability, 24, 31 f.
rigidity, 100 f.
role, 4, 116, 175
role-playing, 175, 182

same-level theories, 66 f.
sample, 52 f.
satisfaction, 121 f., 125 f., 130 f., 165 ff.
scale, attitude, 20 f., 60 f.
  interval, 26 f.
  nominal, 26
  ordinal, 26
scalogram, 8
schedule, 16
science, 56 f.
scientific procedures, 6 ff.
selection methods, 96, 177 f.
  validity, 181 f.
self-perception, 102 ff.
self-recording, 25
set, 98
sexual behaviour, 14
size of groups, 118 ff.
  of organisations, 191 f.
social facts, 83
  field, 90 f.
  norms, 53
  organisation, 160
  psychology, 5
  status, 37
  survey, 6, 17
  techniques, 114 f.
sociological theories, 59
sociology, 6, 21, 73, 160

sociometry, 21, 168
span of control, 191 f.
stability of groups, 159 f.
statistical significance, 41, 48, 51
statistics, 28, 42 f.
  non-parametric, 28
status, 142 ff., 168 f.
  informal, 144 f.
stereotype, 101 f.
structure, of authority, 189 ff.
  social, 160
  sociometric, 158 f.
students, studies of, 194 f.
subception, 87
suggestibility, 110
suggestion, 110 ff.
suicide, 83 f.
supervision, 169 f.
Survey Research Centre, 195
sympathy, 108

Tavistock Institute of Human Relations, 19 f., 38, 161
teaching methods, 194
Thematic Appercention Test, 16
theory, 9, 54 ff., 58 f.
  of games, 79 f., 113
threat, 148 f.
time-study, 162 f.
topology, 79 f.

unconscious, 42, 87
unemployment, fear of, 188

validity, 20, 31 ff.
variable, dependent, 47
  independent, 47

wages, 186
work teams, 7

Yale, 67
Yankee City, 168